Deborah Jeanne Weitzman has touched people around the world with her work as a performer and teacher of voice, expression and the Alexander Technique. She continues to grow and learn from her students and audiences, and from all the people she meets on her travels.

An accomplished singer-songwriter, originally from New York City, and recipient of numerous ASCAP awards, her recordings Beneath Your Moon, Right Here and Touch the Sky are available on iTunes. *Pandora Learns to Sing* is her first book. She currently lives with her husband in Oslo and Berlin.

www.deborahjeanne.com

PANDORA LEARNS TO SING

A JOURNEY TOWARD WHOLENESS

DEBORAH JEANNE WEITZMAN

Library of Congress Control Number: 2013952145

Paperback edition: ISBN-13: 978-0-9826077-8-7

eBook edition: ISBN-13: 978-0-9826077-9-4

Deborah Jeanne Weitzman
Web site: www.deborahjeanne.com

Stream of Experience Productions
Web site: www.stream-of-experience.com

Front Cover Image: *She Who Knows*
Copyright © 2011 by Rowan Farrell (more info at end page)
Web site: www.rowanfarrell.com

Back Cover Image: photo of Deborah by Joachim Gillert, Copyright © 2012 by Joachim Gillert and Deborah Jeanne Weitzman

For Harold

Whoever can see through all fear will always be safe.
- Tao Te Ching

Be patient toward all that is unsolved in your heart and try to love the questions themselves, like locked rooms and like books that are now written in a very foreign tongue. Do not now seek the answers, which cannot be given you because you would not be able to live them. And the point is, to live everything. Live the questions now. Perhaps you will then gradually, without noticing it, live along some distant day into the answer.
- Rainer Maria Rilke

PROLOGUE

The wait seems forever at Miami International. I'm starving, as they only served pretzels during the flight from Boston, which went okay because I took two *Xanax*. Anxious about the long flight, I swallow one more. This too makes me anxious, but the doctor who renewed my prescription said it was okay to take more, especially for the long haul to Buenos Aires — the one I'm so afraid of as it flies over the Amazon with lots of turbulence.

With still half an hour to go, I walk slowly away from the gate and then quickly back again and again and again. I stretch; do some yoga; meditate; but nothing helps.

Impulsively I phone Harold, telling him that I want to cancel the whole trip and come home. He reminds me how unhappy I'll be if I change my ticket and come back to Oslo.

- Stick to the plan, he says. Think about how much you love dancing tango in Buenos Aires.

- But I'm… what if…

- You'll be all right, he says in his soothing voice. You're lucky that you're getting away at the darkest, coldest time.

But I don't feel lucky. I feel scared, very scared.

As I board the plane, I think of the slogan *there is nothing to fear but fear itself*. How quaint that sounds when the *fear itself* is quiet, like a sleeping child. But this is no sleeping child and I am no David to fight this Goliath of terror.

My hands tremble as I struggle to fit my guitar in the overhead bin. The aisle is packed with people. I want to push past them, to get out. Instead, I sit down and fasten my seat belt, like a good girl.

We are airborne, but I still can't stop shaking. I ring for a flight attendant and take another *Xanax*. Still no calm. My heart beats faster and faster, like it will beat itself to death. A not-so-friendly flight attendant comes over; she doesn't even look at me.

- What do you want? she asks. She clearly doesn't want to know, and I start to cry.

- I've never felt like this... I'm really scared...

- I can see, *jeez*. Try to calm down.

- I... I... I need to get off this plane.

- A therapist is what you need, she says, and starts to leave.

- Wait! PLEASE help me.

- No, *you* wait! she says, and then she's gone.

The man sitting next to me has seen all this. He looks over with a sympathetic smile.

- She was not very nice, he says, which is comforting to hear. Are you okay? he asks.

- I... my medicine isn't working.

The fear escalates. I ring the bell again. This time a man comes.

- What do you want? he asks impatiently.

- I... I need a doctor. I feel so strange. I HAVE to get off...

But I am crying too much to continue. He says nothing but exhales the sound of *shit* between his teeth then rushes back with a bottle of red wine.

- Here, for God's sake, drink this. The captain can't stop the plane for every passenger who has a funny feeling. This isn't a bus.

I grab hold of his hand. It has never been this bad and never have the flight attendants been so cruel.

- Please, I beg him. Don't go! I...

- Madame, this is a very full flight.

Now the man sitting beside me is very concerned. He leans over gently. His eyes are soft brown; his face is wrinkled and covered in freckles. He hands me a freshly ironed handkerchief.

- *He* was not very nice either, he says, with a heavy accent that I cannot place. Immediately I feel his warmth and wish he were the flight attendant. The panic has taken over: it builds and builds without end. I open the wine and drink it in compulsive sips.

- It's my heart... it's...

But I cannot breathe, and cannot form words. I take his hand and place it on my chest, so he can feel it himself.

- Oh my, he says.

With a hand rubbing my back, slowly, gently, he tries to calm me down. My heart is still racing, but a tiny bit less so it gives courage, that I am at the peak of velocity.

I am from Brazil... going back to see my family for Christmas... it's been a long time. Yeah, my accent... Brooklyn... twenty years... with Italians all day...

I lean against this stranger and feel the vibration of his words for a long time. The next thing I know we have landed.

Like a zombie, I follow the others through passport control, to the baggage claim. I exit and see my name on a sign. The driver sent to fetch me picks up my suitcase, my guitar and leads me to his car parked outside.

The car stops. Time has lost all sequence. I have no idea where I am except that I somehow recognize the street. The driver, a very kind man, opens the door and nudges me softly.

- *Señora, señora... estamos acá... Señora we are here.*

PART ONE:
THE SESSIONS

Buenos Aires

Every day I see Ana. I've been going for weeks and weeks, like a job, furious at having to do this. How many therapists does a person have to have in her lifetime?

- Why is this happening to me? I ask, because I have no idea how to make sense of anything. My skin, my breath, my eyes, my face, nothing is familiar, nothing is mine and it scares me to death.

- We carry things, Ana says, and we hide behind them. But one day the load becomes too much. The way you've learned to live, to survive, will not work anymore. Your inner intention has taken over and begs you to see what is buried within. Only then will your entire self come together in a new and healthy way.

- It will take too long, I say. There will never be enough time.

And she, with that amazing laugh of hers, insists there's plenty of time. Then she wraps around me, with all her love and conviction. With her funny English and irresistible power she brings me to where I'd never dare go on my own.

Session One

As a child I was very good at one thing: holding my breath and playing dead. I think I was four when my Russian paternal grandmother told me how she held her breath for so long that the Cossacks — assuming she was already dead — left her alone on the floor. After that story, it seemed holding one's breath was a necessary skill to survive the dangers of the world.

My mother's father, Sam, who came to New York from Poland (less traumatized but no less hungry) worked as a carpenter. I think he worked hardest at our house as my mother was not just his favorite, but the one with the least money and the most children and the biggest dreams. I was sure his back hunched over because of us. Sawdust was always on him: his hair, his arms, his smell. But I loved him most of all, much more than my parents or his strange wife, my weird grandmother, who came to New York much later and never learned to speak English properly, who had had such a hard life that she'd rock in a chair (not meant for rocking) and sing strange haunted melodies while staring at my mother as if jealous of her existence.

My grandfather built everything in our house including an *Anne Frank* hiding place between my bedroom and my brothers'. The opening was disguised as a bookcase. If you asked my mother she'd say, *What hiding place? That was for storage.* After my parents sent me to bed, I'd slide through the hidden door into the secret room and practice not breathing. At the first sound of my parents coming up the stairs, I'd jump back into bed, seemingly fast asleep.

While expert at holding my breath, I was not very good at breathing, especially not in public and I hated to be in front of the class. When the inevitable school project or book report was due, terror broke out in the form of flu, fever, bellyaches or hives. At first these symptoms kept me home, but soon my parents wised up to these tricks and as my no-nonsense mother worked as a teacher, we had to be nearly dying before she'd let us stay home.

- Get up my darling Sarah Bernhardt! She'd laugh, yank one of my long braids and drag me out of bed. We lived right by Kennedy Airport and I'd remind her about the planes flying over the school, that with my sore throat no one would hear me.

- Then you will just have to shout, she'd say with a swift push.

In front of the class, my throat would close even more; my breath fast and furious and my heart beating like a captured sparrow. And then there was the peeing, even if I ate and drank almost nothing before going to school. As soon as my name was called, I'd leap to the front of the class, read my book report like lightening, run back to my seat, then ask to be excused. I'd walk to the girl's room, feeling so stupid, convinced that something was dreadfully wrong with me. Everyone else seemed so fine, so positively fine.

I was nine years old when there was a serious blackout in Queens. I remember sitting in the basement of a friend's house gluing and pasting a shoebox replica of Henry Hudson sailing up the river, due the next day in school, when the lights went out. We yelled for her mother to turn them back on. She yelled back that she couldn't and told me to go home before it was completely dark.

The strange thing about memories, at least mine, is how often there's a mixture of the wonderful and terrible. I remember fearing the trouble I'd be in for waiting until the last minute to do my project and yet the minute I entered the house, it was so lovely, so magical, with the glow of candles everywhere, so unlike the usual hectic pulse of activities, that no one even noticed me, but in a good way. As if we'd all slipped back in time. I finished my project romantically by candlelight and totally forgot about having to be — and *talk* — in front of the class the next day.

My father was in a festive mood, like we were camping in the mountains. He dug out the camping lantern and stove and even helped prepare dinner. And after we'd eaten, with no news to watch, he took us outside to look at the stars.

- Where do they come from? My little brother Andy asked.

- They have always been there. We just never see them when all the lights are on. My father spoke in a soft resonant voice he hardly used. But it was strange to see him like this, so warm and friendly, so *other*.

The blackout lasted most of the night, yet with sunlight pouring in the next day it vanished like a dream. Andy and I wanted this special feeling to continue, to never use lights again, our father in such a good mood, but alas we still had school. It was Thursday, the day I was forced to wear my brown Girl Scout uniform, also the day our book reports were due. I really hated the idea of having to stand up in front of the class in that dorky outfit.

The special reading teacher was late; everyone was restless and jittery. By the time she called my name, I was so nervous, nearly unable to stand up. I needed to pee so badly, but was too terrified to ask, and thought I'd race through my presentation like other times. I rushed up in front of the class to get it over with when suddenly the teacher was called away for a moment. In that instant of sheer panic my eyes were drawn to the back of the room where my almost boyfriend, Wayne, stared at me. His blond hair, usually slicked back with Brylcreem, was loose, a lock falling over his eyes — his blue penetrating eyes.

When the teacher came back, I was so nervous that nothing came out of my mouth. All I could see was my almost-boyfriend staring at me as if he knew something terrible was about to happen. My knees went all wobbly and then it happened. I started running down the hall to the bathroom. But it was too late. The line of pee followed me everywhere. It wouldn't stop.

Hidden in the cubicle, scheming where to run so I'd never have to see my friends or my stupid family or my almost-boyfriend ever again, I recognized the heavy footsteps of my 4th grade teacher approaching.

- Debbie, are you in there?

- *No.*

- You have to come out.

- *No.*

- You can go home if you want. I will take you out the back way — no one will see you. It's OK, it was only an accident — it's not the end of the world.

- *Yes it is, I've never had an accident, not even in my own bed. EVER.*

- You made a good box. Your Henry was a very 'lifelike' representation. I will keep your book report. It was very well done. You must come to school tomorrow. The kids will forget.

- *No they won't,* I yelled. *They'll never forget. Wayne'll never forget. But it doesn't matter. I will die tonight and never come to school again anyway.*

*

I wasn't always afraid of flying. At the beginning I adored planes, their sound, their gush of movement, the sense of freedom. Our house was so close to the runway it was nearly part of Kennedy Airport. I'd open the window in my brothers' bedroom, so close to the flight path, and almost touch the passing planes, see the faces inside. Oh to fly somewhere, anywhere! My dreams overflowed with tropical islands and exotic places impossible to pronounce — just the idea of being far, far away from my family. Why? Why did I long to go and my brothers were so content to stay? What was possible in the distant location that just wasn't allowed at home?

When at last I had a chance to travel, at age fifteen, with my aunt and cousins to visit relatives in Mexico City, I couldn't believe it! Finally to get on a plane from my beloved airport and get away from dull and drab Queens and go to a far off land, colorful and exotic. That my mother actually let me go, encouraged my aunt to take me along, made me feel so lucky, so happy! My cousin Amy, just a little older, was the perfect combination of sister and friend. It was her first trip as well, both of us so excited to be on a plane that we touched every knob, pressed every button, opened every plastic package of foldable slippers, eye shades, doll-size combs, toothbrushes and the smallest tubes of toothpaste we'd ever seen. Thrilled to see the stewardesses (there were no flight attendants then) just like Barbie dolls with their little hats balancing on their perfect hairdos as they sashayed down the isles. What a different time it was then, arriving in Mexico City, walking off the plane into a brilliant light, even a Mariachi band playing on the tarmac to greet us — just like in the movies. Far more glamorous than any flight to anywhere I'd ever imagined.

Five stories high, the room that Amy and I shared looked down upon a symphony of life: the donkeys and wagons, the ladies with their colorful embroidered tops and flowing skirts, the music and sounds and smells straight from my dreams. Such a contrast from my regular life! The most exciting thing to ever see from a window at home was my best friend falling off her bicycle.

I had no idea of the significance being fifteen in Mexico has — it's a time of coming out, of falling in love. The moment we met our very animated cousin Pepe, who was around my mother's age but acted years younger, with his handlebar mustache that seemed to dance on its own, he sang out how gorgeous Amy and I were, like he meant it. And it felt good to be seen, to be fussed over.

- But where are your boyfriends? he shouted. This is Meh-khee-ko, the land of love! Tomorrow I will arrange something!

God only knows where Pepe found those boys. Boys, my father would never have let me go out with, but this was Mexico and he was far, far away. Amy was paired with the older, more likeable one, but it was the first real date we'd ever been on, and they both seemed grand as they treated us to everything — ice creams, boat rides and big wide sombreros.

As dusk came, the boys led us back to their car, parked hidden behind a tree. The older one, who'd been holding hands with my cousin all afternoon, took her into the front seat and went straight to kissing. My guy was a little creepy, so as soon as my head touched the backseat I pretended to fall asleep. He nudged me, even asked if I was sleeping and when no reaction came, began touching me under my tee shirt. When I still didn't move he slid his hand further down, opening the button of my shorts and slipping under my panties. No one had ever done this before, and I was so curious what he would do, what he would try. It felt good, even if I didn't like him, but I made a secret vow to myself to stop him if he went too far (I wasn't even sure what that meant). Deeper and deeper down he traveled. It surprised me, how he kept doing the same thing over and over. Maybe he was busy with his other hand, hard to know. The only thing I felt for sure was his finger moving inside me. It seemed to last forever and kept feeling better and better. I had no idea a feeling could be that good. Maybe because I didn't know him, didn't have to say a thing, I didn't have to own this. My cousin Amy suddenly stopped the action in the front seat and shouted:

- Holy cow! It's really late… We have to get back.

We never saw those boys again, but we met two brothers that we both fell madly in love with, that we saw as much as we could and did all the things we had never done before, had only seen in the movies. We didn't want to leave them even when my aunt organized a trip to Acapulco.

It was a short flight from Mexico City, forty-five minutes at most. This second plane came as a disappointment; it was small and rickety with nothing fun to play with, no little packages to open, but also intriguing (at first) to be able to feel every movement.

Drinks had been served when all of a sudden an exploding white lit up the sky and flashed through the windows. The flash happened again, and then a terrible sound and a hard slam as if the plane had crashed into something fierce, like a wall in the sky. I didn't know the Spanish word for lightning that many shouted, but from the terrible screaming I knew we had been hit.

I wasn't scared, not at the beginning. It just seemed so unreal, so exciting, so alive-making. Even as a young person I loved when life jumped off the page and forced people to act differently, when you could see their secret selves.

The turbulence made the orange soda I had ordered spill all over me, and I remember worrying that it would stain. When I tried to call the stewardess to ask for some water to get it out, no one appeared. The only one left standing in the aisle was a nun who struggled up and down to bless everyone. I let her, as she was so determined and I figured God would understand she didn't know I was Jewish. There were tears on her cheeks, but she was very beautiful. She held my hand and touched my head.

The pilot came on and said to remain in our seats, that one propeller had been damaged, that he was going to make an emergency landing. Then it was awfully quiet as if time had stopped, and we were just floating – at times heading down, and then as if caught on a gust of wind, lifted up again. Amy and I kept looking at each other, neither of us crying, but we heard weeping all around. We crouched down and peeked through the spaces between the seats to look at my aunt sitting behind us. She couldn't see us watching her cry. My aunt, who always had a pretentious way of speaking, as if more dignified and cultured than the rest of us, suddenly became a small, frightened girl. I couldn't stop watching her as if, finally, just before we all were going to die, I really *saw* my aunt. Perhaps this was even scarier for Amy. It was then, seeing tears on my cousin's face, that I too became scared.

They say your whole life flashes by just before you die. Instead, what popped up for me was a memory of the previous summer, of the family camping trip across America. We were in New Mexico on a dirt road in the middle of nowhere. My father loved that — to drive off the main road and *discover America*. We had a collapsible trailer attached to a hitch at the back of our Dodge station wagon. Suddenly there was a terrible sound, a pop and then a bump-bump-bump. My father braked and jumped out.

- Son of a gun! he said.

That was big cursing for him so we knew something was very wrong. My brothers and I looked at each other and then looked around. It was the end of the world — not a house, not a store, not even a lamppost, only dust and sand and dried-out shrubs as far as the eye could see. Nothing. We grew up in New York City; we had never seen nothing before.

My father worked fast, getting out the spare tire and jack. There was a metallic slipping sound. I got out of the car desperate to know what was happening.

- Son of a gun! my father said again. The jack won't hold.

The sky was a burning blue but you could tell it would soon turn red and then get dark. Really dark.

- It's going to get very cold when the sun sets, my father said.

My mother, still in the car, had her face down in her hands, shaking her head. But my parents didn't even start fighting. That was bad! I went to sit at the side of the road. The air was so dry it hurt to breathe, but it smelled good. Typical teenager that I was, and not wanting to be on this trip in the first place, all I could think about was where I'd find any friends in this wilderness.

I was staring down an endless dirt road when out of nowhere came a donkey pulling a wagon. Slowly the wagon came closer and closer. Sitting high holding the reins was a grizzly-looking man with very brown skin. The man spoke Spanish, but there weren't many words that passed between him and my father. He had everything in his wagon — every single tool needed to fix anything and the exact size jack that fit perfectly under our trailer.

-This is a miracle! my father sang out.

Maybe that was it, I recall thinking on the plane to Acapulco, one miracle per family, that's what you get. Maybe if you pray you get more, but I always forgot to pray.

Just when the plane was dipping down fast, when it really seemed like the end was coming, a man directly in front of Amy leaned over his chair and in a drunken Texas accent started telling jokes. Funny ones too.

- I know the pilot, he said. We have a poker game to play right after we land and he ain't gonna crash this plane. We owe *him* money. Now if it was the other way, say, he owed us, maybe he'd let this sucker sink, but we owe him more than this fuddy-duddy airline pays him, so he sure wants his money. You are damn pretty girls, he said, rambling on.

- C'mon. Gimme your hands, he said, leaning over his seat to get hold of ours. He didn't have his seat belt fastened. We mentioned this to him.

- Don't worry girls, I'm holdin' on with my feet.

This monkey-like Texas cowboy kept saying over and over that he was a good friend of the pilot and that we were definitely not going to crash. (That was his opinion; everyone else was preparing to die.)

- It's a right pity, my pretty little girls, that people never have faith in anythin', except the thing that smacks them in the nose. They just give up believin' at the first sign of doubt. You're not like that, pointing his finger at us.

- You believe me! I can see it. God bless you girls!

Then suddenly, with a power completely new to me, I was convinced the man was right, that we were not going to crash. That by some miracle the propeller would start up again, or the pilot would find a way to land. That I wasn't meant to die yet, like God needed me for something even if I had no idea what that something was. I had to stay alert, had to pay attention. Me, who never believed I was worth the few pennies that I kept in my pocket for luck, leaned over and made Amy do the same and we gave that man our hands and all our will.

- That's my girls! Hold on... hold on... just keep on holdin' on. Don't you dare let go of my hands!

I held on so tightly that when we finally landed, it took a long time for the blood to return to my fingers. Once safely down in Acapulco, there was such cheer and so much clapping. As we left the plane, we all fell to the ground and kissed the tarmac.

It wasn't directly after that trip to Acapulco that I developed a fear of flying, absolutely not. I had no trouble getting back on the plane for home — well, besides hating to leave our boyfriends in Mexico. We knew, Amy and I, that besides the almost-crash we'd had the best summer of our lives.

Session Two

I wonder what my life would have been like if I'd never seen a movie, because as long as I can remember, I've lived my life as though it were a movie being filmed on location. Never sure who I was, only concerned with how my character came across. Certainly, I was not the first young girl who tried to pump herself up and out of her unhappy childhood with dreams of fame.

One time on that cross-country family trip, somewhere in South Dakota, wanting desperately to be 'discovered,' I waited outside, alone on a street corner, while my family went shopping. With my long dark hair blowing ever so dramatically in the wind, so sure all those passing blonde and blue-eyed people would see an enchanting gypsy princess. When nobody stopped and nobody looked, I couldn't believe it! *I'll be famous one day and you'll all be sorry!* I preened even more, twisting my torso like Marilyn Monroe, when my father emerged from the shop and watched me. The way he looked gave me the creeps, and immediately I closed down and became invisible.

Strange paradox: being shy yet wanting desperately to be seen. Even if I didn't get the best parts in the school plays, *I* knew my potential. Hadn't I become an expert at arranging my face in the mirror to create the expressions my parents wanted, a smiling child, the sweet lovely girl? Hadn't I also practiced with the door locked the less desired moods as well? It was just a matter of being cast in the right movie.

When I got the chance, several years later, to finally study acting with Lee Strasberg, I was thrilled. Loved the school from the start; the large black rooms where we took big gulps of space, moved freely and explored our voices, ourselves.

Luckily there was no audition, you just had to want to act more than anything and be able to pay, which I managed by working the front desk in exchange for class fees. Lee Strasberg was really famous then. When I first met him, safely behind the counter, he seemed just like my grandfather. It was not just his Jewishness, but the warmth and piercing intensity of his eyes, his fascination in your existence without your doing anything special, not giving a hoot if you were shy. In class he gave me so much attention, often more than the famous actors, which confused me — so sure he mistook my endless supply of tears with talent. But I loved every second of it.

One time, while working the front desk, he watched as a young man holding a script leaned over the counter to tell me something. Lee obviously could feel the attraction between us. The moment this student left, Lee's eyes burned into me as he spoke.

- *Don't do it*, he said, *use it in the scene. And, if you have to, wait until you're finished. You'll see how quickly the feeling vanishes when there are no lines to say. But if I were you, I wouldn't do it in any case; I don't think he's worth it.*

Those words would haunt me often, as I was lousy at waiting, and most of the men were not, as Lee had said, worth it.

An important exercise we did in class was the 'emotional memory.' It had to be something from your distant past that had stayed with you for years and years. For this exercise I chose anger, using the memory of when my father unexpectedly hit me. I'd always hated my father, his burly size, his unpredictable rage; I had enough pent-up anger for years on Broadway.

The idea was not to conjure up the *cause* of his fury (the wrongly placed lid on a pot, a juice bottle not tightly closed), but the specific sensory elements that surrounded the event. Like the feel of the staircase he dragged me up before hitting me, the feel of his hands on my little body struggling to break free — exactly what I needed for the character I was rehearsing. Yet no matter how hard I focused on the touch of that railing, that carpet, those walls, my brain kept snapping to the sensory elements of the house we moved to when I turned fifteen.

It was old and broken-down with *Fair Oaks* painted on a piece of wood on the driveway. Built for the wealthy, which we were not, it motivated my mother with her rose-colored glasses to restore it. She kept my grandfather and the rest of us busy scraping, sanding and painting for years.

I should have loved that house, all mysterious and colorful, but there was something mournful and lonely about it. Plus the snazzy new neighborhood was wrong and phony, living as we were in our ramshackle white elephant. My father had to get a new job and earn more money; there were new people to meet and new standards to measure up to. My parents fought every night. It was impossible for me to sleep.

My mother thrived on it all — working three jobs, feeding her large family, and yelling at my father. At the end of the day, it was amazing how a stillness would permeate the house after her last angry words. With everyone asleep, the hallways seemed to fill with a creepy, eerie silence. And then the sounds would come — the groan of wooden floors, loose joints, as if the house was haunted by ghosts.

One night, feeling very afraid (maybe there *really* were ghosts) I heard the creek of opening cupboards, of hushed footsteps. Slipping out of bed and down the stairs, I entered the big hallway and saw the kitchen light on. Even more slowly, one toe at a time I went towards the kitchen and jumped when a looming shadow crossed the floor. I peeked my head around the wall and there stood my father holding a box of cereal.

My mother was forever trying to get my father to lose weight, and he had started yet another of his wrenching diets — ten glasses of water per day, hard boiled eggs for breakfast, cottage cheese for lunch, and a big piece of meat for dinner. He would eat his meat swiftly, get a fruit and a cup of black coffee, and go hungrily and unhappily into the den to watch the news. I always wondered (and so did my mother) how it was possible to be on such a strict diet and yet gain weight.

I don't know, my father would say harshly. *I don't know, and don't ask me.*

But he did know, I thought, unless he was a sleepwalker. That's it, that's what he is. He doesn't even know he's standing in the kitchen eating. That's the reason *he didn't know* why the diet wasn't working. I'll help him, I thought. I'll gently wake him up and lead him back to bed.

- Dad? I said as softly as I could, and yet still he jumped. Dad... What are you doing here?

- What are YOU doing here? he shouted. GET BACK TO BED THIS INSTANT.

I ran up the stairs as fast as I could, so sure he'd come after and hit me. He didn't, but it took forever to fall asleep. The next day, my father gave such a look of warning, letting me know if I said a peep to my mother, I was truly going to 'get it.' Always terrified of my father, I knew he meant it.

Every night I'd listen for when he'd sneak down. Not long afterward, I'd wait until he finished his midnight binge then go down and have one of my own. My mother must have noticed the food diminishing faster, but she never said a thing.

My father didn't know about my binges, but even if he did that wasn't the reason he started hitting me more often and with more un-controllable aggression. It had to do more with frustration over money, the endless fights with my mother and the fact that his daughter was no longer a little girl.

This confusing memory broke my concentration in the acting class. I had to start the exercise all over again, this time using the sense-elements of the staircase in our new house, the antique banister, my father's breath-ing and heavy footsteps on the old wooden floor as he dragged me onto my bed to hit me.

During the exercise, I expected to feel anger, all the rage never ex-pressed at home. But instead, only a soft erotic whimper came out of my mouth and a feeling so disgusting, so shocking that I had to get away from the class and out of the building immediately. I ran straight into the nearest shop, bought the fastest thing to rip open and shoved it into my mouth — anything to block that shameful feeling. I hated my father, how could I feel *that*? How could I ever live with myself?

We had been asked never to leave the class, that if it were too much we could stop, sit on the bleachers, go to the toilet or call the teacher for help. An outrageous reaction to a potent combination of elements was not unusual, especially a strong emotional memory, yet no one else had ever run away. No one else, it seemed to me, had ever felt something so repulsive, so revolting. There was something very, very wrong with me, and no one, no one ever should know about this.

Ana makes clear how connected they are -- anger and shame, viola-tion and the erotic. The reaction my brain produced that day in act-ing class wasn't so 'crazy' after all.

- Can I tell you the rest? I ask.

- Absolutely! Remember, Ana says, you are not here to take care of me. Nothing you say will make me stop caring for you, if that's what worries you.

- Yes, I say, I always worry about that.

But now, wanting so much to get well, I tell her what finally happened that stopped my father from hitting me, in his very peculiar fashion, once and for all.

It was a hot day, and we were all at my uncle's house. A seriously dieting teenager then, I was quite skinny and wore a really short summer dress. I sat on the floor cross-legged slumped over, teenage style, and my father was in a chair at the opposite end of the room. I never thought about this before, but my father probably had a clear view between my legs, to my white panties.

There was a fan by the window, right near me and I remember struggling to keep the sides of my dress down. But I also remember feeling okay that day, enjoying laughing with my cousins, not worrying about anything when all at once my father grabbed me and dragged me outside. It was so scary and so startling, cause there was really no reason at all, nothing I could have done wrong. He was livid, like a mad man and he really hurt me as he dragged me outside onto the porch.

'What's wrong with you!' I shouted at him. The anger came up in me like a volcano. Always so afraid of my father, I didn't care if he killed me because I was going to kill him first. 'Don't you dare touch me,' I screamed. 'If you ever touch me again, I will never ever see you. Do you understand? I will go to the police and tell them everything. Keep away from me!'

It came out so fast. The force in my words must have shocked him, for he let me go and fell over in a slump. 'I mean it,' I said, 'don't you ever come near me again.'

I slammed the door and ran back into the house, past my mother and all my relatives, not looking at anyone, furious at all of them for not helping me. I ran up to my cousin's room and jumped into her bed, pulling the covers over my head, even though it felt like a hundred degrees. And then I began to shake.

When I leave it on the floor in Buenos Aires, when I throw away the mountain of tissues I've cried and blown my nose into, and when Ana comes over to wrap her arms around me, even if I try to push her away, something heavy lifts out of my bones. A tightness I've grown so accustomed to heaves open, and I look at her without words. For at times there are no words, despite the effort to find them.

- You did good work, she says, this is how you get well, really well. And then she asks:

- He never did touch you again?

- No, he never did, but that wasn't the end of it.

- I can imagine, she says. Things don't go away that fast, they just take on other forms.

*

At the end of my three years' acting training, they invited me to an audition at the Actor's Studio. It was a great chance; many famous actors came through that place. But I was so nervous right before the audition, that instead of preparing, I gulped down two pints of ice cream so quickly I almost got frostbite. You can get pretty wasted on two pints of Häagen-Dazs! The girl who walked onto the stage was a bloated impostor, while the real actress was bound in rope and her mouth gagged. Lee arranged another audition, but this time I didn't even show up. And a few months later he died.

I was working then as a waitress in a new French café on the Upper East Side.

It was a very chichi place, very trendy, one of the first that opened in New York, with tables outside like Europe. Everyone who came looked perfect. God only knows what they did with the buttery croissants they seemed to eat because they all weighed like three pounds.

The pastry chef, straight from Paris, had just arrived. He was so cute, had such a lovely face, his lips shaped from all those luscious French words but I never dared talk to him. One day out of the blue he asked me out and I nearly dropped my serving tray. Why would he want to take me out? Me, sneaking into the kitchen between orders to stuff a pain au chocolat into my mouth when he wasn't there. And how mortified, when he'd return before I could finish swallowing. He'd seen me with my cheeks puffed, my face red with shame — why in heaven's name would he want to spend time with me, and if so what was wrong with him? Yet still he kept asking.

Finally I agreed to meet him, or rather to let him come meet me, in Central Park where I went folk dancing on Sunday afternoons in the summer. There was no fee, only a box for donations, so even when I'd spent all my money on a recent binge, I could still go. At least two hundred people came to dance and another large crowd gathered to watch and take pictures.

I was having a bad morning the day I was to meet the chef. I can't remember what triggered the eating binge the night before. I could go for weeks doing well with food, following a regime of swimming and yoga, acting classes, rehearsals and concerts, not eating anything extra at the café, just having my café au lait and Perrier water. Then something would set me off — a phone call from my mother, a comment from someone in the audience, a lousy audition, a bad dream, a sleepless night, my period. And then off to the races I'd go, eating to satiate a hunger that no amount of food could fill, forced to wear my baggy 'fat' clothes.

Maybe it was just the idea of meeting this amazingly handsome, normal man who not only was a great chef but was always calm and centered, something I could never be. I wanted to phone him to tell him not to come. Now I cannot recall his name, maybe Pierre or François, he was that French. Back then we didn't have cell phones and I hadn't the heart not to show up, so I put on the best of my formless, concealing, dresses and forced myself out.

The walk itself did me good: movement, no matter what, jiggled that rotten thing inside me and shifted or at least postponed plans for suicide. Even when I felt enormously fat, I was never *that* fat, and even if I was, it was not against the law to dance. But I didn't have such thoughts back then. It was more along the lines of deserving life imprisonment for my trespasses and self-indulgences, for being so impossibly far from perfect.

I turned down East 91st street and headed for the entrance to Central Park. It was a beautiful walk, around the bridle path to the west side, across the playing fields to the concrete circle that served as dance floor. I heard the music a long way off — the Greek melodies, the Romanian fast and noodling violin, the mournful Serbian and Macedonian songs, and my mood began to change.

He was there, the chef, standing around the periphery with the others, enjoying it as I knew he would. It was just as I told him: high-level dancers, people from all over, so quintessential New York — this gathering and celebration in a way no longer done in the countries of origin. As though New York were the true guardian of lost cultures.

We gave the French greeting, a quick kiss on both cheeks, but didn't stop to talk. Still wrapped in self-loathing, I dared not open my mouth and chance something awful coming forth. Instead, I let myself be pulled into the line by one of the dancers, they all knew me by sight as a regular, and did not stop dancing for at least an hour. My mood and sense of self had completely altered (those beloved endorphins!) and when my heart was pounding from the exercise, feeling assured that I'd not say anything depressive, I went over to talk to the chef. But not for long, I needed to keep dancing.

What I truly love about social dancing, besides the actual dancing, is that it is deep and profound and yet superficial all at the same time. You are with people, but you don't have to talk or really be with them. They don't get to know you and you don't have to know them. And yet when the power surged through the line and the music burned a hole directly into you and you saw the same in the other's eyes, it was like knowing some secret about them, at least for the three and half minutes of the dance.

I found myself searching for him as I danced, to see if he was still there, to see if he was watching me. He seemed to like that I looked over at him, giving him at least some attention. After a while, with my cheeks completely flushed, I stopped dancing and went over to chat a bit more. He greeted me again; enough time had passed to warrant a fresh kiss on the cheeks, but this time he held me a bit longer, his hands gently on my shoulders.

- You change, he said. You are beautiful now.
- I love to dance, I said breathlessly.
- Yes, I can see it. You are very different from how you are in the restaurant. I have taken a picture of you, and when I get the picture, you must have it; you must remember who you are, really.

He was probably right in what he said, in what he saw, but after that day I lapsed into feeling ashamed of myself again and continued overeating, so I never did go out with him. Back then as soon as people really saw *me*, it was reason enough to never ever see *them* again.

I gained so much weight at that café (stealing pastries to binge on later didn't help my cause), and had to quit the job. And only when I'd lost enough, on one of my severe diets, and my eating was under control and I was fitting into my clothing of choice, did I go to the café, as a normal person, a customer. I asked after the chef and was told that he no longer worked there. He had found New York too lonely and had gone back to France.

Session Three

Smack in the middle of a song I can get so homesick that I want to break open the wall of the song and crawl inside. Like now, alone, in Buenos Aires singing The Boxer, a song I've never sung, don't even know why I started playing it. All at once I long for New York, my New York -- not as poor as the boy in the song but starved for something I couldn't name, not then anyhow. I can almost name it now, though hardly without crying.

I want to go back, not scared or hungry, or so quick to give up the things I worked so hard for. Please never let me walk down the streets of New York again as a waif, stuffing the wrong food in my mouth, the wrong men in my body, the wrong thoughts in my head. Who could know it would go so fast? That some chances come around only once, and that in the end no one can rescue you, for even if they do, you don't believe you're worth it.

Someone had to believe in me. A look, a smile, words saying *I could*, made all the difference. Way before Lee Strasberg, it was my music professor at college, when I was seventeen, who told me how much he loved my songs that made it okay to sit for hours upon hours in the stairwell scribbling words, creating melodies; shifting my unsettled feelings into something beautiful. But the moment I got a wrong look, or felt nakedly judged — like around my highly competitive family — I froze. Instantly my voice became a limp reed, my inspiration vanished and I filled the aching void with food.

At college, I survived easily on carrot sticks and fruits. The instant I came home and felt lost and lonely and stupid in my loneliness my overeating — the only friend for my wretchedness — spiraled out of control. Amazing that no one noticed how much weight I gained, but no one said a thing. I dreaded coming home, but you couldn't stay at the college all the time.

During my second year, my music professor advised me to take time off and travel, to get new impulses and write songs — just the words needed to convince my parents to let me go. What hopes that young girl had! Nineteen years old, a guitar slung over her shoulders, off to the places where no one knew her. She could become anyone!

In 1973, not so many people played like today, where just having a guitar and writing songs made you special and exotic in Europe. It was the age of Bob Dylan and Joni Mitchell, Judy Collins and Jacque Brel, and my voice sounded the time. So easy to get gigs, to earn money that I fooled myself into believing it would continue when I came home again. That whatever had caused the overeating was long gone, I was cured. Yet the instant the plane touched down in Kennedy, my self-esteem plummeted and the whole show started up with a vengeance. All I could do, to keep my body from exploding, was finish my degree and leave again.

Two years later, bags packed for London, to study music more seriously, I went to say goodbye to my Grandfather Sam. He'd always been the most important person in my life, the only one I'd dare sing to as a child when it was just the two of us, alone. That he really wanted to listen, even asked for a song, made me feel like a million dollars! As soon as my mother got home, she'd charge into the room with something urgent, taking him away. The start, I am sure, of the habit I still have of looking around while singing, checking for permission to go on.

My grandfather had just moved to Miami, to Collins Avenue (when it was still rundown) across from the beach. The weather was beautiful and we took long walks along the sea. He told stories about his life; stories there'd never been time for. It was intimate, special, like two grownups sharing secrets. I told him about my dreams and plans, my big hopes for my music.

Maybe hearing about Europe reminded him of the life he'd escaped. But all of a sudden he came down so hard on me.

- How old are you now? He asked, with his heavy Yiddish accent.
- Almost twenty-two.
- That's much too old! If you are not a famous musician already (his look reminding me that I wasn't), it's too late! You have to find another job.

- No Grandpa! That was in the old days, the world has changed.

- No Debala, about *this* the world will never change.

We walked home to prepare dinner and when we'd finished, I kissed my grandfather good night and went back to the beach, totally devastated. The winds picked up, the palm trees bent and the waves smashed on the shore as if expressing my angst. What was even more upsetting, was the *resignation* I felt and my willingness to throw away my dreams and my music. How could I continue to love and respect my grandfather and at the same time imagine him wrong? It was all or nothing, black or white.

This dilemma followed me to London, and even if much went well — determined to become a better musician, I practiced like mad — the gnawing sensation that my grandfather was right persisted, that I'd never be a real musician. Another part of me refused to believe him so there waged a constant battle. And at times of losing that battle what better way to *soothe the aching breast* than with food?

However, by the second year, on such a fierce regime of lessons and hours of practicing, a daily class of either ballet or modern, and a rigid eating plan learned from the serious ballerinas, my period stopped coming for months and my weight hit an all time low.

Everything now depended on being thin, everything. With nothing female in my appearance, I landed a well-paying job in a swank West End restaurant that only hired men. My inherent acting skills helped me mimic the other waiters, so besides being a bit too clean-shaven, I was more than acceptable. So good at it, I imagined myself a gay man. But when the other waiters (who loved me so during our shift, who laughed hysterically at my *shenanigans*) left for their exclusive male clubs… I couldn't go. A brutal emptiness hit, an emptiness that without food to fill was unbearable.

Two years of this highly disciplined life convinced me that my eating was under control, that I was ready to return home to New York, to find fame and fortune or at least work as a musician. But once again, faced with the intimidating presence of my family, and the real world as I imagined it, food, like a faithful lover was waiting to embrace me, distract me… *consume* me.

*

Twenty-four years old, lost in New York, no longer writing songs or practicing and no clue how to get through a day without stuffing my face, I got a job waiting tables in a corner diner. Unlike the trendy French café, or the hip restaurant in London, this was safer in terms of food as the crowd *really* came to eat, hardly any leftovers to shovel in my mouth on my way to the kitchen. Besides, the cook — you could hardly call him a chef — kept a keen eye on me, letting me know how much he *liked* my ever-changing hips.

- *A bit more, he'd say*, in his Jamaican English, *and I'll feel you as you rush by!*

Ever the chameleon, I once again recreated my persona. In this diner, working with tough gals, union waitresses who'd crack their gum so loud like little bullets shot from their mouths, you had to learn a whole new language. *Time is money, little missy, and our patrons are hungry fuckers.* For an order of grilled American cheese with bacon on toasted rye without tomato you shouted — *Jack, back, whisky down, hold the tommy.* I thought it would serve me well playing opposite Al Pacino in a movie.

Two years later, still working the diner, still studying with Lee Strasberg, I got my first real acting part in a weekend production of *Hansel and Gretel*. As my character was supposed to be very hungry, I really had to starve each week to fit into my costume. But come Sunday, boy did I eat. On Monday, I'd wobble into work, bloated, trying to avoid the smiling Jamaican cook, licking his lips like he wanted to eat me.

It was at this diner, on the corner of 63rd and 2nd where I first learned about the secret life holding sway in church basements all over Manhattan. A group of ten or so would come in every Monday around eight o'clock. They never ordered much: coffee, tea, seltzers and cokes, maybe a piece of pie. Mondays after the dinner rush were slow, and they sort of fascinated me. I'd sit on the counter stool close enough to catch a glimpse and simply observe.

They were a most unusual group — a mix of ages, sex, and race. Each week brought different people who all seemed delightfully engaged in whatever the heck they were engaged in. Impossible to figure out the context, I was utterly intrigued. One night when one of them wanted more coffee, I could hold my tongue no longer.

- Can I ask what kind of group you are?

- Sure you can ask! We are from A.A! That's Alcoholics Anonymous. We have a meeting across the street at six, and then we come here to continue, you know... talk to the newcomers, get them into it. But me, he said, patting his stomach, I've gained so much weight since getting sober that I *also* go to O.A.

- O.A.?

- That's Overeaters Anonymous. I've switched addictions you see, eighty pounds worth! My doctor says I am nearly as unhealthy as when I was drinking!

Before I could say no-I'm-not-interested-but-perhaps-a-friend-of-mine-might-be, he handed me the list. Luckily I'm not fair-skinned, so he couldn't see the blood gushing into my face. I shoved the list into my apron and got the coffee pot to refill his cup, trying desperately to act normal. I felt humiliated. That man knew! The minute I came home I wanted to throw the list away, but couldn't and stuck it far in the back of a drawer.

When I first started going to OA — after one of those awful binges when you swear: THIS IS THE LAST PIECE OF PIZZA I WILL EVER EAT, but later that night, you rummage like a raccoon through the garbage and you don't care about anything except shoveling more into your mouth – and learned there were lots of people like me doing terrible things to themselves, I felt a strange mix of relief and disappointment. I wasn't alone, fine, but I also wasn't special. I hated the meetings at first; hated *fessing* up to an eating addiction, would rather have been alcoholic — that was glamorous, poetic! All the famous people drank, all those dramatic alcoholic scenes in the movies! But food, ugh.

It's basically the same 12-step program. In A.A *you lock the lion up once and for all*, while in O.A. *you have to walk the lion around the cage three times a day.* The O.A. meetings felt like a Tupperware party, until I got into it. In the program they tell you that you have to hit bottom before you're willing to do the work, and it seemed my addiction was bottomless.

For years I couldn't stay abstinent for 90 days in a row, the magic number, blowing it on day 88 or 89. At 90 days you got a *chip*, a symbolic coin, like you made your first mile on a long and tortuous climb, and you had to tell the group, who clapped and made a fuss over you. The newcomers rushed over like you were one of the Beatles and asked for your number and how in the hell did you do it. It jinxed me — all that attention and responsibility.

As a child, I could spend hours stringing tiny beads onto a thread to make a necklace that no one wore, but gently adding one day after the other of balanced living was impossibly hard. I burnt through sponsors like a bush fire, but finally found one who encouraged me to stop counting; to not weigh myself daily, and if there was a little slip — like a helping too much — to not call out the perfection police and set myself up for a *what the hell I might as well keep on eating since I've already messed up* binge.

All the starving I'd done over the years, between binges, had kept my weight from ballooning too high, yet when after six months I stepped on a scale and had lost twenty-five pounds, I was ecstatic. Still, my sponsor did nothing different, no celebration, just encouraged the continuation of one baby step after another. As my weight stabilized, it was more about bad habits to shed than pounds to lose and it actually became easier. I had reluctantly stopped doing all artistic endeavors to stay abstinent, but my sponsor encouraged me — *that I was not giving up on my singing and acting forever; to trust it would all come back when I was ready.*

Unfortunately I had no trust. It became clear that I was weak and wimpy and prone to stage fright. Unable to brandish the artistic sword, nor enter the dark, lonely cave of creation, it was time to admit defeat. Time to brush myself off and be normal. No more reaching for the stars. At last my grandfather won. And I had to quit working around food, which meant doing far more time-consuming jobs, like teaching and cutting hair.

Yet I stayed abstinent and my sponsor told me that was more than enough. My days were now filled with program phone calls and meetings, with swimming and yoga and long walks. And endless cups of coffee with my sponsor and new program friends. With the extra money — food is not free and bingeing is expensive — I bought new clothes, new bras, new shoes. Amazing, how when you lose weight everything shifts, everything changes and how much more time there is when an obsession lifts.

We were taught to stay away from 'civilians' so I rarely saw my family. In trying to be *normal,* ordinary, I'd sometimes burst out crying just thinking that yes it was nice to be thin, but I'd never be able to sustain such a boring existence.

In the twelve-step program, they encourage you *not* to change your life too much in your first abstinent year, that boring was not so bad and to keep things as simple as possible. In my desire to bend and break rules and suggestions — as I am a *special* person — I became engaged to a man I'd recently met and moved away before completing this first year of abstinence. As it had taken me so many years already and I'd *finally* lost my weight for good and really acted normal, I figured everything would be OK, that I'd be able to keep my new life going without ever bingeing again. Nope. In the twelve-step program, no matter how special you think yourself to be, you still have to follow the rules.

Session Four

I wonder if other people torment themselves as I do, especially with nonsense decisions like whether to swim or eat dinner first. I can easily waste a whole afternoon deciding what to have for dinner yet for the really important things, like where to live or with whom, I do no more than flip a coin. Not exactly letting heads or tails decide per se, but the *feeling* the instant the coin lands — that helps me decide. It was such a feeling that came over, when my boyfriend Josh, offered a good job outside Detroit, asked me to marry him that made me say: Yes! Of course I'll leave New York with you! The *feeling* assuring me how much easier it would be to stick to my rigid eating plan away from the temptations of Manhattan, and having someone to love and to be loved would remove the need to overeat once and for all!

What I hadn't counted on was the wretched quiet in Ann Arbor, Michigan, that Josh would work late all the time, and that I'd be far lonelier *engaged* than ever before. All well and good to finally have health insurance and not worry about money, yet away from my program friends, my routine and potent striving to become *something* in New York I had no idea how to get through the long tedious hours between meals. (This was the early eighties, before Internet and Facebook could fill all your time.)

A part of the twelve-step program that I'd so far avoided — because I found it impossible to sit still that long — was meditation. Now with oceans of empty hours I forced myself to start a meditation class at a nearby ashram. In addition, I joined a yoga group, had a part-time job teaching music at a private school and went once a week to an OA meeting in Michigan. But this vacuous stimulation compared to New York was like being dead.

The best option, to use myself up after my meager dinner and short talk with my sponsor, was to walk and walk, to discover every tiny cove and alley, every hill and dale. On one evening prowl, I stumbled upon the Ann Arbor Civic Theater where an audition notice for *Cabaret* was posted.

Come prepared with two songs, a short monologue, and wear dance clothes — all parts open. My heart pounded as I read the announcement; the heart is always beating but when suddenly you *feel* it, it reminds you that you won't be alive forever. *Cabaret* was one of my favorite scripts, no way to let this chance pass by. I ran home, pored through the box of acting books and papers that I'd hidden from Josh — as I'd promised him to give it all up and be *normal* — and quickly chose a monologue best suited for the lead role of Sally Bowles, the only part I wanted. Impulsively, I changed into an outfit that helped me be *her* and began rehearsing. When Josh came home I was so deep into it, prancing loudly in the back room, that I didn't hear him; hadn't a chance to put anything away.

- Who are you talking to? he called.

- No one.

- Then why are you talking to yourself? He walked into the back room and saw my not-exactly-every-day outfit and the papers spread all over.

- I'm not.

- What's going on? He asked, his face glowing red, his lips tightening. You brought this stuff here? I thought you were…

- It's just an audition, Josh. I mostly mess up at auditions. Don't worry I won't get the part.

- Please. Don't audition.

- Why not, what does it hurt? It's good for me to stay in shape. I'm...

- You said you were doing yoga.

- I am, but...

- I'm begging you. Don't do it.

I didn't understand why he was so against it. Until then, nothing had come up so far to test us and we still didn't know each other that well. He was huffing and puffing as he pulled out the futon, almost ripping the top sheet.

- I know you're gonna get the part, he growled. You're going to get the lead, and I'll never see you. You'll rehearse every fucking night and every weekend and then the show will run… it's going to ruin us, it's going to ruin what we have.

- What do we have, Josh? I shouted back. Cause if you ask me, all we have is a big heap of nothing! I never see you anyway, just on Sundays.

And we're supposed to get married and have kids that I'm supposed to love because that's the way it's supposed to go, and those kids will grow up hating me anyway because I'll blame them for the career I never had!

- You're terrible, he said. Go do your fucking play!

He took off his clothes and threw them in the corner, pulled the blankets over his head and went to sleep. Infuriating, how quickly he fell asleep. I was all geared up to fight more. In spite of my selfishness — he had incredibly long days, got up at the crack of dawn — I let him sleep. Josh was a good man, one of the best you could find in New York: honest, hard working and open to many things. And funny. That he could make me laugh seemed as much a guarantee of being a good partner as anything and when I agreed to marry him and move to Ann Arbor, I said on one condition, that we never stop laughing. He said no problem, he knew a lot of jokes. What he didn't know was that there'd be no time to tell them. He was amazingly supportive and patient of my twelve-step thing, especially with my foul after-dinner moods when I always, always, always wanted to eat more. He'd seen me in New York stressed and discouraged after auditions, so he was right to urge me not to go. But I had to; there was no choice. Watching him sleep, I felt just like the scorpion that begged the frog to take him on his back across the river.

'Why should I carry you?' asked the frog. 'You will sting me and I will die.'

'No, no,' swore the scorpion, 'why would I do that? If I sting you, I will also die.'

So the innocent frog took the scorpion on his back and away they went. Halfway across the river, the scorpion stung the frog.

'Why did you do that?' cried the frog. 'Now we will both die.'

'I had no choice,' said the scorpion. 'It is my nature.'

The audition was a grueling five hours: I pushed and dared myself like it was truly a matter of survival. Often I hold back, fearing my voice will crack, but when I sang: 'Maybe This Time' from the movie version of *Cabaret* a mighty power — the power of being unused — erupted. I gave everything, and on my way home I felt wretched and drained and terrified with the thought that I might get the lead.

Josh didn't say anything, but at the start of the play, I was so happy and on my best behavior that he actually seemed relieved, like maybe being busy *was* better. Plus I'd found a therapist, Colin, at the ashram so all was calm on the home front. But alas, even if not so evil as a scorpion, you can force a restless bird to sit still for only so long before it has to fly away.

Maybe what came out of me the night of the audition was just a fluke. I kept overhearing at rehearsals that I shouldn't have gotten the part; hadn't the *balls* to play Sally. Tom, my co-star who played Cliff, knew everyone.

- Don't listen, Tom said, they're jealous. Everyone wanted to play Sally.

Tom opened his hands as he spoke; he had huge hands and towered high over me as we rehearsed our duets. His voice was big and powerful and he carved the path for me to sing on. The rehearsals went late into the night. I loved it and dreaded going home.

Sally was *supposed* to fall in love with Cliff, yet it was frightening how attracted *I* was to *Tom*. Suddenly Lee Strasberg's words of warning — *Don't do it, use it in the scene! You'll see how quickly the feeling vanishes once there are no lines to say* — came back to haunt me. Colin, my therapist, thought it the wrong time to be in a play. It would have been better to be grounded in meditation *and in myself* first. He didn't know and I didn't tell him that getting 'grounded first' would take the rest of my life.

-You worry too much about your life, Colin said, and you have no trust. Can't you see it doesn't matter what you do? Just meditate.

- I've heard that before, I told him. Maybe it works for some people, but not for me.

- Love God, he said. Let yourself be an open channel.

- No way... I'll just overeat.

- Don't worry about your eating!

But I did; I worried about everything. Just because Colin saw me in pretty good form, he hadn't a clue of the monster inside me. He was a nice man, but easy to fool. And he had no idea how many people were needed to help me, so I divided the task and also started meeting the Swami at the ashram. Both were kind men. Colin was tall and lanky with a full head of blond hair whereas the Swami was compact with a shaved head and he laughed all the time, even more than Colin. It felt embarrassing to need to talk to them both and I hoped they didn't com-pare notes as I rarely told the same things. But for some reason, I was more honest around the Swami.

In between, when I actually saw Josh awake, we made love. It was nice, but I didn't want nice, so I couldn't sleep. And when I finally did, the dreams were terrible. I dreamt about Colin, that he couldn't help me. That no one could.

In the morning I called Colin and left a message that I was too scared and wanted to quit the play. He called back:

- GO! he said, even if you feel anxious.

- But you told me it wasn't such a good idea...

- Yes, but quitting now is even worse. You have a commitment to the play.

- But I —

- See you in a few days. GO.

Sally collected men: she needed them to adore her. Her loneliness was unquenchable; she hated quiet, despised being still. She would never meditate; she wanted to dance! She opened her arms wide at the center of the carousel and sang, *Come celebrate! Come to the cabaret, life is a cabaret.*

It was Berlin in the late 30's and the theaters were closing down. Sally couldn't perform anymore; Cliff couldn't get work teaching and spent all day looking for work, he had no time to write. They drank way too much. Sally became more and more agitated, hysterical as the carousel slowed down, as people jumped off. They feared what was coming, no longer sure what to celebrate. *Things will work out!* she screamed. *They must. I will make them. If life were a cabaret, there would be no war. Come everyone, please come to the cabaret.*

In rehearsal, the passion flew madly between Sally and Cliff, and backstage — because it wasn't just *Sally* who felt that way. (Never in my life had I felt that sexually charged.) Cliff adored Sally (far more than Josh ever loved me), but my *Sally* was much too shy, too ashamed of what she felt, of her guilt (or was it mine?).

If only we could have rehearsed forever. I just needed more time to get courage, to dare. But the play was opening soon and there was no time to help an insecure actress. I feared the other cast members in the wings, their looks of disapproval, of disappointment.

Tom (Cliff) was great. He kept reassuring me that I was doing fine. Yet the more Sally lived inside me the more I clung to Tom between our scenes.

We'd beg Margo, the director, to let us do our scenes over and over.

- Why? She'd say. It was fine.

- It could be better.

- No! Margo snapped. We have a whole play to run through!

Waiting backstage, *Tom* kept flirting with me and it got really confusing.

- I'm not used to this, I said to him, in the English accent cultivated for the part.

- Used to what? he said.

- All these emotional shifts, these feelings…

- But it's all *you*, Tom said, it's through you that Sally lives.

- Then why do *I* want to kiss you all the time? Why do *I* never want this feeling to stop? Why do *I* lie in bed next to my fiancé and only think of you?

I hadn't told any of this to Colin, or to the Swami. Hadn't mentioned to either of them that I didn't want to get married, not to Josh, not to anyone. I wasn't overeating. I was getting thinner and thinner. I loved it. Meanwhile, with the delicate balance between fantasy and reality shifting, it pissed me off that I couldn't kiss Tom every second. Not even in the play.

- Don't sulk! Margo shouted to me. It's spoiling the scene.

Fuck the scene and this stupid play. Fuck everyone in the entire world. Why can't Tom just hold me and make it quiet under my skin?

Now furious, I charged onstage for my scene and Margo cheered:

- Yes! Yes, that's it, that's perfect!

After rehearsing, Tom and I spent hours in his pick-up truck, kissing. He wanted to sleep with me badly, was sure he was in love with me. Lee Strasberg jumped on top of my head shouting: *no, no, no, no, you must wait, you will ruin the play.*

I was ruining everything, and the anxiety was killing me. I begged Colin to see me, and trudged through the heavy snow like a madwoman for a therapy session.

- Wow girl… Slow down!

So much to tell him that my words flew off my tongue like hot cakes, yet all he said was:

- Slow down, don't make any decisions. Finish the play.

I paid him for a whole hour and all he could say was *slow down*. What kind of lousy therapy was that?

Terrified of losing Josh yet hating him, I couldn't sleep. Terrified of how I felt towards Tom, or what I might do, on- or off-stage, Margo was now afraid that maybe I'd mess up the show.

Performing jitters are normal, she kept saying.

But the amount I had?

Finally opening night: so nervous my lips were glued to my teeth, I rushed home for a prop I'd forgotten and caught Josh standing in the bathroom with my diaphragm case in his hands.

- You didn't know, did you? I check every night if you've taken *this* with you.

- My diaphragm? I shouted. Are you crazy?

- You're sleeping with him, aren't you?

- No.

- But you want to. I know you want to. I touch you and you're not there.

- Oh Josh, the rehearsals end so late. I'm --

- You're full of shit, he said, slapping me hard across the face. It hurt, but not as bad as the shock of being hit by the man you were supposed to marry.

- OK, I shouted, grabbing the diaphragm case. Since you're so sure, why don't I just take it with me, why don't I just not come home tonight?

Josh was livid. He lunged at me, dragged me into the living room with his hands wrapped around my neck and threw me down onto the carpet shaking me violently. If it wasn't for the play I'm not sure he would've let me go. He fell over crying and I ran out of the house.

So in the end Josh was right, it had all gone wrong. Perhaps everything is just a game of dominoes, one action triggering the next. If Josh hadn't done what he did, I never would have slept with Tom. But he did. And I felt justified, almost giddy as I gave over to Sally. I hated the fight with Josh, yet it was so dramatic that when the curtain lifted and the play began, I felt like a true actress. And by the end of the evening, with the rush of applause, I thought I'd done great.

Tom wouldn't let me see the reviews until the run of the play was over. He kept reassuring me how well I was doing, but when I finally read the reviews, I couldn't focus on the positive part that called me a *'stunning, vivacious actress'* but rather, ripped my guts out on the: *'but no Liza Minnelli'*.

It killed me at the cast party to see the 'I told you so' looks on everyone's face as we watched the video of the show. So ashamed of my feeble performance, I ran into the bathroom and threw up. Tom ran after me, saying how well I'd done, how beautiful I looked, that videos always make it worse, the sound shit. But nothing he said helped. I saw what I saw — my *fear* in full Technicolor — and it was horrible. Tom kept saying that Sally Bowles *was* afraid and confused, that it was good you could see *her* fear. But he couldn't convince me.

To act, you have to learn that when you *open the door for something, an emotion needed for the scene, all the rest will tumble out. The actress must permit this and use the whole mess of feelings, like wood for a fire, in the play; to not dissipate the energy by protecting herself* — that will only smother the character. Even without a Tom or Josh to confuse me, I was far too afraid, too subjective — like Pandora, who slammed her box shut when aspects too frightening escaped — all my controlled feelings made for a weak and wimpy Sally.

- You are judging yourself again, Ana says. Can you learn without judging? The doubt in yourself was unfortunately the strongest force at the time, but you did it the best you could. This is our work --to challenge that doubt, that look you thought you saw in everyone's eyes and see it for what it is and was: an imposter.
- A mighty imposter, I say sadly. I never acted again.

I didn't go home opening night. Instead, I stayed with Tom and suffered the guilt of being a horrible person, yet it was the best sex I'd ever had. We were together every second, well for a few weeks anyway, until it became more and more apparent what a great actor Tom had been. More and more apparent that it was *Cliff* I'd fallen in love with, not Tom. I tried holding on, just like Sally had, tried to prevent the carousel from stopping.

I canceled appointments with Colin, but kept going to the Swami. He didn't judge me. He tried to help me see that *it was time to get off the ca-*

rousel and find peace, alone; to stop seeking refuge in food, in people, in men and to find it in God. To give myself three months of time out, to have no sex, no relationships whatsoever, and to find the love in myself, only then would I truly feel better. The Swami also suggested taking a break from talking to my family. *Wear the world like a loose garment,* he said laughing, *including your mother. Don't think of it as being forever, just take it 'one day at a time.'*

I hated those words; it was impossible to take anything one day at a time.

The Swami's words went round and round in my head so many times I swear it woke Tom up. It was New Years' morning, and he'd slept over at the room I'd rented.

- What, he said, what is it?

- I can't do this anymore.

- What? What are you talking about? We have the best sex this side of the Mississippi.

- I can't stop thinking, and after you fall asleep I just lie awake and cry.

- I cry too sometimes. What's wrong with that? Tom asked, sitting up. You're sensitive, that's why you're a good actress.

- I'm a lousy actress. Beside, I'll just fuck this up like I did with Josh. I can't let anyone really close to me. I can't bear it.

I was sure Tom would be furious, just as Josh had been. Dark, Josh had called me, dark and depressing.

- Ah come on, Tom said, putting his arm around me. Josh wasn't the right guy for you anyway. It's awkward now, but you'll be fine.

- I don't think I've ever been fine. It's like I'm always waiting behind a door, not sure how to open it, not sure if I am allowed in.

- Everybody feels like that.

- No they don't.

- Still… that's no reason to break up.

- Sorry, I said, sliding far down under the covers.

I kept hoping it was a dream, that I hadn't said anything; that we could make love and it would all go away. But he'd heard me.

- Are you sure? he asked. You don't want to think about it?

I whispered no from under the blankets.

- Should I take my things?

- I… guess so.

He grumbled as he gathered up the articles of clothing, shoes he'd left in the closet.

When I heard his truck pull away, it felt as if everything I'd ever known, loved or wanted was on that truck. I wanted to run after him and take it all back.

I will tie my rubber boots on tightly and trudge through the snow. I will arrive at Tom's house and knock on his door. He will be surprised yet pleased to see me. He will pull me close into his strong thick arms. We will go upstairs to his room, to the mattress on the floor. He will take off my clothes and I will let him, going weak at the knees as he reaches for my breasts. I won't have to think about anything. The passion of wanting him will fill me deeply; my whole world will be him. He will get hard and I will stroke him how he has shown me, rhythmically, so that he jerks his belly in, tightens his thighs. I will get wet and he will feel it. He will enter me deeply; it will hurt, but it will also be good. We will build more and more, like we are building a house, higher and higher. But then it will be over, and the house will fall down. He will sigh with contentment and roll to the side. I will ache with loneliness, wanting more and more, and more. For him to hold me and caress me, to tell me how much he loves me. But even when he does, eventually it will be over. He will fall asleep and I will wonder what is wrong with me that I cannot sleep. I will try to wake him.

- Tom? Tom? I will ask. But he will not hear me.

I didn't go to his house. I just stayed there under the covers. Each time I heard a truck, I thought it might be Tom. But it wasn't. The next day I moved into the ashram. I had to spend most of the day with the Swami; I was shaking so badly, aching for Tom something fierce… like a junkie.

Session Five

I'm having a good day, even slept a little. That alone makes me so happy, so incredibly grateful there's a skip in my step as I head for Ana's. Today it feels good to be here in Buenos Aires. May even try some tango tonight!

Going to Ana has become a sort of ritual. I join the rhythm on the street; the way people walk. Not so fast as in New York, but with a sway and sensuality that's catchy. I'm in no hurry to get well, could stay here forever.

-You're in a good mood, Ana says, when I arrive.

- I feel great today and the sky is such a lovely blue. It reminds me of sky in San Francisco when the fog would lift.

- Did you also live in San Francisco? Ana asks. Weren't you living in, what was it -- Ann Arbor, in the ashram?

- I was, but just for another year.

- Why did you move? Too boring? Ana asks, laughing.

Maybe, especially as everything got easier and easier. The Swami was kind and incredibly patient, helping me sort through the chaos and confusion so my life could unfold more gently. Yet this *gentle unfolding*, I must confess, was not very exciting. Instead of blissfully meditating, my head cluttered with a thousand schemes of what I *should* be doing instead.

The following year, hired as a full-time music teacher in Ann Arbor but still struggling with my voice, I had to find a singing teacher.

A true need leads to a true action, the Swami always said, *and there are no coincidences!* But coincidentally my roommate in the ashram had a boyfriend whose mother was a singing teacher, and a good one too. She introduced me to the Alexander Technique,[*] work I'd heard about earlier in London but was not ready for then.

I shall never forget my first lesson: the way her fingers touched my jaw and head in such a delicate, penetrating way that all at once a voice — surely not mine — burst forth. So unknown, this powerful sensation of 'letting go,' of letting the song sing me. If only I'd had lessons with her years before! But at last I found what I'd been desperately seeking. All my bumbling years suddenly made sense; even if I'd never succeeded in any apparent form, I could help another on the road behind me. This teacher not only taught me how to sing with a freedom I never even knew existed, but took me under her wings and prepared me to become a singing/Alexander teacher like herself. That meant training as soon as possible to learn the Alexander Technique, just as she had done.

Moving to San Francisco wasn't necessary, there were closer training programs, but I was growing restless. It was far more appealing to venture into the unknown and recreate myself again! When a tempting chance came along at a spring folk dance festival in Michigan, I could think of nothing else but moving to California. Everyone was sad to have me leave, but at least I listened when the Swami urged me *not* to move in with the man I'd met dancing, who'd invited me to California and made it very easy to move there, *and* to continue meditating. There was an ashram near San Francisco and I was accepted into the Alexander Training program starting in the fall. The pieces fit so perfectly that in the end the Swami slapped his thigh in amazement.

- You are one heck of a story, he said, laughing.

In San Francisco, the adrenaline rush of change put me in a fabulous mood. I found a cozy place to live, a great job teaching drama at a performing-arts high school with a beautiful commute over the Golden Gate Bridge, went to twelve-step meetings, keeping my weight down like a pro — even imagined the others wondering why someone so *perfect* as me would even need a program.

The first months went fine, without a hitch. The Alexander training was tough, but since we students all had breakdowns, and crying was as

---

[*] The Alexander Technique is a remarkably effective means for changing habitual patterns of tension and improving coordination. It is extremely beneficial for musicians dealing with excessive stress, often due to performance anxiety, and can enhance freedom and power of expression.

common as drinking coffee — the work itself encouraged release — there was no chance to store up my usual volcanic material. In addition, floating on the grace the Swami sent me off with, I landed an amazing job on Saturdays teaching at the best theater school in San Francisco. Everyone commented on my luck, how smoothly everything had fallen into place. But unfortunately this was *the catch*: life working, flowing, scared me to death. No way could I keep it up.

It began as a typical Saturday, but instead of teaching my regular class, we were ushered across the street to the main theater for an open audition. My task was to supervise all the kids to move swiftly onstage with their song, then off again. I hadn't been to an audition since Ann Arbor. Maybe that was the trigger, jealousy: all these rich kids who sang great, with no fear, with parents devoted to their development. Or boredom — the kids were so good they didn't need me at all.

I'll just slip out for a minute; no one will notice. I suddenly feel peckish, just need a little pick-me-up: something small, a tiny piece of chocolate will do. Like in Ireland, they stop by the pub for a *quick one* that lasts until the pub closes. They warn you in the twelve-step program about these insidious slips that begin passively in your thoughts. I had no idea how long I was 'out there.' It's the addict's trick to assume the time actually stops when you go out for a 'fix.' Not true, especially not that day. When I got back the director stood holding the ends of the curtain, like God herself, just where I was meant to be. What cruel universe made her pop in just then and not during the previous hours and hours when I *was* there? She fired me on the spot. No excuses, no more chances.

I can still feel her words like sharp icicles pricking my skin:

- Go. Right now. Your services are no longer needed. I will stay. You shall never teach again at this school, *ever*. Not. With. Anyone. Of. Any. Age.

- But I…

- Go. Now.

Storming out of the theater, ever so dramatically, to seek revenge for every unjust moment that ever was, I headed straight into the worst binge of my life. And — knock on wood — the last. Most binges were shrouded in denial, but this LAST one, with its funny tag, will always be impossible to forget. Had the ending been different who knows if I'd *ever* have stopped! People, including famous ones, have died stuffing food in their mouths.

No longer the sixties, there were still plenty of burnt-out, drug-destroyed hippies left in the infamous Haight-Ashbury. Stuck in time, they spent their days up and down the street begging for money. Ashbury — no longer just 'groovy' shops, but filled with pizzerias, ice cream parlors and fancy eateries — was the chosen site for this most exquisite binge. Zigzagging the street, stuffing all and sundry into my mouth, so many drug-destroyed hippies asked for money — precious money *I* needed — that I nearly went mad. *I was a person besieged, on a mission; get the hell out of my way!* Finally, one ragged fellow asked for the umpteenth time that I took him by the shoulders and shouted:

- I HAVE NO MONEY.

The clincher was his response:

- YOU MIDDLE-CLASS HOUSEWIFE!

Don't ask me why this woke me from the trance. This outrageous comment, so disconnected to anything in my life, except the few months with Josh, startled me so fiercely that I screamed with such rage all the other hippies rushed over to help, offering me *real* drugs. The smell of them so toxic, so disgusting, I started to gag. Crying hysterically, I ran as fast as my wretched body could manage.

I was sick as a dog for days, scared that I'd ruptured my innards. The program taunts you about hitting bottom: unless you're willing to admit complete defeat, the bottom will keep lowering. Truly terrified, I went to meetings like crazy, taking the *disease* even more seriously, terrified of what I could do to myself. Once again, O.A. meetings were my life, family, sustenance. Luckily I still had the high school teaching job and the daily Alexander training — if anything the Alexander work helped dissipate my destructive urges — my days were scrupulously planned with school, teaching, meetings, the ashram and all the walking between. No moment left unscheduled, no time unchecked.

My California *sponsor* was cool and strict, no-nonsense like an army sergeant. By now it was crystal clear that I was sneaky and fickle, resentment my devil and food my drug. I loved being impulsive — who knew what might pop up along the path of life? I called it spontaneity; she called it bullshit. In America, food is everywhere: dressed up in shop windows like crown jewels. It intoxicated me. This sponsor wouldn't even let me go *window-shopping.*

The twelve-step program is built on *twelve steps* that you take whether you're ready or not, because some of us are never ready. If done thoroughly, you are meant to experience a shift of being, a 'Spiritual Awakening,' — leading you to a saner, less destructive and an ultimately happier way of life.

Besides my sojourn at the ashram, I was, like many in the program, furious with God. Yet in my secret self, I couldn't *not* believe in something no matter how hard I'd tried for years to be agnostic, atheistic and anorexic, failing at all three. A sense of humor is always good and you'd hear pretty funny things at meetings, especially concerning the Higher Power. I tried summoning images of ancient trees, redwoods or sequoias, or an old woman with her hair long and flowing like Jesus' beard. I even tried Jesus for a while, but nothing worked, nothing stayed.

It was the punishing idea of God from my childhood that always tripped me up: A God that watched and judged and found me lacking. A God, concerned with big drama like parting seas and plaguing Pharaohs... why should he help some pathetic human not stuff food into her mouth? Surely he had better things to do.

It seemed impossible to conjure this friendly God-like connection, but since my *eating* was okay, I was more than satisfied. My sponsor was not. She was adamant about finding this Higher Power — like a mean mother who forces her child to keep looking for a pair of socks that just are not there. The idea was to find these *socks* and keep them on as you walked the remaining *steps* over and over for the rest of your life. Without this higher power connection, a true spiritual awakening and permanent shift of being could never happen. But I couldn't find those damn socks.

It was in the middle of a holiday week, a beautiful blue-sky day; I was totally free, no private students and no Alexander classes. All that unscheduled time used to kill me. My plan was to spend the afternoon walking and *singing* in Golden Gate Park — I was writing songs again and found inspiration on the isolated trails.

The area of dense palm trees was my favorite. Usually empty and the acoustics were great. I was deep into a mystical trance of singing when out of nowhere a very old man slammed into me. Truly bizarre, there hadn't been a person anywhere. This man said not a word, no: *Oh pardon me,* or *Gee, I'm sorry,* he just stood there grinning, almost thanking me for rescuing him from some invisible force.

- Are you all right? I asked.

- No, he said, tears falling down his face.

- What's wrong?

- I don't know. Where am I?

And then, switching on his brain from confusion to sanity he looked very sensibly at his watch and said:

- Oh my God, it's really late. My daughter's going to have a fit. Do you know the way back to 16th?

San Francisco is basically a grid, but you have to know if it's a street or avenue and on which side of the park. When I asked these specifics, he went all funny again. He opened his wallet, letting items fly into the breeze.

- Wait, I yelped, catching loose bills and receipts.

I quickly found an address. It was an avenue. But I still needed to know on which side of the park and when I asked this, he waved his arms towards the Richmond district.

- Do you want to go home? I asked, assuming he'd just gotten lost.

- Home? Home? he asked, bewildered. You can take me home? It's such a long way from here.

- It's not far. I'll drive you.

- You cannot get there by car.

His Italian name, his accent... did he mean...? Or...? The way the breeze suddenly stopped, the way he looked through me with a profound presence... from the deeper world that has no form; just feeling. And all at once I became feeling and love and knowingness. *Oh my God,* I thought, *this is it, my spiritual awakening. Pay attention! Don't miss a moment.* But I was already disappointed. *Was this it? Nothing grander?*

The intensity was broken: there stood before me, beyond doubt, just an old confused man whose wallet I was holding. *At least be a Good Samaritan and drive the poor man home.* I took his hand and led him to a bench along the main path. Amazing how light he was; so easy to lead.

- Sit here, and don't move. I'll be right back, I said and tucked his wallet deep into his pocket.

- Oh thank you, thank you!

- Just wait here, I said.

And there it was again: the glow in his eyes, the hum of vibration. But this time the message came louder:

Good girl. You're awake and listening. Soon you will no longer feel lonely or afraid, or need anything to fill the empty void... for there will no longer be an empty void. Trust me. But first bring this man home.

I ran to get my car, fearing the man would've wandered off. But he was still there, just where I'd left him. So happy to see me, he leaped up with the energy of a three year old. When we pulled up to his address, he smiled with recognition.

-Yes! This is it! This is my house!

New tears rolled down his cheeks as he reached for his wallet to pay me.

- No, I said. I don't want any money.

The little show was over and he clicked his brain back on:

- Thank you very much, he said. You are so kind. I wish for you everything, everything you ever hope for.

When I came back, it was nearly two P.M. The sun was still bright, the air warm. No sign of the usual afternoon fog. I took the phone outside and called my sponsor.

- Can I talk to you? I asked.

- What is it?

- I had it.

- What? she asked, in a don't-waste-my-time voice.

- You know the... umm... the spiritual thing. But I'm... not entirely sure.

- Either you had it or you didn't.

- Well that's why I'm calling... How do you know for sure? Isn't it easy to imagine the whole thing because you want it so badly?

- Time will tell, she said. How's your food?

- Fine, I said, I am not hungry at all.

- Well you'd better eat lunch, and then she hung up.

After that day in Golden Gate Park, there definitely was a shift and a kindling into the notion of connection. Plus, after the last binge on Ashbury, I was more stubborn than ever to get well. Those words I thought I'd heard, about *not needing anything to fill the empty void, for there'd no longer be an empty void,* those words stayed with me. The choice was actually simple: either fill the void immediately and block the chance of a higher connection — which I'd always done because I was powerless to not grab, like a drowning person, the thing that would save me or at least numb the terrible feeling — or hang in there and endure the horribly awkward, nerve-crackling seconds, or minutes, or sometimes even hours distracting the 'king-baby' by a meeting, a phone-call, breathing, praying, jumping up and down and whistling Dixie, anything but reaching for your drug... until the obsessive need finally passed! And it would, that was the miracle after that day in the park, it really would pass. I wouldn't die from it... if only I had the courage to wait!

The war of resistance that I'd need daily to battle was going to take everything, everything I was still hopeless at — discipline, diligence and patience. But at least I was making a start with the Alexander work and the 12-step program, and the therapy I was nearly always doing. My God, did I need help to get through a day.

We'd all laugh at one of Mr. Alexander's quotes: *how the hardest thing about changing is that you really have to change.*

Or like the joke:

How many therapists does it take to change a light bulb?

Only one — but the light bulb has to really want to change.

*

I was so grateful to have 'recovered' from the food thing but why wasn't it enough? Why did I soon start panicking on the highway, or in the middle of a bridge? It got so bad, I could hardly drive on my own through a tunnel... would pull over on the side of the road and cry hysterically.

- It's all the same core. Ana says. The little girl in you just wanted to feel safe and be loved...

- But she still wasn't...why, why was that? My childhood wasn't that bad? God Ana, I see the children here, on the subte, on the streets picking through the garbage. They have horrible childhoods...

Why always this undertow of anxiety? It would attack at the most unlikely times. Suddenly, with friends, or in the middle of a totally mundane activity I'd need to rush out for air, or I'd wake in the night sweating with terror for no apparent reason. It was exhausting to never know what triggered these monstrous feelings especially when things were going so well. What to do? Keep constant vigil? Seal the box of my hidden desires, my creativity forever? Even with rigid control, a storm might brew outside my radar and I was powerless to prevent it. The key was to not aim too high, not be overly ambitious. And this recipe worked for a long time… and everything was so fine…

I'd finished my Alexander training, had tons of students and moved to a larger apartment so near the ocean you could hear the waves crashing while lying in bed. My students loved the place: the air was good and clean and hearing the ocean gave a profound sense of space. I really loved teaching, enjoyed a life without overeating, wearing the same size clothing day after day and I felt, at least consciously, totally satisfied. I'd wake with a sense of wonder, of what might happen, of who may call.

One bright morning the phone rang and it was a new student referred to me by the teacher in Ann Arbor. His name was Steven. He had recently moved to Berkeley, from Michigan, had his own recording studio in the basement of his house and was looking for an Alexander/singing teacher. In those days, I was the only one offering this combination, so he was delighted to find me. Steven was thin, about my height, with piercing black eyes, was highly neurotic just like me and we instantly became friends. Once, at the end of a lesson I'd mentioned writing songs and my long buried dream of singing, of recording. So we agreed to exchange recording for lessons. The Ashram was so near Steven's studio that before or after a recording session, I'd stop by to meditate.

A few months later I attended a meditation weekend at the ashram. The main *guru* had arrived from India to lead us. She was so pretty, her skin a lovely shade of brown and her eyes bursting with life, it was impossible not to feel 'enlightened' in her presence.

At the end of the weekend we were invited to come up and get a gift. Whatever she handed you was supposedly rich with significance, even if it took ages to comprehend the *intention* behind the gift. When at last it was my turn, and was handed a cheap five-and-dime pin of three monkeys: *hearing, seeing* and *speaking* no evil, I nearly cried out with disappointment. Later, when I complained of this, my friends laughed at me, saying: *the guru didn't work like that, but appearances were always deceiving. Wait, and do not give in to the obvious, and you will be very surprised.*

About a week later, at the community center where I swam, the director, who saw me leaving with my guitar, asked if by chance I sang for kids. They urgently needed a new music teacher. I said yes. And that job led to another job singing at birthday parties, where the child would pick a theme and I'd write songs accordingly. I had never tried writing children songs before — it was pulling rabbits from the hat, it came so easily. The children loved the inventive way I drummed on my chest, played the guitar and the kazoo. Suddenly it struck me to record these playful children's songs in the studio with Steven. After hours of meditating on the significance of the three monkeys pin, it hit me that it was not the obvious *Hear, See and Speak* no evil, but rather I was meant to sing and record the three monkeys *song*!

When we listened in the control booth Steven was so delighted he immediately contacted enough musicians to make a real recording — for kids. Before leaving that night, I pulled the monkey pin out of my pocket and said: *I know this is bullshit but maybe, just maybe, it will bring me luck.*

Once under way the recording rolled along so smoothly that it took some getting used to. I was almost relieved one morning when the bass player didn't show: *now this is more like it.*

- Funny, Steven said, as we waited in the studio. I'm sure I saw his truck out front. Where can he be?

We went outside to start looking, and just then Steven noticed his front door open.

- Go in, Steven said. He's terrible with food... he knew my mother came last night with leftovers and he loves her cooking. I'll get the mikes ready... just bring him down.

And there he was, this bear of a man. Overeating is so private, nothing like drinking at the bar with your mates. Aside from my father, I'd rarely seen another compulsive overeater in *action*. It felt intrusive, intimate to walk in and nudge him gently on the shoulder. I knew he'd lost all track of time. Disgusting to see the mix he had consumed: green Jell-O with little square marshmallows, a pile of chicken bones, a burnt noodle pudding, and a plate of crumbs that must have been a chocolate cake. Probably more, as Steven ate very little and each dish was probably full.

- Can you still play? I asked, thinking how I felt after a binge.

- Oh sure, he said. And just like that, with a bite or two more, he brushed himself off and back to the studio we went.

After completing this recording entitled *Three Monkeys*, which sold surprisingly well, we had a lot of concerts. Just seeing him binge had made the bass player *safe* for me, one person not to worry about impressing, and we played great together, joking on stage in such a relaxed way that thrilled the kids. What a pity that his main band got famous so he was no longer available for my gigs.

Yet a *flow* had started, so even with the bass player gone other musicians quickly appeared. Amongst them was a fabulous guitar player who encouraged me further. He took me to open *mics* to do the most terrifying — to play my own songs for my peers. It scared me to death to sing for an audience other than children. Yet being in a room with everyone just as scared, gave courage. After a few weeks, I — who loathed competition — was chosen out of the heap for the 'best of the open-mic' series and from that to the 'best of the best' and from *that*, to my own night: a whole show with just me, a percussionist and the fabulous guitar player.

And then, busy with all this, the earthquake came: The *Loma Prieta earthquake* — the largest in San Francisco since 1906 — the *World Series Quake*, that struck just as the third game of the 1989 World Series was about to begin.

At exactly 5:04 P.M. — while most of San Francisco was already watching the game — I was with the photographer, who had recently taken my headshots, deciding which was best for my press kit. I remember admiring my beautiful face when a violent *shove* knocked out the lights and threw us on the ground. I will also never forget the next fifteen seconds. Funny how fast time usually goes, yet those fifteen seconds went slow as molasses: like the building was a ship on the high seas in a terrible storm, in total darkness getting beaten by one huge wave after another. Before realizing it was an earthquake, I actually imagined being *hit*, punished as it were, for admiring my own reflection, for thinking how *good* I looked in the photos. When it became apparent it was a genuine and long lasting earthquake, it was really scary; nothing compares with the power of the Earth slamming into itself.

That I survived was great, yet the months following would prove even more challenging. You rarely hear about this aspect of a serious earthquake, how people cancel all activities except the most urgent. If

not for sales of the Three Monkeys, and the recording made directly following of my 'grown-up' songs, I'd have starved. Now, it was not just
the fantasy of being a recording artist, but the urgent need of income
that inspired me, with the help of the fabulous guitarist who had a long
list of booking agents to send out my recording to the world at large.

When I got a response — an offer to play in Holland, Wales, Scotland
and Norway — I couldn't stop jumping up and down for at least a week.
Not ready to go out on my own, but desperate for money, I left for my
first international tour.

Session Six

I started my 'singing tour' in Holland, that summer of 1990. Such a different world! No earthquake, no Oliver North trials, no former President Reagan and no George Bush. Life seemed as good as it gets; it was June, hot — a *hot* that rarely happened in San Francisco especially not at night, so balmy that everyone sat outside eating and drinking and talking, and half of those people wanted to buy me a drink. It seemed the whole town of Nijmegen had heard me sing. And they, in their Dutch style of poking fun instead of saying straight out that you were good, thought it *impressive* how someone so small as me could stand alone with a guitar and make *real* music. Honest, they called it and powerful, especially from someone so short. For Holland is the land of giants; no place could you find so many tall people!

Despite terrible jitters, once the shows started my energy and voice poured right out. It was thrilling at the end to hear the passionate applause of the audience, and the asking for more. People lined up to buy recordings, even some asked for my autograph. On my last night a few musicians asked if I'd like to return in August to do concerts with *them*. YES, of course I would! Those first successful nights helped alleviate some of the trepidation for the tour ahead, but alas, not enough.

Next, I was booked to play at two folk festivals in Wales. The weather continued to be great: sunny, no rain. Singing through a humungous sound system to thousands of people was like performing to the heavens. I was nervous, but it went fine. Next came the smaller venues, folk clubs, where you could see everyone's face as they listened; *that* was scary. The hardest concert of all was in a folk club near Cardiff. The agent had warned me of the great singing tradition in Wales, of how tough the audience could be. By the time we arrived the place was packed with, so I imagined, fabulous singers; I truly panicked. All at once I regressed to the nine-year-old girl in her 'Girl Scout' uniform who had peed in front of her whole class. My name was announced... I made it to the stage... I reached for the microphone. No sound came out, nothing, my knees wobbled, my mouth dry and my throat clenched. The audience, and what I'd imagined them thinking, had paralyzed me.

Standing there adjusting my capo, pretending that any moment a song would start, I finally looked at them with full recognition of my plight. In an instance of grace I remembered that in Wales, as in England and Ireland, they loved country music. Awakening my best acting skills, and with a southern twang my voice sprang out loud and clear:

- You're scaring me to death! I know *yah'all* sing great, much better than me... but help me now, come on get me going.

I chose a rather known Nanci Griffith tune, and just like that one hundred and ten people stopped holding their breath, laughed as one and started singing along: *Rita was sixteen years, hazel eyes and nut-brown hair* ... They sang the whole song through and by the end I'd found my voice. Not all of it, but enough. I was crying a little, and some of them were crying too, and even when I did my own songs, which was most of the program, they kept right on singing.

From there I traveled to England, Scotland, Norway and Germany. Everyone treated me great, like a celebrity. Just flying in from the US was enough to draw crowds. And the fact that my looks were slightly ethnic, dark enough to be exotic then, and my nervousness made me funny in a Woody Allen sort of way, the audiences found me charming. All so much more comfortable than I'd thought, than I'd feared, that at last it seemed that I'd found my way. When I returned to Holland, now booked to play with other musicians, it was like being in heaven!

It was nearly tropical *again*, when I arrived, that people actually thanked me for making it so, as if I'd carried the California sun in my suitcase — the normal Dutch weather can be quite dreadful. From all the nervousness of performing regularly, I'd lost so much weight that my collarbones were sticking out, my features more prominent and my clothes hung nice and loosely. So many people from earlier in the summer came to hear me again, and I really felt like a star! I was invited to dinners and parties and had a sense of homecoming. One of these new friends, who came to hear me sing many times and was very encouraging in setting up even more gigs was Wil. He lived alone in a big house and offered me a room to sleep and another for practicing. That made it easy to come back to Holland again and again. And — we stayed just friends, really and truly just friends!

After that first tour and the ones that followed, I went back and forth between Europe and San Francisco, resuming as much of my life in California that still waited for me there. But when you travel away, nothing really waits for you, especially not in America. Each time returning, I'd feel less able to keep up and found myself longing more and more to get back to Europe.

Once again in Steven's studio, in California, I'd made another (my third) recording and had sent out packages to other parts of the States and more countries. My next tours included the US, Belgium, Switzerland, Great Britain, Scandinavia and naturally Holland. The times in San Francisco continued to be difficult after the earthquake and being so much away made it harder to keep my remaining students, so I finally had to move from my lovely apartment near the ocean. I became a real musician, constantly on the road.

During these *gypsy* years I stayed with friends in London and in Germany, but my real sense of a home was Wil's house in Nijmegen. In addition to our friendship, there was something special about Nijmegen, a university town that I really liked — the intimacy, the beautiful old houses and town square, the location along the river Rhine with all the barges coming and going and the atmosphere of tolerance. The Dutch really seemed refreshingly less materialistic than Americans, not thinking that bigger or *famous* was necessarily better. Perhaps not speaking Dutch helped create this illusion, but it really was perfect for me: small, friendly, one charming village after the next, the authentic café life, how accessible everything was by bicycle and train — such a welcome change after all the driving in the United States — and how much easier it was to be *special*, at least then.

Wonderful and exciting, all the music, the different countries and the people to meet, I was finally living the life I'd always dreamt of. Yet with all the flying between countries my fear of flying really kicked in; I thought then, that must be the cause of an ever-worsening undertow of anxiety.

- *Is that when you started taking the pills to help you fly? Ana asks.*

- *Not yet, but soon. My flights were getting worse and worse, and eventually I couldn't stand it anymore.*

Funny, how ever since coming to Holland I've used the idea of being on the David Letterman show as a marker of my nervousness. Hearing David's voice welcoming me... I can tell immediately how I am doing. And that got started because of Karen, who introduced me, besides to the David Letterman thing, to the fear-of-flying pills — to *Xanax*.

I first met Karen at a New Year's Eve party in Nijmegen. Her clipped New England words, her cropped blond hair, her perfectly trimmed pants should have warned me, yet I saw the best of her that night and found her charming. It was language deprivation that most seduced me; I ached for her fluency. Meeting not just another American, but someone highly intelligent like Karen, who could banter away at the speed of light, was irresistible. And Karen was the perfect match for me. Besides flirting, and dancing, it is talking up a storm that I most love. We had so much to tell each other, I swear we could have been shipwrecked and not even noticed, we didn't stop until three in the morning.

Karen was also a traveler, but she, I later found out, lived her own *myth* even more thoroughly than I ever could live mine. In order to become fast friends, especially short term, there must be at least one strong factor in common. We soon discovered that we shared a dreadful fear of flying! Boy did we talk that up, especially when neither of us had a flight coming up. I had funnier stories — some I'd started sharing with my concert audiences, discovering my hidden talent as a comedian and a way of managing the panic — but Karen had stronger theories. I was actually surprised that she was afraid; she managed everything else so well.

When you tell people of your fear, they assume you are afraid of crashing, and maybe the flight to Acapulco as a teenager did have a lasting effect: knowing full well what *can* happen in the sky. All well before today's preoccupation with terrorism, it was more about where I was heading and what was expected of me that made me petrified to get on a plane. Not surprising that during my singing tours the fear became most unmanageable.

Perhaps the most incredible incident was on board a British Airways flight, heading for London from San Francisco. Usually upon entering the plane I'd seek the kindest of the flight attendants, mention my fear and ask if they'd come to check on me. *Just to make sure you're breathing?* On this specific flight, it was a youngish man with a heavy Welsh accent who came to my aid. Just after he finished the safety instructions, he rushed to my aisle seat, knelt beside me and took my hand in his so tenderly and asked if I was okay.

- No, I said, I have it bad today.

As with all things, phobias have their better and worse days. And before he had a chance to respond, the girl sitting beside me leaned forward and blurted out *her* fear, and before he could say anything kindly to *her*, the woman sitting by the window reached over, with a tear splashing onto my thigh, also confessed hers.

- Let's all hold hands! the kind flight attendant instructed.

And so we did, with me still holding his. Just then the captain's voice came on: *Flight attendants please take your seats.* He didn't move.

- Shouldn't you go to your seat? I said in another form of panic.

- No dear, I am fine here. It is a good day for flying. There will be no turbulence, not to worry, love.

It felt like a prayer meeting. We, the three frightened ladies, all looked at each other in such a state of wonder that somehow we were up and airborne and hardly felt a thing. He stayed there kneeling beside me until the first ping was heard — when the crew starts handing out little bags of peanuts. Like a jackrabbit he popped up.

- I'll be back soon, love, promise.

I am not sure I would have struck up a conversation with these women, but as we all had the *fear* we were suddenly related and had lots to talk of. A true phobic person does not like to discuss the phobia while in its grip, so we talked about everything else. I learned every detail about these women, especially the one by the window, whose fear made her garrulous. I'm usually quiet, at least for the first half hour when the symptoms are strongest.

He was right, the charming flight attendant, it was a smooth take-off, good weather, no bad pockets of air. We floated up light as a feather and very soon reached cruising altitude. That of course is bliss for fear-of-flying people. Once cruising, you can almost forget that you're on a plane. By the time our friendly flight attendant returned, I was already much better, but clearly he had a mission. He knelt once more on his knees, took my hand and whispered:

- I knew it!

- You knew what? I asked, also in a whisper.

- I prayed for you and Jesus has taken you into his fold. You have changed! You have completely changed. Look at her! he said, leaning over so that the other two fear-of-flying ladies could hear, can't you see how she's changed, her face has opened. She has received the Lord!

- Well I...

- No need to thank me, he said. You were ready.

It was all I could do to keep myself from shouting 'Praise the Lord!' Luckily, someone else had rung the bell for assistance and he had to go.

Karen didn't like these kind of stories. She never held anyone's hand, never had to; she took medication.

One hour before departure you take a half, Karen advised, *once on board another half, or a whole, depending on how you feel. Once the flight is under-way, you decide whether you are OK. If not, you pop one more half. It doesn't put you to sleep, just takes the edge off.*

Despite Karen's theories, I was still not convinced. On one of my next trips, with the flight attendants too busy to appease my fear, I had it very bad. Barely able to get on the plane, I prayed for a kind seatmate, when a young girl came to the seat beside me. She recognized the look on my face, the look that screamed HELP and turned immediately to an overweight woman in the next row and shouted:

- Mom, we have to change seats! And then, like a receptionist in a therapeutic office, she said to me: My mother will be able to handle you much better than I. You'll be happy to sit next to her.

Her mother, it turned out, was a professor who specialized in phobi-as. It was embarrassing for me how her daughter reacted, but she was right, her mother was great. Despite Karen's theories, I was afraid to take medication; it seemed the wrong road to go down. However, when this professor, with her impressive diagrams and hypnotic way of speaking insisted that medication was the way to go, all meshing with what I'd already heard from Karen, it suddenly seemed without doubt like the best option.

- The artistic brain, the professor explained, is wired differently. You are a sensitive artist, a songwriter, therefore the right side of your brain is enlarged. We *should* be afraid of flying, so your reaction is more nor-mal than the people who find it perfectly okay to fly. Of course most people, who are not phobic, process it sensibly as a means of travel. In a way you are doing that, just to a lesser degree, because you are after all on this plane. You could be much worse! Some people have it so badly they can't even go to an airport. But you'll find it so much more pleasant, even enjoyable, with medication.

- Isn't there a risk of getting addicted? That's what's always stopped me.

- Oh no! she insisted. It's better, in fact, to *take* medication for it helps set up another experience in your brain. With *Xanax*, for instance, you moderate the uncomfortable effect of your animal nature, the part that recognizes what is abnormal and against the human instinct. We, being *animals*, want our two feet on the ground. We react harshly, with anxiety symptoms, as a warning if we're suddenly exposed to danger, like a lion leaping out of the woods, or if a situation *seems* frightening — like a plane lifting off the ground! It is the way our system warns us to take care or some action to prevent further harm, a warning to remove yourself from the dangerous stimulus.

- I guess that's why, I confessed to her, just at the peak of acceleration, I want to call the captain to stop and let me off!

- Right, she said, that's it. With medication you won't feel that. Not to mention the harm this type of stress does to your whole system. It is important to avoid *this* stress at all costs.

I was convinced.

When next I saw Karen and told her all this she only nodded and said: *I told you, I've done enormous research. But okay, you had to hear it from a professor, but now you believe me.* So I started taking the pills just as Karen and the woman on the plane advised and the take off *was* much easier. No longer anxious days before a flight. The sad thing was, with both of us taking *Xanax*, we had less and less to talk about. Maybe the *Xanax* made it harder to know each other. Anyhow, Karen lived with such a degree of secrecy that it took me time to know that I did not ever know her at all.

Way before cell phones and e-mail, you really had to make an effort to stay in touch. I'd return between tours, leave messages, and when I didn't hear back just assumed she was okay, was just busy like me. Then she vanished altogether, some say to Amsterdam, others back to the States. She left no forwarding address, no way to find her. But she had apparently followed up on one thing she'd offered to do during our last meeting: to give my newest CD — one I'd recorded in Holland — to her mother, who lived across the street from David Letterman.

Session Seven

- Did you ever meet David Letterman?
- No, but can I tell you something else first, something incredible that...
- About a man? Ana asks, with that smile of hers.
- Why do you assume that?
- Because I'm beginning to know you.
- You meet a lot of people when you play music.
- I'm sure you do!

It was hot when I'd returned to Holland in June of 1993, the year before meeting Karen. So hot, you wanted to strip off your clothes and jump into anything cool, even a muddy Dutch pond. I was touring with the percussionist I'd met the first summer and a clarinet player named Jan. The gig, on this fateful hot and steamy night when I met Bouke, was in Den Bosch.

We had driven to the gig with the windows wide open — no air-conditioning in those days; the feel of summer infectious. The car was so loaded with extra gear that I had to keep my guitar between my legs and my knee kept hitting Jan's at every turn. After a short time, he gently put his hand on my thigh to steady it and kept it there for the rest of the trip. He'd never done that before and even if it made me uncomfortable, I couldn't blame *that* for making me more nervous than usual.

Setting up on stage, I kept dropping things, plugged cables in wrong, even knocked over my guitar. Finally the percussionist, who was always more cool than both Jan and myself, grabbed hold of my hands and asked:
- What's with you tonight? You're so jumpy!
- I don't know... there's so many people waiting outside... I don't want to mess up.
- Don't think about that! You can sing, you talk to the people and get

them to laugh, you write great songs and you're even nice to look at, so why are you afraid? There's nothing to be afraid of.

- It's a bad habit, I said.

- You're a rabbit!

- No... I laughed nervously... it's a *habit*, a bad habit.

- I still think that you're a rabbit, he said. The thing is, he continued, I am not the best drummer in the world and many people can find fault with my playing, but when the audience comes to see our show, it is *me* up there, not *them*, and that means a lot. There are many drummers far better, but I am the only drummer they get, so I play and have fun and there is nothing to worry about. So quit being a rabbit.

- Okay.

If only it was that simple, but I was so used to being a *rabbit*; I didn't know how to stop. Didn't think I ever could — until Bouke's eyes found me, sometime in the second set, then everything shifted. So close he sat, and he listened with such adoring intensity that he became Tony in *West Side Story* and I, his Maria. What energy he poured over me! His face open and gorgeous like he'd searched far and wide his whole life for someone like me. And there I stood, at long last, singing my heart out just for him, only him. He grabbed hold of me and refused to let go, and by the end of the show I wanted to stay glued to him forever. So strong I felt, so grand, soaring high in the sky, no longer a rabbit but an eagle that I could barely fit into the car for the drive home.

Now living rather permanently at Wil's house, where in addition to the little room to sleep in and the attic for practice, Wil let me use his office to organize gigs and contracts. In turn, I respected his rhythm and never interfered with his work... or his sleep, well not until that night.

It was nearly three in the morning when I returned from the gig in Den Bosch and the phone was ringing itself off the hook. Wil usually turned off the ringer at night, but had apparently forgotten.

It was Bouke, and he was on fire.

- I fell in love with you, he said. I told my friends there was something incredible about you... that I want to leave everything and go on tour with you. You said you didn't do a good show but I felt your openness and that's so special. When you drove away, I went crazy. I miss you so much already. Can I see you tomorrow?

- Don't you have work? I asked.

- I'll cancel my lessons. I have to see you. I'll meet you at the station.

- Will you recognize me? Cause I don't wear make-up except when I'm performing.

- Do you wear make-up on your inside?

- No, I laughed.

- Then I'll find you from your inside.

My friend Wil was a bad sleeper, so it wasn't surprising that he asked the next morning who had phoned — no one dared phone *him* that late. He'd heard me talking until the wee hours for which I apologized at least a zillion times. Luckily, he was more curious than angry.

- What happened to you? he asked, for I'd lost five kilos overnight and my eyes bulged like Bette Davis'.

- I crashed into a major wall of the universe.

- What? he asked. (Wil's English was good, but not that good.)

- I met somebody last night at the gig…

- Is he the one who phoned so late? That was fast.

- This has never happened to me before.

Wil's eyes rolled straight at me, and his eyebrows arched high: *You, the biggest flirt in the world, this happens to you all the time.*

- No really, I insisted, not like this.

- You're gonna meet a lot of people when you play, you can't…

But I was no longer listening, no longer capable of a conversation. The feeling had taken over, that weak-in-the-belly sensation. I swam through a sea of Bouke: his voice, deep and round as he said his name over and over so I could get it right (Bowkuh); his gray-blue eyes, small and almond shaped that I couldn't stop looking into, and his legs brushing against mine and the charge up my whole body again and again as I cleared my things from the stage; his long, sexy legs everywhere… and later in the back — when the guys were clearing the equipment — the way his fingers slid through his straight brown hair, sweeping it off his forehead and his hairless chest that I touched as he grabbed and kissed me. So tall, he was two men wrapping around me, but soft and sensual and so amazingly safe that I could have spent the rest of my life leaning against him, kissing.

If they'd phoned just then and told me David Letterman was ready to have me on his show, my reply would have been: *I'm so sorry, please tell Mr. Letterman that I am busy and will contact him when I am free.*

It was Jan, the clarinet player, who interrupted us backstage. The guys were ready to leave. He looked at me as if I'd sinned.

- What the hell are you doing? Jan asked. He grabbed my arm and pulled me away. He said something in Dutch to Bouke, and Bouke said something back.

- O.K. Jan said, his voice tense. And you! he shouted to me. If you are not at the car in two minutes, we're leaving without you.

- Is that your boyfriend? Bouke asked, laughing, after Jan ran out.

- No!

- Give me your number, quick, he said (we couldn't stop kissing), and then you'd better go. I think your *boyfriend* is going to kill you.

- Deborah? Wil called out. Hello? Deborah, are you there?

- I don't know, I said, landing back into the present.

- You keep looking at your watch.

- I do?

- I have to leave now for a meeting at school, Wil said. I'll be back about eight. Shall we make dinner together?

- I don't know. I... don't think I can eat.

- You are going to see him today?

- Yeah.

- Then I'll stay with my colleagues for dinner, but... you have to eat. Make sure you eat something...

- I will, I said, I promise.

Then Wil took me by the hand and led me into the living room.

- Sit down, he said. I just bought this CD of 'Thelonius Monster' you have to hear this song 'Adios Lounge.' Especially the part where Tom Waits sings, it's incredible.

After Wil left I played it over and over. The song referred to exactly what Bouke had said on the phone about my singing. How I was almost great but wasn't because I was holding something back...

- *What is that?* Bouke asked me. *You've got to find that thing that stops you. No one wants a safe musician.*

And the song that Wil made me listen to, could've been the sound track for my life at that moment. First Thelonius Monster singing:

Now I lie here alone in my bed,

With his words running wild in my head, he said:

Then came Tom Waits and I lost it completely — the power of feeling in his voice made me choke. Not since the emotional memory at the Lee Strasberg school had I cracked open that fast and that much. The chorus came around again and again like a whip, with all the brokenness, the truth in Tom Waits' voice…

> DON'T LET NOBODY GO THERE FOR YOU
> DON'T BE SATISFIED WITH A SECOND HAND LIFE
> DON'T LET NOBODY LIVE YOUR LIFE FOR YOU
> NOT YOUR FRIENDS, NOT YOUR KIDS, NO NOT
> EVEN YOUR WIFE
> IF YOU WANT TO KNOW WHERE THE RAINBOW ENDS
> IT'S YOU GOT TO GO THERE AND FIND IT MY FRIEND.

Over and over I played that part, crying so hard that I scared myself, thinking a person could literally drown in her own tears. My eyes were so bad that I had to put cucumber slices on the lids to bring the swelling down enough to open them, enough to see on my bike as I rode to the station. But then I started crying all over again as I thought of Bouke's words on the telephone.

- *I have to warn you,* he'd said right before we'd hung up, *I have trouble with relationships. Well mostly because of the music. It means everything to me, my music… But sometimes it's not enough, sometimes it makes more confusion and it can be so lonely. Sometimes you just want to meet someone who understands it all without having to explain it.*

Me, me! I wanted to shout out, you have just met me. I understand all of it!

He had called me again during the day, when Wil was out.

- Everything you feel, Bouke said, I feel too; everything you fear I fear too. And when you go back to America I will go crazy, just crazy. Sure I am afraid of this.

- So maybe I won't go back to America, maybe I'll stay here. I'm getting enough work.

- We can't control this, he said.

I wasn't sure if he was glad or not. He just kept asking about my feelings…

What are my feelings? You want to know my feelings? They get me in trouble these damn feelings — they are like juvenile delinquents.

And all the way to the station I feared he wouldn't show up, that I'd said too much, that I hadn't really listened to his words; that I'd dreamt it all. But there he was! Like the actor Sam Shepherd: tall and strangely handsome, odd, even a bit ugly, and yet so sexy.

- Hi Sam, I called out as he stepped off the train.

- Hi! He said long and slow, with a big smile. I think he liked me calling him Sam.

It was the fault of the song repeating in my head almost directing my movements that made me jump Bouke's bones. I'd never taken anyone home to Wil's house before, not even the musicians, and I felt totally out of control.

My hand trembled, opening Wil's door slowly making sure he was out. Bouke and I kept banging into each other like we had magnets in our pockets, and because we stopped every second to kiss it took forever to get up the three flights of stairs to my attic room. He wanted me to sing, really sing for him, to express, to communicate from every cell in my body. After I poured my heart out, trying to be intense like Tom Waits, he reached over and kissed me. It was our first moment alone since we'd met just the night before — a thousand years ago — and I lunged on top of him. Me, always hesitating, always doubting, I ripped off his clothes like in the movies. I grabbed him everywhere and did not think a single thought, because I no longer had a head.

All those sensible talks before sex, like who's been with whom: *Are you safe? Are you healthy?* None of that mattered because it wasn't *me* pressing into Bouke, wasn't *me* not asking him a thing; wasn't *me* not caring that *he* didn't ask either. It all was so big, so huge, so much larger than life that it transcended all rules. And besides if it was me that this amazing passion raged through, I didn't care if I died the next day for the world had ceased to exist. No longer alone, I became a giant. A powerful giant that made love to *him* and he loved it!

And when he left, his smell, the musk scent he used, filled the room, the carpet, *my* clothes — all that touching, feeling, kissing, so much kissing, my mouth was sore.

When Wil came home, he asked how it went. I couldn't speak, couldn't form sentences.

- Enjoy it while it lasts, Wil said. It never does. I'm going to bed and shutting the ringer!

It scared me, this passion. I couldn't sleep, couldn't eat, I lost so much weight that even my skinny clothes were falling off. Every night Bouke and I spoke for hours. I used the feelings, the *Bouke feelings*, and the gigs went better and my singing got stronger. I could tell by the audience's reaction; by the number of CD's I sold. But it was too much, all that power, containing it, owning it; so I gave it back to him. But he didn't want it. Nobody does. And I couldn't stop myself from turning back into the lost, sweet little *rabbit* girl, the one who holds most of it in, the one who needs someone to save her. Addicted as ever, I didn't turn my life and my will over to a Higher Power... I gave it to Bouke. I made him re-sponsible... to *do* me, to *be* me.

No way could I remain the charming mysterious girl he'd seen on stage, the one he'd fallen in love with. And even as we talked and talked and did all what true-lovers do, he refused to have a real relationship so our love hung in the air like a branch without a tree. But he also refused to let me go.

- Of course I want to kidnap you. What do you think? But it will nev-er work, you must go back to America, face yourself and decide your life.

- But I don't want to go home. It's too big in America. I get lost there, forever on highways and dingy motel rooms.

- But America is *great*. Everyone wants to play in America.

- You don't even drive Bouke, how can you know what it's like? The songs make it romantic, but it isn't. It's lonely, really lonely. And besides, I sing so much better not near my family.

- Why does your family mess you up? You've got to be free of your family.

- I know, I said. That's why I'm here!

- No, that's cheating. You're not free; you're just further away. You got to stop running away.

- Can't a person also run towards something?

I had this book with me from America — John Bradshaw's 'Healing the Shame that Binds You,' but had never read it. Then suddenly in the middle of practicing it fell off the shelf. Really. So I picked it up and read where it had opened. It was all about the irony of making your life topsy-turvy in order to do an activity but having so much shame that you destroy the activity. *If you are going to do something,* Bradshaw wrote, *you might as well do it...*

'We humans are essentially limited. The unlimited power that many gurus offer us is false hope. Grave problems result from refusing to accept our limits. There is a joke about a man 'who gets on his horse and rides in all directions.' Without boundaries we have no limits and easily get confused. We lose our way and become addicted because we don't know when to stop. Healthy shame grounds us. It is the emotional energy that says we are not God; that we have made and will make mistakes.'

That's it!! I must stop my life... get off the horse... NO MORE BOUKE!

I flipped randomly to another page: 'In order to be healed we must come out of isolation and hiding, and this means finding people we can trust. The only way out of toxic shame is to embrace the shame; we must come out of hiding.'

So... I need MORE BOUKE! That's why I met him, to come out hiding. He is my mirror! He wants to see ME.

Except he hadn't called in a few days and I was going mad. The weather was still so hot, so I stopped practicing (and watching the phone) and went for a swim.

The water was good and comforting and the swimming helped... until the obsession started again. One lap I'd imagine Bouke never phoning again, another lap that he did. Into a momentum, I had this conversation with myself.

- And if you never saw him again, what would happen?
- Terrible disappointment.
- Of what?
- Of never feeling happy again.
- Can there be happiness only with Bouke?
- Yes.
- Can't you give this to yourself?

The answer came so fast that I lost my stroke and water shot up my nose. It is a stupid thing to start crying while you are swimming. I reminded myself of my younger brother Andy who was able to play football against himself and actually lose. He'd come sadly into the house, dirty and beaten. *Andy* I'd tell him, *since you played against yourself, you've also won.* No, he'd answer, *the team I was really on, lost.*

A few days later, Bouke finally phoned and we met for a bike ride along the river Rhine. The weather was perfect, a warm breeze and plenty of sunshine. I was deliriously happy. We talked and laughed and time-to-time he'd reach over to kiss me. Even if I couldn't bike as well as the Dutch, the accident was not entirely my fault. It was the *energy* swirling with such force that caused our handlebars to entangle and shoot Bouke up into the air and flat down on his head. I was sure he was killed.

Luckily a man working in his garden saw it happen, and rushed to our aid with ice, bandages, a glass of water and a few pills. After a bit, Bouke opened his eyes and they spoke some Dutch and I understood enough to know it wasn't serious. His hair was completely wet from both blood and water, and the ice had melted onto his leather jacket.

- You are going to kill me, Bouke said, laughing.

- I didn't mean to.

- I know, and please don't cry. If you start then I'm going to start, and my head is already splitting.

- Do you want to go home? I asked.

- No, come on, Bouke said, I'm strong.

We thanked the helpful man, who reminded us to not bike *that* close together and rode on until we came to the café Bouke wanted me to see. It was a beautiful old mansion situated on a small lake, a place where people came to swim. We sat outside drinking coffee and he ate his apple pie with one hand, the other arm around me. We didn't say anything. After the accident we were quiet, careful — but I felt such a strong love for him, so amazingly strong, more than I'd ever loved anyone.

Maybe in the end Bouke wasn't that strong. Maybe all that power opening in me wasn't so good, if so much power can hurt someone you love, it can't be a good thing. That accident — and the one that followed a couple of days later when we crashed into each other again and this time I was thrown and hurt — made it impossible to deny that too much love *was* dangerous and that *something*, whether we liked it or not, was tearing us apart.

*

They say that when one shines a light, the 'thing' can no longer stay hidden and will change. What they don't ever tell you is when!

Because of Bouke, I definitely wanted to stay in Holland, and in a frenzy had organized enough gigs for nearly six months, but I'd given myself a break in August, hoping to spend time with him. Go on 'holiday' together. It was the end of June and I had a tour planned from before to Scotland, Wales and Ireland. I hated to leave him, but he was all lovey-dovey and wanted to take me to Amsterdam, to his favorite market where he bought his clothes, before my trip. He wanted to pick out the perfect outfit for me and we spent hours trying on everything. In the end, he bought me a black velvet jacket and a pair of hanging earrings that sparkled in the light that made me feel so lucky, I wore them at every concert. When I felt the Bouke earrings hanging from my ears it was so good and comforting, like he was with me. It had been so nice, just before I left, that I couldn't help but fantasize him missing me, aching for me — well before cell phones and email, you really had a break from someone — that he'd decide to live together with me, like he would with a real Dutch girl!

On the plane home from Ireland, I reached to touch the earrings and realized they were gone! With only a few minutes before landing, I searched frantically but no luck. And then came the sinking feeling that Bouke, too, was gone from my life forever.

I came into Wil's empty house, and it was cold and damp and unhappy — as if the house already knew. There were no phone messages… still I dialed Bouke immediately. Hard to say if my insecurities had triggered his coldness, but the sound in his voice was totally different. He had gotten used to me being away, was well into himself, so he said, doing his music, playing his new guitar, obeying his list; that list of things he'd been promising himself to attend to (like having no relationship, that he had told me about but I'd refused to believe him).

No, I can't see you now. I'm practicing for a concert, so I can't really talk, but I'll call you next week.

It should be against the law to make someone wait for a phone call. I was losing it… even phoned information to see if there were any OA meetings in Nijmegen, in Holland. When the person asked me what OA stood for and I foolishly told her *Overeaters Anonymous* she burst out laughing, saying it was the funniest thing she'd ever heard.

And then it started raining, like the end of the world. I walked in the rain and I cried in the rain and I read the John Bradshaw book cover to cover. Finally I got so mad that I phoned Bouke. I was rough and ragged, tough and weary and didn't give a shit anymore so we had this great conversation with lots of laughing and insights and realizations, just like the old days. Should've left it at that; should have wished him a good life and hung up the phone and counted to four million and eighty and never spoken with him again! It's like he knew it... and the second before we hung up he seductively asked if Wil was still away and would I make him dinner. And me, stupid, stupid me, said yes.

I prepared a beautiful dinner of Spaghetti Bolognese with an expensive bottle of wine. I knew the sex messed me up — when I let someone in, I become insatiable. So, the deal with myself was: dinner, some laughs, some talking, maybe a song and a wee kiss goodnight and away he will go...

Oh how life happens when we fool ourselves with our plans! Even before we ate, Bouke wanted me to listen to *him*, all the Beatles songs he'd learnt. I don't even like Beatles songs but I was so happy he was having a good time. And it surprised him how good a cook I was... and the wine; he had seconds and thirds... and then it was too late to catch the train. He was so affectionate and really wanted to be with me, and we made love and it was great...

But then he wanted his cigarettes and to be left alone, in peace, to sleep.

And then like the biggest idiot that ever was I asked him:

- Will I see you this weekend, or are you too busy?

- I am too busy, he said.

I was furious and teary-eyed, but this time he wanted to talk it out, to make things *clear* once and for all. He admitted to leading me on, not on purpose, but he wasn't ready to make the commitment to help me stay, it was too complicated and...

- Shut up, I screamed and ran out of the room.

Just because I hadn't listened, that wasn't his fault. He'd told me from the start, from the very first day we met, that he didn't want a relationship. He told me about the *list* he'd made way before meeting me, where having a relationship had a big X next to it. It's cruel when someone tells you they don't want to see you, but then kisses you like you're the Queen of Sheba. How can you not try like mad to please that person? Like I was on trial at home, as a kid, with everything conditional. He made me so hungry, not for food, but for love and I hated how much I wanted it, wanted him, that I totally understood why he wanted to get rid of me. Wish I could've gotten rid of myself too.

After he left, the whole house reeked of his musk scent. I stripped the bed, washed the sheets, opened the windows and scrubbed the floors. I felt tempted to set the house on fire in an act of cleansing but my friend Wil trusted me with his house and burning it down is not what a responsible person does.

It was worse than giving up food — the idea of never seeing him again, never the fantastic feeling of being alive when he touched me and kissed me and saw me... I'd never met anyone *that* open before. Why did I ask those stupid questions? Why couldn't I trust just a tiny bit and give him space? Why corner him like a rat? I asked for too much and then I got nothing, absolutely nothing.

The house was squeaky clean when the phone rang. I almost didn't answer it, but knew it wasn't Bouke. It was my father. The strange thing about my father over the years is how easily we'd talk on the phone; something I didn't have with my mother. Usually I didn't talk with him about personal stuff. I remember once, he came to a therapy session of mine in New York a long time ago, and he just started crying. The therapist hardly said anything but my father couldn't stop. I'd never seen my Dad cry before, and it was pretty weird. The therapist asked him why he was crying and he said he didn't know, he really didn't know why.

My father heard it in my voice and asked if I was okay. So I told him about Bouke and the Bradshaw book on shame and how everything was connected; that it felt important to be able to forgive him, my Dad, for what happened when I was a kid. He cleared his throat a few times, but I think he understood. He got quiet on the other end and then I asked him to say that he loved me, that I was okay and worth loving. And he did, but it made him sad.

- Did I really do things to upset you as a child? he asked.

- I was traumatized by your rage.

- Were you really? he asked in shock. (It's incredible what people forget, but maybe that's the only way to live with yourself.)

We hung up and I wished I could be in one of those great O.A. meetings in New York and bathe in the love and support. I felt swamped in loneliness, but I thought of what I'd hear in the rooms: *that loneliness is just a feeling and it won't kill you, and this too shall pass.*

It was actually okay that Wil wasn't there, that no one came by and I had no gigs. I went into the living room and put on the song again, and this time when I heard it, it felt different, like I'd traveled some kind of light years. But it hit me that I'd avoided doing the deep work of feeling secure in myself no matter what: whether I do a great gig, or the guy loves me. It was time. Everything rests upon it. Jesus, if only I had the courage to sing this pain. I'm not surprised that Janis Joplin died; I'd be dead too if I had the courage to show my feelings, to sing it out. Or maybe you really do have to take all those drugs.

Then I thought of what Bouke had said about 'using' me or not: *If I were to use you, then I'd come fuck you every single night.*

But it wasn't in my body where I felt used… it was in my heart. All the time he kept asking about my feelings. Well, he stuffed his pockets with those feelings, my feelings! Right before he left, he finally showed me his famous list. I was number 15 on it. He was not supposed to have anything after number 10 — like the cigarettes he wanted to quit smoking, which he never did, which were, by the way, number 11.

Session Eight

Not just with men did I crave the impossible. Only the most remarkable life could redeem my phantom suffering and the raw injustice flooding my veins. I dared the Gods at every turn, because at good moments I felt high and lofty, *god-like*, inspired with a mission. Yet at the worst moments — which sadly felt more trustworthy — I knew I was an imposter, a cute, seductive imposter: a magician. And when someone in the audience actually knew, I could hear their *knowing* like a shot to my brain: *What the hell do you think you're doing up there? I paid to see this crap!* Like parents who suddenly arrive home and find you dressed in your mother's flowing scarves acting the rightful princess, who rip off those scarves double-quick and leave you standing in your baby pajamas with those rubber feet and you know to the root of your bones that you never will be a real princess. The disappointment is overwhelming and it feeds that raw injustice like a delta creating ever-new land.

One night I'd dream of Joni Mitchell coming to me for advice and we'd exchange tales of the road, and the next of my walking onto the stage of a packed house and forgetting every single one of my lines. Performers like myself who suffer stage fright take workshops where you learn to make the audience into a roomful of children, who want to be entertained, soothed, comforted and inspired. One teacher even coached putting the entire audience on the toilet bowl. Yet for me, the audience, those first moments until proven wrong, was a group of restless Nazis or Cossacks ready to shoot. The only chance was to keep them so amused that they didn't notice who I *really* was.

The key was keeping myself pumped up and to be around those who did the pumping. Of course I didn't see this then, maybe just a glimpse; it was all about surviving. In my mid-thirties now, living under-the-cuff at Wil's house in Holland, on the road towards becoming a famous musician, I finally knew a few things about myself — that I had no idea how to love without going mad; that I dissolved in the competitive arena of America; that my mother was a truck that ran me over (even if her truck was mostly virtual, by phone, her power to disintegrate was impressive); that my father scared me to death; that I felt completely ill-equipped to manage daily life; that I needed constant reassurance; that if I didn't write songs and sing them I'd end up in the loony bin... yet if I didn't find a way to start taking cocaine or the drugs of rock-stars I'd never make it. The musicians I played with (wisely so) forbid me to try any of it. *You'll become hopelessly addicted,* they warned. But I'd lie awake at night in a cold sweat of panic over how the hell to do the life that was looming before me.

And even how I got from Wil's house to the next place, where I'd live the next four years, and yes to the next man — who at least arranged it so that I could live legally, with health insurance for the first time in my adult life, and who gave me a home to feel 'settled' in — that bulging thread of fear was already manipulating everything. Was already leading me, even then, even before David Letterman, to here, to Buenos Aires.

I never did see Bouke again, but I missed him terribly. There's no word thick enough for the devastation I felt without him. Without the dream of him, everything changed. He had reached his long beautiful arm into the sky and plucked out the sun. I mean it. A person can do that; the God of your own making *can* be that powerful. The moment Bouke walked out of my life, it started raining and it kept on raining so much that little Holland, let alone me, started drowning in all that rain.

And after that, everybody in Holland *looked* exactly like Bouke; every time I turned he was coming back to get me. But it was never him — ever. Only once, a year later, he came to hear me play but I was already living with that other man, and felt terrified to be near him as the other man forbid me to see him. Because I needed someone to do that for me, to make it so clear that I'd never see him again. Because I was, after all, a small child who had no idea how the morning ever became night and how the night ever turned itself back into morning.

You hardly need to know who this other man was, a rose does smell the same by any other name, and a man that comes to rescue you on a bicycle instead of a horse could be called so many things. Shall we dub him Henk? Because that's a typical Dutch name even if he didn't look typically Dutch, and not anything (thank the Lord) like Bouke. His eyes were the sad blue like my Grandfather and Lee Strasberg, even like my own father on that strange day in therapy when he couldn't stop crying. Henk was not an arrogant man, more bruised and beaten by life, which was a comfort for me, sharing the bruise of living. He had a sweet house in Nijmegen, on the other side of town from Wil and also worked, like Wil, as a teacher. He'd seen me in newspapers and posters around town, but had never come to hear me sing. I looked too beautiful, he said, and that scared him. But when he found me, one rainy summer's day at a café, some weeks AB (after Bouke) under a stack of papers — I'd written a hole through my diary and realms of loose sheets grew around me like a rain-forest, with song bits and stories and dark tragedies — he thought I might be thirsty. And I was, and also very hungry, because I mostly couldn't eat AB. And he fed me, this Henk, who really looked like my grandfather, bent over and hunched, whose teeth were not good because he was the youngest of thirteen children when the Dutch were still hav- ing huge families, and he hadn't enough milk as a child. And when he saw me, with ink all over my fingers and my hair a mess and no make- up, my eyes swollen from crying, he didn't find me scary at all. And be- cause I always love singing for one person who really wants to hear me more than anything, he started inviting me over to sing my new songs for him. He loved them and they made him cry (telling me the same: that he could only cry in front of one person at a time; that when you grow up in so large a family, it's too dangerous to let anyone see you weeping.) Maybe that's not the worst exchange to have, and maybe if I could've stayed happy with that, we'd still be together because much of it worked okay. Being 'settled' made everything easier, suddenly I was able to book concerts way into the future, and my musical life charged full steam ahead.

And so did my fear. And the look that Henk would sometimes give me, the look I remember from Margo (the director of *Cabaret*) that I was going to mess up. I'm not sure if Henk knew how badly he wanted me to get famous. He'd say all kind of kooky things: for example at one of my good gigs — when the crowd was swinging their hips and spilling their beers and singing their raw and throaty Dutch voices and he knew I'd sell a lot of recordings at the end and that a line of men and woman would want my number — Henk stuck his wobbly chest out all proud and pompous.

- Don't you mind all the flirting? I asked him.

Because it was part of it, part of selling CD's, part of the encores, part of getting booked again at the same place the next year.

- I love it! Henk said. They all want to fuck you, but I actually do!

Henk knew that most of the best songs were written about Bouke. One of the more poignant became Henk's favorite; every time I sang it he cried. Ironically, it was this song, *Fly*, that led to my first recording contract in the Netherlands and my fourth CD, the one that David Letterman would hear, with *Fly* as the title. The intention of the song, was using the word fly metaphorically as 'fuck off.' Ironically — the more well-known I became, now doing bigger and better concerts and festivals, the more nervous I got — I was always being asked about *flying* because of the CD's title. Literally trembling, during one live-aired performance (a mini-David Letterman) and interview, I was asked why I was *so* nervous and all I could say was:

- *I have always been afraid to fly.*

*

Henk got along great with the musicians and loved when we rehearsed at the house. He'd set out cold bottles of beer, snacks, telling the guys to just help themselves, American style. He even started driving us to the concerts, helping set up, like our roadie. It thrilled him, all the places we'd travel to and the *schmoozing* at the end — the part I also loved best, especially if the gig went well — drinking beer, talking into the wee hours, staying in the cute hotels in the story-book towns.

Once during my *almost famous* years, playing at a great festival in Ghent, in the Flemish part of Belgium, we had a huge suite overlooking the city. *This is unbelievable,* Henk said over and over as he popped the bottle of champagne chilled to perfection, compliments of the hotel. It was a balmy night and with all the hoopla and the relaxed Belgium style I wasn't nervous and truly enjoyed the whole event. All those virile, young men setting up the sound, giving me a big, fat, luscious voice. Making me larger-than-life as our music went out to thousands. I wore a white tango hat and a sexy tee shirt that said: *getting strong*. It was the closest I ever came to being Madonna and Henk loved it. But alas that night in Ghent was the peak. You really need to not be afraid of heights if you want to keep climbing, and the music business is vicious: there are no rest stops along the way.

Henk had been the answer to many of my prayers, and he did provide everything needed to live as normal a musical life as possible, yet I never fell for Henk as I did Bouke, which was a relief; another obsessive affair would have killed me. But perhaps not for Henk, who, while watching me write my heart out that rainy day in the market square had an idea of who he thought I was — and had unfortunately learned everything about Bouke those first weeks — and knew that I'd once loved a man with every ounce of me and that *that* man was not, nor ever would be him, had finally eroded the fabric of his kindness.

Or maybe it was just *me* being more and more who I really was and less the sweet, skinny girl whom he'd rescued that summer's day. Maybe no matter how hard you try, you can't pretend in the long run to be someone else, even if all the parts line up. True, Henk helped sort out the details of my life, still I'd never stopped *wanting* whatever it was that Bouke made me feel. Or maybe I was too busy missing what I didn't have, to notice what I had.

But it was a huge disappointment that my career didn't blast to the moon, even with his help. When my new CD got some notoriety and airplay but not enough and I decided to rent a piano and give lessons again, he was dead against it — as if teaching was the ultimate sign of failure. The lessons were taught while he was at work so he never saw the students. What he did notice, however, was how good and grounded it was for me to teach, and the extra money didn't hurt.

Usually with a student, I'd turn off the ringer of the telephone, which was on the bookshelf in the dining room, and leave the answering machine with the volume off to take messages.

One day with Henk at work, I was giving a lesson to a good singer, a young man, who loved the singing/Alexander combination. The lessons always started with some Alexander work. He was lying on the table at the point of the *directions* tingling through his nervous system, like a sauce simmering. To leave it a moment without stirring is not only okay, but essential. It was not a bad moment when the phone rang but it surprised me, as I thought the ringer was off. It actually rang *differently*, more aggressive, calling out to be answered — even more than when my mother phoned — like in a cartoon, how the ringing vibration causes it to leap about on the shelf. Startled, I picked up the phone and did not say the usual Dutch greeting of stating my name, but rather the American response of just hello.

- Can I speak with Deborah Jeanne?
- Yeah, that's me.
- We are phoning you from the office of the David Letterman show.
- From the where? Is this a …?
- Hello?
- Yes, yes, I am still here. Is it true, are you phoning about the …?
- Yes, that is correct.
- Am I…? Are you…? Is he thinking of having me on his …?
- This phone call is to inform you that you are under consideration to be on the David Letterman show.
- I am in Holland now, but I could…
- Can we reach you at this number? Will you be able to fly out immediately?
- Uhh yeah. He, umm, David Letterman, he liked my CD?
- Mr. Letterman always decides who comes onto his show, so he must have. We will contact you. Do not phone us.

There are different ways to end a phone call in Holland, but I said nothing, only heard the echo of the click on the other side of the phone. At first I thought it was a phony-phone call, the sort we made as kids, squishing our little heads around the phone, with someone giggling at the end. There was no laughter on the line. This was an official call! But how in heaven's name did David Letterman get my CD? Then I remembered Karen, who'd promised to give my CD to her mother — who must have gone across the street and placed it in Mr. Letterman's mailbox. That David Letterman actually listened to my CD and *liked* it was so startling and so scary that I almost forgot my student. All at once he sat up in amazement, for the show had just started airing in Holland.

- Wow!! Are you going to be on the David Letterman show? he asked, in a vibrantly rich voice.
- I don't know, I said. (My voice trembling.) Maybe.

There is a saying in Dutch: *don't stick your head above the fence or someone will chop it off.* This student was not in the head chopping business.

- I can't wait to tell my friends that my singing teacher is going to be on the David Letterman show! That's so cool! You're gonna be famous, and everyone will know you... and I'll tell them that you actually taught me how to sing... then I'll get famous too! This is so...

- Wait, wait! I begged, Don't say anything yet.

Trying desperately to not let him see that just the *idea* of being on the show made me so nervous I could hardly breathe. What if they phoned back? What if they really wanted me on the show? I'd have to fly out immediately; I'd have to do it. You can't say no to David Letterman.

*

When Henk came home from work that day, he was so excited about my possible appearance on the Letterman show that he nearly built a shrine for the phone. The ringer was now always on. But the call never came. And sadly, I see now, I did nothing, absolutely nothing to help my cause; didn't even tell my agent. There are things a performer can do, things of gentle persuasion that keep you in the limelight, but you must *want* to be in that light.

It was Henk who was most disappointed; I was so terrified of being on the show, of singing one song 'live,' certain I'd faint, or worse — pee. But that damned call triggered something rotten between us, and we never found our way back. Our fights became vicious. Henk couldn't forgive me for almost, but not, getting famous. Little by little, reminiscent of Josh, Henk started working late, reminding me yet again how incapable I was of anything remotely human like a steady relationship. We saw each other less and less; he stopped coming to the gigs and on nights with no gigs, I returned to my old habit of walking.

They say 'Necessity is the Mother of Invention'. Who then is the father — longing? It has to be. It has to be that nagging emptiness that leads you on; that led my feet, one gloomy fall night, down an unfamiliar street where I heard, unexpectedly, the mournful strands of Greek folk music, music from my old dancing days in Central Park. Familiar tears rattled my cheeks and just like a movie scene where the character's beloved returns and she drops everything to run towards him, my body ran towards the warm, rhythmic sound. Into an old schoolhouse, I dashed down the hall and burst into the room and automatically linked arms with the other dancers with tears like needed water for dry and parched Greece splashing down my face. The leader smiled, for he knew that feeling and he welcomed me; he welcomed me home.

I hadn't realized just how much I missed dancing. Since coming to Europe there'd been no time nor occasion, but suddenly there in that shabby schoolroom, dancing steps that my feet totally remembered, the need to dance was so strong, urgent. This little Greek class that met once a week for an hour was sweet but not enough to satisfy my craving.

At the same time, with things falling apart with Henk and me, I'd started taking yoga. I really liked the teacher who had lived abroad and knew about being displaced, about homesickness so vague that you can search and search but never find whatever it was you longed for. After the class I'd linger, help collect the mats and pillows. We'd talk of all kinds of everything... *chewing the fat*, as my grandfather used to say. I'd mentioned the Greek dance class, that I missed dancing more than anything else in America.

- Have you never been to the Argentine tango here in Nijmegen? he asked.

- No.

- Well! You have to come next weekend, to the *Milonga*. It happens once a month. It's great, really great dancers come.

- What's a *Milonga*?

- The place where people gather to dance tango. But dress well, people come from all over and they really dress up.

With absolutely no idea what to expect, butterflies circled my stomach as I pedaled through the dark, late-night spooky streets that led to the tango 'den'. As I locked my bike, I noticed a few people outside, some smoking, some men airing their shirts. The music seemed to dance out on a wave of smoke. The entrance door was just like any other on that rather bland and unexciting street. It was, however, a very heavy door to open.

Once opened, it led to a magic theater, to a time away from time, to a thousand nights of dreams and love and dark intrigue. Past the entrance space overflowing with coats and scarves and the paraphernalia of the mundane world, the room became tropical, the women were stripped down to the sultry, bare-sleeves, bare-back clothing of the movies — and the men in so many shades of black that I hadn't seen since acting school.

Once truly in, the owner and teacher greeted me, knowing immediately that I was new. He inquired where I was from and my name, which he never asked for again, as he had that rare talent of remembering. Tango is a whole other world than folk dancing; it is not for peasants. I now felt far, far away from home, but intriguingly, mysteriously so. Slowly I breathed in the smell, the scent of something erotic; powerful, dangerous: of sweat, perfume, coffee, of exclusive leather shoes, so many shoes, and smoke, an amazing amount of cigarette smoke. The room was dark, like entering a cave, a womb, into the Roaring Twenties, a speak-easy perhaps.

The tango music: nearly classical but pulsating, passionate, completely its own, filling the space perfectly. Perfect for all the elegance, the glamorous black clothing and all those high-heeled shoes. The tables overflowed with ashtrays, wine glasses, coffee cups. And the soft possessive hum of deep conversation, as if the room were divided into invisible cubicles where the various couples almost embraced as they spoke.

A sloping archway led to the main dance hall. My first look at the Argentine tango literally took my breath away. I'd learnt ballroom tango, the silly dance with the rose in your teeth, had danced salsa in the clubs in New York and San Francisco. But *this* tango was something Other. I wanted to be in it, to know it immediately. Yet I, who had never feared dancing, felt in awe: like the black diamond ski slope, for experts only. The movement of dance was so impressive, so improvisational with no two couples doing the same steps, yet all part of a flowing symmetry. Like a snowstorm with each snowflake unique yet connected, where the wind and interplay of the delicate flakes is what creates the design.

As in all dancing the music is master, yet in tango with its varying rhythms and moods it appeared even more so, demanding more concentration. After listening for a while I could distinguish the variation: the waltz and a faster almost salsa rhythm called *Milonga* (the same word used for the night itself), and what I'd soon learn was the true tango, much slower and charged with melancholy. At the start of each song was a moment of motionless attention, and then one by one the couples began to move. The leader pulled the partner close, while the follower, draped one arm luxuriously over the leader's shoulder; their eyes did not meet. No talking. This was serious, amazingly serious and sensual. I had never seen anything like this in Holland and as I looked more closely everyone seemed passionately *southern*. Even my yoga teacher, he too became *Latin* as he danced.

I was transfixed: my mouth must have been gaping open. At a moment when I was truly lost in this dream world, someone gave me a *look*, such an inviting look, that it was clear he was asking me to dance. I quickly stammered that I had no idea how to do it.

- But can you dance? this man asked, in heavily accented English.

- Well I...

- Come, just follow me and listen to the music.

He took hold of my hand and led me, reassuringly, onto the dance floor. As the music started he wrapped one arm lovingly around my back while his other hand opened to receive mine. He moved his feet gently from side to side letting the rhythm take over and then, invigorating me with his essence we began to move. I watched and mirrored a woman beside me and tried to imitate her movements but within seconds I was spun away and lost sight of her. The dance captured me, and my partner, with whom I barely spoke, was so present of body, so demanding, that it took all my attention to remember to breathe and to follow his movements.

The dance was a precious and precise conversation that asked for an open heart and soul, a complete surrendering of the body's deep balance and poise to the shifting sway of the music. To listen as if it were the only thing that ever was or would be important.

That one dance couldn't have lasted more than three minutes yet the dimensions were so vast it seemed forever. And yet, even forever comes to an end, but he just held onto me and waited until a few bars had passed of the next song, which was faster and in a way easier. I laughed out loud from the sheer joy of it, but caught myself quickly as laughing seemed sacrilegious. After a few dances, with a look of gracious thanks, this man walked me back from whence I had come. To never again be who I once was; it changes you, such a dance.

I felt like a million dollars: beaming and so sure, now that I dared the diamond slope, that someone else would come ask me to dance. But no one did. I waited and watched for hours, really hours, for the tango is like Las Vegas: you can burn a hole through an entire night and hardly notice it. It was around midnight when I'd first danced and four in the morning when I next glanced at a clock.

The evening had been like a drink that at first makes you feel good and charmed and beautiful, but without freshening makes you feel washed up, unused and unwanted. But I'd already caught the bug. *Fuck,*

fuck, fuck, I remember thinking, *why can't something in life be easy!* There were enough hard things, enough challenges. The dance was going to be dangerous! The last time I'd felt anything like that was when Bouke — a lifetime ago — had brushed his legs against mine one steamy night and I hadn't forgotten all the trouble *that* had got me into.

Almost too tired to get on my bicycle and ride home, knowing that Henk would be relentless with me for being so late, I wanted, needed, one more dance so badly, but who would dance with me, such a rank beginner? I wobbled, defeated, out of the womb towards the entrance, when an arm grabbed me.

- Where are you going? she asked.

But she knew, of course she knew. I had already seen my face on a few other dejected women waiting, hoping.

- Dance with me, she said.

- With you?

- Don't worry, she laughed. Like it was her job to catch the strays before they fell out the window.

- Just follow me, she said. I watched you before. You can dance; don't try to do anything, just walk.

- Walk?

- Yes, without thinking. Let your body follow me and just listen to the music, there is nothing to get right.

She did the same as the man had done, except her touch and feel were harder, more severe. She was very skinny, but incredibly strong. It felt good to dance with her. Very good. We danced a few in a row, not on the dance floor, just there in the other space, the practice space.

- There's a dance in another month, she said. Take a few lessons. You'll be surprised how much you can learn in a few weeks. Especially someone like you... for you've clearly danced before. It'll be a piece of cake. (That infamous *piece of cake.*)

- Yes I have danced other styles, I told her, but the tango is so hard, and then the shoes... Everyone wears these high heels.

- You don't have to, she said.

Immediately I signed up for private lessons with her, and with the other teachers. But she was wrong about two things: it wasn't a piece of cake and I did have to wear high heels and those shoes were in some ways the hardest part, and the feeling in my stomach that scared the shit out of me, the feeling of being *there*, of being seen, what I've always struggled against. Yet still I wanted, needed, *loved* the dance more than anything at that moment — because it made me so incredibly alive.

Soon the tango had my heart, had swooped me off my feet; a relief to be infatuated by something not connected to any special man! Yet like all obsession, it would quickly change my life. Soon all my money was going to take lessons, classes, *practicas*; all my free time spent at *Milongas*.

The tango was the final straw with Henk. He quickly came to hate it since unlike the Bouke obsession — a thing he was able to control by forbidding me to see him — there was no way he could keep me from dancing. The tango became everything I'd ever longed for and as selfish as that sounds, not he, not anyone, neither food nor shelter would keep me from dancing. Within a few months it quickly became my strongest addiction ever. I was willing to give up everything, even my music.

Because really in the end, I just wanted to feel free: to be free of myself, the bondage of self. After a night of dancing, I'd feel marvelous, perfect; completely exempt from humanity. I could finally live in the day, be in the moment. I have the gift of raw talent and when I decide on something I can do it. Within a short time I'd come into a *Milonga* and mostly dance myself into a froth of endorphins, so happy, so deliriously happy that the rest — the whole goddamn rest of it, who I was, who I married, getting famous, failing miserably, it really and truly didn't matter a jot! I was free of the whole expectation of life! If, on my bike-ride home I were killed, it all wouldn't matter. For I had lived! I had gobbled down a big fat chunk of delicious life and no one could ever take that from me! I even wondered if David Letterman had known so delicious a moment!

Bulging with gratitude, for the incredible twists and turns that made it possible to be where I was — smiling away through the damp and cold early morning streets of Nijmegen after a splendid night of dancing — realizing (even if I had no idea what would happen next, now that my relationship with Henk had ended), it is rare and wondrous to feel so happy.

Session Nine

I could scream. The fear is bad today: demanding, aggressive, unrelenting. I start squirming on my seat.

- I need to move... I can't sit still.

- So move, it's okay.

- It's crazy to be here in Buenos Aires and not be able to dance tango. You can't imagine how many dancers dream of coming here.

- You will dance again, I promise!

My body starts jerking; I shake my hands as if to get rid of them.

- What's happening, Ana asks.

- What am I, just an object for dissection? Have I only been a stupid self-centered person trying desperately to get free? I know it takes 'two to tango' but when I think of how I acted with Henk and with everyone, how easily I dismissed people if they didn't serve my cause. It's like bile in my mouth. I'm just like my mother and father... it sickens me. Is that it? No matter how far you think you've traveled you'll always be an apple from that same goddamn tree! It's why I never had a child! I had to break the chain.

- I thought I was pregnant, with Henk, I tell Ana. But it never happened. And maybe it was for the best. I had no business being a mother. (I'm jumping around the room now, ranting and raving.) It's too easy to become a parent. Would it have been such a tragedy in the way of the world to make sure everyone learned HOW to take care of themselves FIRST before getting the task of caring for another? Like some hormone that stopped you from getting pregnant! When I think of all the suffering -- and I realize mine is just a speck. My father, he was just a small child when his father nearly destroyed him, and did his father only mean him harm? Wasn't he just trying to feel free, hopelessly frustrated that he couldn't? And my mother, she didn't ask to be born at a time when her own mother

hadn't the energy, couldn't speak English. It was her older sister who mostly raised her.

- And I wonder if in the end anybody knows anything. Yet those who convince, who intimidate, they're the winners, or so it seems, or so we make them. And me, what pill would I have to swallow to stop being so gullible, so willing to believe the others? So willing to believe there's a place where I may be safe and a person who is going to take care of me. Is it wrong to want to be safe?

- No, Ana says. It is only wrong to expect the impossible from other people. It is only wrong when we are unable to forgive and let go.

- I think it's complete bullshit, all this letting go. I want to hold on, I want to hold on with all my might.

- I know, Ana says. And it's killing you. But please try to stay with me now... we need to do this.

She has put a pillow on the floor and has asked me to think of that pillow as my mother and speak to her.

- I can't do this, I tell Ana. Not today. This is too stupid. My mother is not a pillow; I'd not have feared her if she were just a pillow.

But therapy is like little ants that tickle your feet. It keeps tickling and then -- like a crack in a gray and miserable sky -- I all at once start singing in a New York accent:

I got ants in my pants and I wanna dance...

I've got ants in my pants and I wanna dance...

I'm moving my hips and acting as we used to as kids, pretending to be black, pretending to be cool. And Ana starts laughing because I'm becoming as crazy as the Argentine people... and somehow she sees this as a sign of health.

Even being best friends with the most popular girl in school — the one brave enough to get that 'ant' song started when we were in line waiting for some activity to start — wasn't at all as it should have been; what a dork and stupid girl I was. And what should I do with all that: turn Naomi, my best friend, into a pillow and smash her against the wall? It wasn't her fault that I was such a gullible fool to believe her, so many, many years ago.

Naomi was the most popular girl at school because she wasn't afraid of anyone; was just that bit taller than the rest of us and had that thing, that ability to convince others. After my Henry Hudson debacle in the fourth grade, I was transferred into the class for the brightest kids. My mother claims it was because of getting smarter, and maybe it was, so ashamed was I to see any of my former friends, I had more time for homework. In any case, in the next class I met a whole new group of kids, including Naomi, none of whom had witnessed the peeing episode.

One day after school, Naomi came up with the brilliant idea of picking a secret admirer. The boys as a group chose one girl, and vice-versa, and we kept sacred vigil about this, not even giving hints, until the certain day (that she'd later decide) when we'd reveal these names.

Weeks went by, notes passed furiously about whom these two secretly *admired* might be. It was such an intense experience that when I look back at this time at school it is all I remember!

Not even hoping to be the one *admired*, it was a terrible shock, on that day of revelation, when the boys announced their choice, and it was *me*. Panicked, I did the only thing I could think of: run like hell as fast and as far away as possible.

Our neighborhood had no hill, no haystack to disappear in and no real tree to climb. I ran home, grabbed some milk and cookies and hid under the living room couch. When my mother came home from school, she shouted:

- Debbie? Debbie… where are you?

- Shh, I whispered, I'm under here.

- Why are you hiding under the couch? And why are all the boys in your class standing outside?

- It's a long story, I whispered. Just tell them I've moved away.

If you'd ask my mother about this today she wouldn't remember, but she was great that afternoon. I can still hear her words:

- I am so sorry, she said to the boys in her loud teacher-like voice, but it seems my daughter doesn't live here anymore.

I have no idea what those boys wanted of me; or how differently my life would have been if I'd walked out onto the lawn making a grand entrance — Scarlett O'Hara style — honoring them for their long vigil, giving each and every one a soft peck on the cheek. Maybe I should have put on a yellow polka-dot bikini and danced the hula-hula.

But my choice of hiding under the couch until the last boy went home was clearly not appreciated, and the next day at school no one would talk to me, not even the girls. Except Naomi — she was delighted that I'd messed up. As if runner up at a beauty pageant, she scooped up those wounded boys, making them special, which in turn made her the most popular girl for years to come. After that, it was like she owned me. She could do whatever she wanted, and I let her. There's an expression for this now: I was her 'wing-girl'. Prettier than her, at the weekend dances she'd set me up as the honeycomb for the boys to come circling around, which they did. Too shy to say a word, Naomi did all the talking. But I could dance with them; the dancing was always okay. After Naomi had done her bidding and found the boy of her choice, I would dance with whomever was left.

I remember once, I heard some boys talking about us: *Well I started with the pretty one, but went for the one with the personality. And what a personality!* I'd already felt that torment — how funny Naomi could be. A personality? I thought. If that is what I lack where do you find a personality? And why didn't I have one?

I even went to the library, a thing I hated doing, and took out a stack of books on the subject. Learning everything I could about personalities, *the social and emotional characteristics of an individual, the visible aspect of one's character as it impresses others*. I set out, at age twelve, with feverish intensity to find one. It was the beginning of my need to 'walk myself out,' so I took on the task of family dog-walker.

At this same time, Kenny — one of the most popular neighborhood boys, two years ahead of Naomi and me — became the designated dog walker in his family. I'd never said a word to him before, but knew who he was. With leash in hand, absorbed with inventive schemes of becoming a well-versed person of character, practicing telling jokes, it wasn't scary when I'd run into Kenny during the walks. Our dogs, meanwhile took a fancy to each other, and this in turn forced us to be more together. After a few weeks of these encounters, I felt comfortable with him, even at school. I suppose he was also shy, popular and all (hadn't I been popular?) and found his own comfort in the familiarity between us, and our dogs.

And then he helped me study for the year-end exams.

And then he broke up with his girlfriend.

And then I was sort of his girlfriend.

And then my mother noticed that I was walking the dog all the time.

And then... Naomi noticed.

July came and I went away to one camp, Kenny to another. And we wrote letters all summer long, beautiful, personality-filled letters. At the end of August, Kenny wrote one last letter about how he couldn't wait to see me in September. Like a fool, I showed this to Naomi, even before I had a chance to see Kenny, even before the first dog-walk.

- Can't you see he is using you! she said.

- Using me? I asked Naomi, for I was as pristine as the whitest snow. How can he be using me?

- Can't you see? she demanded. It's as clear as anything. He doesn't mean what he writes. Can't you read between the lines? He's had another girlfriend at camp... he's lying to you.

- Lying? I asked. Are you sure?

- I am absolutely one thousand percent sure, Naomi said, and if I were you, I'd never talk to him again.

Using. Lying. Those were key words when we were twelve and thirteen, the worst that could happen to you. I went home and read the letter again, the letter I'd already read a hundred times. I liked him so much. I couldn't find the between lines that Naomi referred to, which made me certain that whatever I lacked in my seeing was exactly what I lacked personality-wise. She had to be right.

So I gave the dog-walking job to my brother, explaining to my parents that I was going to have a lot more homework that year. I didn't run into Kenny until school started. Whenever I'd see him in the halls, or on his bike I'd turn the other way, wouldn't stop, not even once.

But now, even more than for myself, I feel sorry for Kenny. The poor guy never knew why I suddenly stopped talking to him. Several years after this episode, after my family had moved to the bigger house where I saw my father binge late at night, I was invited to a party of my old friends. Kenny was there. He had changed a lot, but he was still cute, still had that oriental look to his face, his smile, still had freckles on his nose.

- What actually happened to you that summer? he asked after many slugs of the Blue Nun wine we were all drinking. So I told him.

- That was so stupid, he said. I liked you so much. And Naomi was a jerk.

- Yeah I know, I said, trying to look at him in a way like maybe it wasn't too late, like maybe we could start up again. But he had a girl-friend, and anyway I was no longer the cute dog-walker: I was chubby, bloated from my midnight binges.

Then I heard about him one last time... that he was married and worked as a lawyer somewhere in New Jersey.

- I know. I know... Everyone has such stories. It's completely stu-pid to hang onto such things. Maybe it's not the only reason I chose to live the life of a hobo, but it has to be one of them. How else can you explain why the hell I ended up in Norway? Okay, I tell Ana. I will try the thing with the pillow.

But I can't stop crying and have turned all the tissues into little rings for my fingers and I have nothing to blow my nose with.

- What are you thinking? Ana asks.

- Of my younger brother Andy who, during a long drive when we were kids, took an entire American size box of tissues and created an army of soldiers and when my mother asked him for a tissue to blow her nose, he suddenly noticed that he'd used the entire box and he tried, he really tried to turn one of those twisted soldiers back into a useable tissue. But he couldn't.

I'm on a roll now of feeling wretched and I can't stop my voice from coming out all whiny and childlike.

- You probably think it's a good thing the 'universe' sent me to Norway. The therapist during my last year in Holland thought the same.

- Please don't lump us all together, Ana says. Every therapist is different. But I am curious about Harold. I know that you're angry with him now for not coming here to Buenos Aires.

- I don't give a shit if I never see him again.

- Okay, so you're very angry. But it's not so important that he be here, I think he knows that.

- How can you say that? You don't even know him!

- So tell me, who is he?

- Do you know I actually had to marry him! A letter came in the mail from the Norwegian government... like a bloody dentist appointment.

- But you're still married, so something must have been working.

It pissed me off! Never in my life did I want to marry and then I had to, or leave Europe for good. Even if I dreaded living in Oslo, it was still Europe and closer to Holland, where I still had gigs and all my friends and living officially in Norway made it possible to work anywhere. And I had fallen in love with Harold — whom I met singing on one of the beautiful Dutch Islands, the summer after things had ended with Henk — but hated the idea of a government forcing me to *commit*. On the day of our wedding appointment, precisely two forty-five, I was literally kicking and screaming. An expensive taxi was waiting and Harold had to barrel me down the stairs. I was crying so much, and couldn't stop crying during our whole little ceremony. At one point the Justice of the Peace asked why I was crying:

- I always cry at weddings.

- Even your own? he sweetly asked. Then offered me his tie to dry my tears, which made me laugh; it was good to laugh for a few seconds. I wore black like it was a funeral, cause that's what it felt like: the end of everything. We had two women as witnesses. One, a friend of Harold's and the other, someone I'd just met giving a concert. She came to me after the show and her reaction reminded me of a silly joke I'd heard at an Alexander conference when a speaker from Australia began by offering a taste of his country:

A man was too long in the outback, tired and dusty and very hungry. He walked into a diner in the middle of nowhere, asked for toast and eggs, a cup of tea and some kind words. When his food arrived, the waitress plunked down his food and tea and walked away.

'Hey, hey,' the man asked. 'What about the kind words?'

'I wouldn't eat the eggs if I were you!'

It was the same with this woman. Her kind words: get out of Norway as fast as you can or it will ruin your career!

Doubtful I'd any career left to ruin, I shrugged my shoulders and said something sarcastic that made her laugh and we became fast friends. She was in the middle of a divorce and had no faith in relationships and thought Harold and I had as good a chance as anyone, and it was her pleasure to 'bear witness.' She became a regular at our house for dinner — that was the immediate difference between Holland and Norway; going out in Norway was so costly, that you mostly stayed home. The first months in Oslo, I'd get into a rage by how expensive everything was: a glass of wine, a cup of tea… a bowl of spaghetti. God forbid if you should want all three at the same time, you really had to make an investment. One dark night — that too was dreadful, I'd never known such darkness, such claustrophobic gloom — I'd just returned from Holland and wanted to splurge and treat Harold to an Italian meal by the harbor. I felt like drinking, and not just one glass of wine. When I saw the price for a bottle, I threw down the menu and stormed out. Harold followed me in a very Protestant-controlled, unexpressed rage.

- Why don't you just scream at me and have it out!

- I am almost angry, Harold somberly replied. His lips squished tightly together like an Englishman, though he was from Holland.

- Let's just assume… shall we, that I've done the next wrong thing and you are angry! Let me have it! I know you want to.

You could tell that Harold, poor lad, hadn't banked on a wild gypsy rover like myself; he didn't know what to do. Unless Norwegians — and he'd lived in Norway a good thirty years — are drunk, they're not big on emotional display in public places.

- You make me so angry! he finally shouted. I could smell the door!

- *Smell?*

- … that's Norwegian, it means *slam*.

It was the best thing that could have happened at that moment and we started laughing hysterically. It was drizzling, still I laughed so hard I fell to the ground. When I got up, I made my way down the street, sniffing each door and we'd start laughing out of control again. And whenever we fought — which happened a lot — one of us put our nose instantly to a door and the humor of it really saved us.

It was actually really romantic when I first met Harold, on the boat to Vlieland, the prettiest of the Dutch islands that sprinkle the northern coast, where I used to sing in the summers. He moved like an athlete, but was goofy and playful, had a head of wild hair and seemed in a very good mood; as if life had treated him well. He didn't see me at all and there's something marvelous, genuine, in a person not aware of you looking at them.

But then he did notice me. And as the boat came into the harbor we asked each other how we could find each other again, because we'd both be there for a week. I told him where I was singing, and was happy when he came the next evening to hear me. And after the concert with the weather gloriously warm, we walked into the sandy woods, and though the moon was not full, it was all lovely. Good weather, the wind softly blowing, the sound of surf breaking in the distance and the stars twinkling in the sky, like God winking down, really does make it easy to fall in love. And we did. And the next day, when it was hot and beach-like and we were happy to see each other, we spoke a bit more about our lives. Because when it's not your first time round the block you feel a certain responsibility to at least warn the other what they may be entering into. We shared, besides the daunting sense of dreams well past their sell-by date — Harold had wanted to be a professional speed-skater and his knees had gotten so bad that he'd recently quit skating — the common story of our fathers that created a bond between us; something to hold us together during the many dark days to come.

Harold was born in the north of the Netherlands, had emmigrated to Norway for the nature, the skating and to be away from his past. He'd been divorced a long time, had two teenage children — that he'd taken to see the island of his youth when we met — and had settled into a version of life that was full enough without a steady relationship. I've asked him a million times why he puts up with me and the best he's come up with is: something about me *touches* him. I think it's more about me not boring him! Because I never seem to lose my entertaining knack, even on my worst, worst days. Harold had heard me sing a whole week when we met, and a few more times in the months to come, and then he organized enough concerts for me to come stay for a long while in Oslo once my time in Nijmegen had ended. It was a year later, after going back and forth from Oslo to Holland, when I finally had to marry him.

But it wasn't what I wanted, not just the marrying part. For once, I didn't want to be rescued. I wanted to have been *famous* enough to survive on *that*. To live on my own, all by myself with the sun always shining like Zorba the Greek, eating bread and wine and olives and singing only when I wanted to and mostly to my donkeys. Instead, here I was, dependent on Harold and living oceans away from Zorba's sun. I hated winter and the winter lasted forever in Norway. And if I'd learned anything in my vagrant gypsy life, people — men — loved me at the beginning, when I was funny and charming before my anger woke up to the fact that the me I was forever trying to get away from, was there yet again, and like a skipping record my life was destined to repeat itself *ad infinitum.*

Harold had taken on the role of being father, even mother; I was getting that bad. Despite a myriad of good intentions about meditating and writing new songs, after a short time in Oslo I mostly slept, and slept, and watched movies and American shows all night, like *The Nanny* (that suddenly became outrageously funny) or *Frasier.* those shows became my family, my social-life. I forced myself out each day to walk the icy streets and trails that surrounded the house. I'd pass the blond Norwegians in those few hours of daylight, and feel again that unnoticed fourteen year old with her long dark hair blowing on a street corner in South Dakota. Now almost forty-five years old I still needed to be adored, worshiped; could hardly get out of bed without it.

I used to love it, in my good days, when someone approached me in a restaurant or on a train to tell me how much they loved a concert and could they have my autograph. I blew it all with my nervousness. Still, I wanted another crack at it but obviously not enough or I'd have gotten out of bed. So the question was: *How to find meaning without the world asking, begging for me and my art?*

I had no answer, so I slept and got more depressed. That was what Norway was famous for. I had already learned about that when I was in Oslo on tour years ago. My agent's mother lay in bed all day, hopelessly depressed. So when in Rome, do as the Romans do, when in Norway...

I wrote e-mails like crazy, complained and swore and begged my friends for a clue on how the hell to get out of this one. One day a letter came from my brother Peter. We used to write songs together, do gigs. There was always a kind of competition between us. Though he was a little younger, I often made him the older and wiser one, maybe because of his position as doctor, that he had kids, all the trimmings of a normal life.

The letter he sent was upsetting because of the nerve it hit. When Harold phoned that day my voice was hoarse from crying.

- What happened?

- I got such an unusual letter from my brother.

- About what?

- About me, and a talk he had with our mother! About how my mother never stops and looks back, never really listens to herself, to anyone, and has no idea of her impact. My brother wanted her to know this, to know the effect it has on me… how she sets everything up. All the people she compares me to who have made it in the big league. My brothers being all doctors — for me it was only by becoming a star did I have a chance of measuring up. 'Don't you see,' my brother wrote, 'that we all keep you stuck there in that child-like fantasy place. Everything Mom does, everything she says, just reinforces that. Like if you could just get famous then everything would be okay, and we'd finally love and accept you. And you could finally love and accept yourself. Because everything she says to you, whether she knows it or not, is telling you that you are not good enough. And you've believed it. You've believed it your whole life. It's bullshit, completely bullshit. What counts,' he wrote, 'is living well, having a good relationship, being a real person… You have what it takes, why can't you accept it now? I do.'

- But what am I supposed to do now? I said to Harold, not understanding why I was crying. It was actually a beautiful letter, so why did it feel like sharp knives piercing my skin? Just to realize I had wasted so much of my life trying to please my mother? That I didn't have to? Without the whip of my mother as driver, what should I do instead?

- We'll talk about it when I get home. Harold said, his voice soothing and resonant, the reason I fell in love with him. I'll come home soon, he said. And we'll go skiing.

It was one of the nicest things to do in Oslo… to ski on the lighted cross-country tracks. Like candles in snow-covered trees it made the darkness less daunting. I was getting better at skiing, the balance and momentum, and exercise; any exercise helps a desperate mood. It was good for thinking… but that night nothing helped. That letter was like a bomb set off in my head. If he were right, if my main motivation was to prove myself worthy, how could I learn to do the music for myself, to write a song with all my heart if nobody wanted to hear it? On the way home, the bomb exploded and my words scattered everywhere, but suddenly everything was Norway's fault:

- How could you move here! How can you stand it? How can you not see the vacant look on everyone's face? The only passion here is drinking!

- I have learned not to look, Harold said.

- But when you look, I shouted… do you like what you see? Do you really like it?

- You want me to say that I hate it here, don't you? Well I won't.

- I want you to tell me how you feel.

- No you don't! If you did, you wouldn't ask in such a manipulative fashion.

Again he was right, of course he was right. But I couldn't let him know that; I was an insect, trapped in a box and shipped to the other side of the world.

- C'mon, I taunted. Tell me how you feel.

- I don't like to see the drunks, but I have to live here. I have to work here. If I keep noticing what I don't like all the time it will give me an ulcer, and I don't want one. YOU must have ten ulcers. YOU who feel that you have to SEE every Goddamn thing!

- In Norway, there are two choices: to get drunk or shut down. I don't want either. I want to get the hell out of here!

- So get out of here!

Harold was now also surly, but I couldn't stop myself; I was on a whirlwind of self-destruction. Once home, I wanted to be on a movie set and throw plates at each other, smash the house to bits. Instead, I stormed back outside. But it was fucking cold and there was ice everywhere. I had iron clamps strapped to my shoes otherwise I'd have fallen and broken every bone in my body.

In the weeks that followed, there was so much hate in me I hardly recognized what I'd become. And even when Harold forced me out of the house to do something meaningful, like go to a museum, the Munch for example, I'd meet my terrible rage in all the paintings. I'd look at: *The Scream*, and swallow down my tongue to stop myself screaming back. Munch must have felt exactly the same: GET ME OUT OF HERE. HELP.

At just the point of giving up, the phone rang and it wasn't Harold. A Norwegian student whom I'd taught in Holland and had really liked had come back to Oslo and wanted lessons. In addition she had recommended me to the music college downtown that desperately needed a singing/acting teacher. *They pay well here,* she told me, *much better than Holland.*

It was a chance I had to grab; I'd run out of ideas. And Harold really was the nicest man I'd ever met, and he hadn't kicked me out yet. Getting work was a godsend: in the end, whoever and wherever you are, you just need something to do. After a whole day of teaching talented students, who really liked me and whom I really liked and who were so happy to hear that I hated Oslo — as so many of them, coming from outside Oslo, felt the same! — my mood improved immensely. I'd soon learn that not all Norwegians were so fond of Oslo; that my words gave form and recognition, and humor to their suffering.

Once, giving a private lesson to a talented young singer/pianist from the very North where people are more friendly and spontaneous, a very surprising thing happened. The student played a ballad in English, and as I coached him through several stages of deepening expression, he got better and better. Finally he sang with such feeling that tears welled in my eyes.

- How did you do that? he asked in amazement.

- How did I do what?

- How did you just start crying like that?

- I don't know, I said, you sang so beautifully and it touched me and the tears came.

- You have to stay here in Norway, he said with his face beaming, *and teach us how to do that.*

So I stayed, and got more work, even a long tour singing through the north of Norway. Between every venue was a flight: no train, no bus, no choice. And then my fear of flying *really* took off. Even with *Xanax,* I couldn't get near a plane, let alone on one without white knuckling it. The planes were so small that the only place for my guitar was strapped between my legs. Those planes tossed in the wind, with no chance to forget you were on a plane, seeing the vast stark-white mountains, the dark water of the fjords, all that desolate nature from the window was staggering, terrifying, each flight making me more and more anxious.

Norway — no matter how hard I tried to find my way, to fit in, felt like being banished to Siberia. Despite the exquisite beauty, the people lacked the thing I needed so badly: eye contact, reaction, confirmation and validation of self. Like in Peter Pan — with no one clapping, Tinker Bell didn't know she existed.

Session Ten

- Maybe the one good thing about living in Norway, I tell Ana, was that I could save enough money to come here to Buenos Aires, the Mecca of tango. It was like a dream!

Ana has that look of surprise that is not uncommon with Argentine people who don't dance; they can't believe we travel so far just for the tango.

- When you dance in Europe, I tell her, all you hear is how great Buenos Aires is. And it's true. It was the best time of my life...

I may have overdone it in my zeal to create a *personality*; may have traveled a bit too far, but at least I finally had one. Although still shy with people, I often had something clever, something witty to say that made them laugh, made them open and tell me things they usually didn't speak about. And when *I* met someone who veered off the main road, whose peppery words and view of the world whet my imagination, I liked them. No matter what, I liked them. So when I first met Evelyn in Buenos Aires I was smitten, completely smitten. She was funny and charismatic and flooded with unmentionable stories to tell. The way she sat, the first evening, at her freshly-made table, with flowers and tea-set and a plate of *media lunas* not waiting but anticipating me with all the time in the world. How she rose to greet me, with her long dress flowing, stirred on by the gentle overhead fan. She gazed lovingly at her banana tree that her house was remarkably built around and showed me how beautiful her life was. She knew beauty, because she was an *artist*. A painter in her better days, long before the recent troubles in Argentina, long before she had to rent rooms — *but we shall not speak of that,* she said. She could see that I too was an artist and we could together rise above, because the life worth living was from high above. She sprinkled our mostly English conversation with the soft *shh* that is characteristic of Buenos Aires *Castellano*, it was so lovely to hear, like music, like laughter; you could stay by her side and listen forever.

From the start, I was smitten by everything in Buenos Aires. Not just surviving the longest flight I'd ever taken, but Buenos Aires was heaven: magical, mysterious and exotic like Mexico was for me as a teenager. Coming out of the brutal Norwegian winter, *starved* for human contact and reaction, Buenos Aires was everything I'd longed for. It pulsated life — even with the economy collapsing, the Argentine person lived more fully than anyone I'd ever met before. At last I'd found paradise, where I could dance all day and all night!

The only problem with dancing tango until the wee hours, and staying at a cheap hotel with travelers who woke at those same wee hours, was a dreadful lack of sleep. So I had to find another place to stay. At a *Milonga* I heard about Evelyn's house and how quiet it was.

- Ten dollars a night, a friendly dancer told me, bananas included. There's even a large studio where you can practice dancing, or whatever.

- Whatever? I asked. Even singing?

Where I stayed, it was forbidden to play any type of music, live or otherwise, for the walls were paper-thin. After six weeks of just dancing, I was aching to sing.

- Evelyn lets us all use the studio, this woman replied. There's even a guy from Austria who plays the violin. Here, she said, writing down the number. Just ask for Evelyn, I'll tell her you'll call.

When I phoned, Evelyn knew about me and gave so much warmth in her *oh hello! It's you*, that I knew it was the right decision to move there.

- Come over, she said. Have a cup of tea with me and see the place!

The evening was balmy: the fan on low created a soft and sensual swoosh through the fronds of the banana tree. Like a tropical beach, so South American, this oasis in the center of a house, in the center of an ugly street in San Telmo, one of the oldest neighborhoods in Buenos Aires. The soft yellow lighting created an atmosphere of all things possible. Evelyn was a master at the art of presentation; obviously skilled at *knowing* what a person lacked.

Though I fancied myself special, I wasn't any different from the other tango dancers who arrived with huge hopes and big dreams. All of us intoxicated by Buenos Aires: doing the tango like junkies; practicing, pushing, daring, going deep inside the belly, releasing the body and mind over and over, and then the erotic excitement of actually *dancing* the tango. It wasn't only me who after several weeks of living every moment to the fullest, collapsed in exhaustion. Granted it was wonderful, as we'd never felt so alive, still we were exhausted, aggressively exhausted.

And so confused, we no longer knew who we were nor what guidelines to follow. We had never opened ourselves up that much for a reason: all that chaos has no place in daily life, only on the dance floor... For some of us, it had been too much. Like children, allowed for the first time to be at a grown-up party and having stayed up much too late, we needed our mothers to scoop us up and carry us to bed. Evelyn knew this well — she earned her living from mothering tired travelers and over-danced *Tangueras*.

We sat there, that balmy evening, sipping her most delicious tea and I let Evelyn convince me that it was only with her, at her marvelous guesthouse, that I'd find the rest needed to keep up my pace of dancing, for I had no desire to stop. With a new pot of tea brewing, she knowingly took my hand and led me down the stairs to see the *studio*, whose grandness nearly brought tears to my eyes.

- Sing, she said, let me hear your beautiful voice. I know you have one.

I never *just sing* in front of strangers. I hadn't sung in weeks, was completely out of practice, but unexpectedly the room took hold and expanded me, making my voice full and so easy that I couldn't stop. As if the walls were mountains and the wooden floor trees, my voice resonated like in a perfect forest. What poured out was so connected to *love*, to not caring if it was good or not, something I hungered for, even more than being mothered. It was this I'd searched my entire life for! Finally, finally I had found home. Singing and tango!!

-¡Estupendo! Evelyn cried out. What a voice! You must sing every day! How wonderful to fill my house with even more music. You singing! Sebastian playing his violin — tomorrow you will meet Sebastian! What more could I ask for?

I bowed to her as she led me ceremonially back up the metal staircase to our tea, to the mesmerizing sound of her voice, the vibration like a delightful tickle inside my skin as she arranged everything. She knew Buenos Aires, every pitfall, every source of harm, but she would protect me; she had taken me in, into her magic kingdom. All would be well. The room she showed me, the best one in the house, was perfect. It led onto a patio, a place to soak my aching feet after a night of dancing and to sip a glass of wine under the starry sky.

- Look, she said, turning off the lights. Look at the stars. *Maravilloso, no?*

I began to giggle, felt tipsy with happiness, completely in love. Just then someone bolted up the stairs breaking the spell — although with Evelyn everything held enchanting possibilities.

- Ah, what perfect timing, she said. Come Ginny, come meet Deborah, she's moving in tomorrow!

- *What* room is she moving into, Evelyn? The house is filled up!

- No it is not filled up, Evelyn snapped, showing a glimpse of a side I was not interested in seeing at the moment, so high was I with happiness. The big room, Evelyn sternly said, is still available.

- What about me? Ginny whimpered, *I'm* supposed to move into that room!

- But you have no money! Evelyn replied. I have to earn money.

- I have money, Ginny yelped, her words tighter and tighter, as if she had to pay for the space they consumed. *We* made an agreement, Evelyn. What about our agreement? I will pay you as we agreed and I will move in tomorrow!

- Okay, Evelyn said, not even turning to look at me.

The little balloon I was floating in came crashing to the ground. But I was too far-gone to give it all up. I stood there not knowing what to do, for I'd fallen in love with the house, the atmosphere, with Evelyn, with singing daily in the studio that it was impossible to leave.

- Oh dear, Evelyn said, quickly regaining my confidence. Ginny leads a very confusing life. Not to worry, there's another solution. Follow me.

She took me by the hand yet again and led me into the main house that was directly above the studio, exactly the sort of place I imagined Hemingway living in. Next to a big front room, large kitchen and bathroom was a nice-sized bedroom with a double bed and large wooden closet.

- How about this room? She asked me, what do you think?

- But whose room is this? I asked. It was clearly in use and I didn't want yet another traveler to come bolting up the stairs.

- That doesn't matter, she said, what do you think?

- I think it is lovely, I said, but it's already someone's room.

- Nine dollars a night, even cheaper than the other one. You can use the bathroom here, and the kitchen.

- This is *your* room Evelyn, isn't it?

- It doesn't matter, she said again. I can set up a bed in the living room, but we will share the bathroom and the kitchen, if that's all right with you.

- But is it all right with *you*?

- I really need the money, she said, and Ginny can't pay much, but I did make an agreement with her, and you see how she is.

- I'll be very late with the tango... Won't I disturb you?

- Oh no, she said, I am a great sleeper.

And the part of me that suspected this not to be true went completely unnoticed.

*

A few days later, after I'd moved in, unpacked my clothing and my tango shoes and had two glorious nights of sleep, she came to find me.

- I have to tell you, she said, about Sebastian. I am worried sick about him.

After hearing all about Sebastian, how beautifully he played, but how troubled he was, how Evelyn thought our music would be grand together, the concert she imagined we'd give in a few weeks time, I couldn't wait to meet him. Playing with another musician, especially a good one, is always more inspiring, easier than playing alone.

Later, when she wanted to introduce us, I was eager. She knocked on the door and called his name. A shuffle of steps, like an old man coming slowly to the door, but Sebastian wasn't old at all. In his early twenties maybe, skinny and pale, like a dog that badly needed food. His eyes lacked something, of what exactly I couldn't tell; but the lack was brutal and the room stunk of old cigarette smoke, drink and unwashed clothing. The walls were lined with empty beer bottles, the large ones they sell in Buenos Aires.

Evelyn introduced us. Without opening his lips, he made a soft mmm sound in acknowledgment. He still seemed drunk, and needed his hand for support on the large sagging dresser near the door.

- Deborah is a singer, she said nudging him. Why don't you try to play together? The studio is free in the afternoon.

- Mmm, Sebastian said again, this time nodding.

She said something in German, as they shared that mother tongue, but still no response.

- Why don't I come and knock on your door tomorrow? I suggested. Maybe you'll feel like playing.

All he did was emit another soft sound and then Evelyn led me away.

- It's a tragedy, she said. I have never seen anyone drink as he does. You'll see... he'll be fine tomorrow, but still I worry about him. Please try to get him to play with you.

The next day, with the sun beating down through the roof above the banana tree, I heard violin scales, fast and furious, a professional warming up before a concert. Beautiful tones. My God, I thought. If this guy plays so well after a hangover, he must be incredible.

When I knocked, a different Sebastian greeted me: this one with fast impatient steps. The bottles were gone, the ashtrays emptied, the air fresh.

- Come in, he said.

Words, I thought, he speaks.

- Sorry about yesterday, a bit too much I suppose. His English was accented as if learned in London. Look, he said, I am not sure what you want, but I can't improvise, I only play classically. Evelyn means well, but she pokes into everyone's life here. Shall we get a coffee?

- Well... I... uh... still would like to play with you, you sound great. I could... teach you how to... improvise. I heard your scales. That's all you need. I am sure you have a great ear... if I sang you a line, you could play it. I'm sure.

No words again, but a non-committal nod.

- Come on. Let's give it a go.

There was something about him, how lost he seemed, so broken, that touched me. A character from Hermann Hesse, straight out of the magic theater in *Steppenwolf* that fit into my fantasy of Evelyn and her amazing house that I'd stumbled upon. That he was also staying there, this incredible musician, gave me courage to persist. I smiled, held up my guitar and motioned for him to follow.

- I'll see, he said.

I went into the studio, tuned my guitar and began to sing. Like the first night with Evelyn, my voice poured out. I set up three chairs, one for me, one for the song sheets, and one for Sebastian who I felt would come. What a lovely sensation: to *feel* a thing will happen, even if his violin scales still echoed in the distance. I started practicing and with each song felt more and more conviction; giddy with the sensation that something wonderful was about to happen.

He crept in so silently that I was startled when he spoke.

- You have a nice voice, he said, are these your songs?

- Yes.

- They are pretty, but I can't play this kind of music.

- Actually… I am quite sure… you can.

Not immediately, for he was incredibly shy — even more than me. It didn't seem possible that someone as talented as he could also suffer from fear of being heard. But he did. To start, I sang the song slowly, without words, just the melody, allowing him to find the scales that worked best, to feel the rhythm, tempo. Then adding the lyrics, explaining the subtext of the song briefly. While strumming the chords on the guitar, I'd sing an improvisational line which he played a few times, little by little making it his own.

Within a few days of practicing, he played with ease and grace. Almost excruciating to be that close to such gorgeous playing — he really was the best musician I had ever heard, let alone sat so close to; like any of the great violin players in any orchestra. As he became more comfortable, he invented his own lines, improvising so proficiently that by the second week it was not only me who wanted to practice. He had so much inside him, so much restlessness that you could tell he began to enjoy the freedom of playing a thing not already written, a thing he could create and *change* depending on his mood. The more power and feeling he put into his violin, the better I sang. It was unbelievable what came out of us.

We hardly spoke, for the time in the studio was precious, intimate. In a way it was like the best tango dances; how the stranger came up and embraced you and held you and danced you like a million dollars and returned you to your seat without a peep spoken. So much stronger to not dissipate into mundane details, like who we were and why we were there. By accident — one night when Sebastian was too drunk to play, but wanted company — I learned that he was on leave for a year from the orchestra he played with in Iceland and was delighted, like me, to escape the dark winter. He'd fallen madly in love with someone; that didn't work out, something he was still punishing himself over. His father, a famous violinist, had wanted and expected the world from him; a world Sebastian could never give him.

Mostly, I'd be in the studio first and he'd creep in quietly. We'd tune up and begin. As our playing improved, the hours passed quickly, too quickly. At the end, almost embarrassed by what had come out of us, of what we had expressed in each other's presence, we'd look down, pack our instruments, make a rough plan on our next meeting and go our separate ways. Me, to dance tango, and Sebastian, on a sober day to learn Spanish — he had a rough plan of teaching violin at a music school in Buenos Aires — on a good, light drinking day, to some colorful bar, and on a bad day to his closed-in room. I'd written a few new songs in a style to please him and he seemed delighted. Yet when I wanted to record us here in Buenos Aires, as I knew what we created was beautiful, he refused. Wouldn't even allow me to record our practice sessions on the cheap Walkman I'd traveled with.

- No one must hear this, he warned.
- But it will only be for me, and I've already heard you.
- I can't play if you record me.
- Why?
- Don't ask me.

And then he'd disappear for days. I tried once, to tell him about my eating obsession and the twelve-step program, but he wasn't interested. He'd only tell snippets of his life; his mother, whom he rarely mentioned, unable to give him what he needed. Maybe it's always the same story, even if you change country and language. Maybe, if you've once used something to manage your fear, in the end it takes over. Or maybe the bizarre urge to destroy — at first in protest to high expectations of parents and of the world — gets a life of its own, with its own dark pleasure. It had been his drinking, he told me, that cost him numerous jobs in prestigious orchestras. It was not for nothing that he was in Iceland, a country far more lenient in terms of alcohol. *I like to be*, he said, *where no one knows me, where no one watches over me.*

We'd practice like desperate strangers meeting for sex. The music soared with emotion, his gorgeous lines weaved in and out of every cell in my body, making my songs sound more beautiful than they would ever be again. Evelyn would stand in awe outside the door listening.

After several sober days he'd be manic, glowing with pink, healthy cheeks, wanting to play for hours; in the breaks he'd laugh, tell stories of himself, of what he really wanted. He'd play more beautifully than one could ever imagine. Then he'd disappear again.

I am so sorry to not have a recording of our playing — that really was the best music I ever made; it was also a relief that Sebastian didn't want to play out anywhere, no gigs, nothing. We really did play just for the Gods, blessed by the Gods. If those invisible Gods had paid us I'd have continued playing music with Sebastian until the end of time.

I was running out of money, and Harold was running out of patience. He'd already agreed to my staying a month longer, as he would be abroad at a long conference, but he wrote: *if you stay much longer, I will lose you. I don't think you'll ever come back. And, I won't wait for you forever.*

I was torn. For me, it was the perfect life: playing music so intensely every day and then all night long dancing my heart out. Yet, when I'd see the soggy yellow-look on the *Tangueras* faces that had stayed too long; who had cut all ties — it frightened me. It wasn't only good to be that free, and I feared losing all grip to the 'normal' life waiting in Europe, and to Harold — who I secretly knew was the last of my Mohicans. I'd never find another man like him, who could love me so well and so deep to let me go for so long.

Was it shallow to want to stay? Was playing with so great a musician like Sebastian and all that dangerous tango dancing worth giving up the best relationship I'd ever had? Wasn't it all strangely reminiscent of the resistance in my life to commitment, to being responsible? Was I willing to sacrifice everything, even security, for the sensation of being alive?

Tango is the dance that thrives on such questions, and on all unsettled feelings. It's the dance that places a loving finger on the lips and says: *shh, don't think my darling, feel, only feel and be in this moment, for that is all you ever get.* When danced well, the tango embrace wraps around you and holds you in such a way that you need only that: its sensual, non-threatening embrace.

The longer I stayed in Buenos Aires the better my singing became, the better my dancing. I wasn't betraying Harold with another man, not in the least. I danced with ever-changing partners, rarely getting to know any of them, never going for the infamous *cup of coffee*; even Sebastian, we hardly knew each other. Yet the dance, the music, the giving of myself so fully to another, is a form of betrayal. Of course it is. But how can art come from the bland loving of just one person? I didn't think it worked like that.

Can you blame me for wanting to stay?

Maybe if Harold and I had met earlier, if we'd had children together, such choices would never have arisen. But Harold was in his fifties when we'd met and had his own children with whom he continued to have a close relationship; my going away often made that relationship easier. He had his work, his exercise — about which he was as passionate as I was about dancing. I am not saying that I asked or expected Harold to be everything for me, just as I wasn't for him. If I'd learned anything in my life it was how impossible it is to find everything needed in one person and in one place.

Ironically, it was Sebastian who told me that I *should* go home. In a moment of clarity, he — who had stayed far longer in Buenos Aires — said that something bad was brewing in the country; and there was definitely something dangerous, chaotic, in staying too long, especially when your savings ran out.

- Look at me, Sebastian laughed nervously. If it wasn't for you coming along... I'd do nothing but drink all day.

Session Eleven

- *It was wise that you went back to Europe when you did, Ana said, at our next session. It was a very hard time here... And it's good you didn't lose Harold.*
- *You don't even know him, why do you like him so much?*
- *From what you say... and from how hard it is for any of us to find a good partner.*
- *Even if I don't love him?*
- *I actually think you do. It's just not the love of your dreams. And besides, now everything is darkened by what you feel. Take Evelyn -- it's hard to believe the woman you've just described is the same one that you're struggling with now...*
- *But everything changed, I shouted. Everything...*

Living in Buenos Aires had made me special, as if I'd sprouted wings and could fly above this... this being human. All my overdoing nature, my excess passion and desires had flourished. Yet once back into the functionality of my daily life in Europe those wings failed me and I became more human and fragile than ever. The way my mother could trip me up with her comments about how this one or that one had 'made it', just her tone of voice through the phone reminding me I hadn't. That I still lagged behind; that my latest CD — inspired by Sebastian — was still not good enough to make me a contender. And my father, with his commanding voice convincing me *it was time once and for all to stop TRYING to be an artist, to accept that I've given it a good shot and get a regular job and live like everyone else.*

Can I pinpoint a day when the resonance of my time in Buenos Aires had stopped, or when the disappointment of having climbed to new musical heights, of having worked unbelievably hard on my latest recording and *still* not 'making it' nearly broke my heart? No, I don't think so.

When I look back, that magical time in Buenos Aires was the end of an era, the end of my youth. Even if my life had been a series of mid-life

crises, I had been able until then to flow in the river of girlish playful-
ness, to bathe in the sensation only youth provides — that it was all still
to come.

Then one day you wake up and are shocked by who greets you in the
mirror. *This can't be possible* you yell at this stranger. *Who the hell are you?
Not yet!* To the face that won't leave, *this can't be happening yet!* Away
from the mirror you feel the same as before, or so you think, or so you
tell yourself. It's the mirror to blame.

Suddenly there's empathy for the wicked Queen in the fairy tale, for
her need to destroy the beautiful young Snow White. If there were no
Snow Whites, she'd still be the most beautiful. When we first hear this
story we love Snow White and we take her side because she is so young
and pretty, and she can't help being pretty. Yet the Queen also couldn't
help getting old. Of course she hates Snow White; of course she wants
her dead. If I were the only one left in the world who could sing, people
would hire me! They'd have to. There'd be no competition; no chance of
finding someone *better.*

Just like the wicked Queen I too needed constant reassurance, but
nothing worked because there's no way to reassure anyone in this most
impossible request. No way to reassure you that you are not getting old,
that you are the only *special one.* It hit me like a bullet. Suddenly everyone was so young, on the streets, at the tango, all the clever new sing-
er-songwriters with their perfect teeth and their belly-button rings.

Is this what many artists cannot come to terms with? When the world
no longer notices or needs them? Why so many put a gun to their heads?
It's a sort of revenge. Because you are angry! Oh boy are you angry.

And yet, despite grand suicidal thoughts I wasn't ready to give up.
Stupid perhaps, but I couldn't forget the small plaque one of my singing
teachers used to keep on her piano: *Success is the best revenge.*

- *Revenge for what?* I asked her once.

- *What do you think?* she asked me back. We spent the rest of the lesson talking about the great desire many of us had to get back at those
who made us suffer. Sure, to succeed *is* the best way to show them — if
you're lucky and courageous enough. For me, seething under the crush
of disillusionment after the release of my latest CD, I was further from
success than ever.

Nothing made any sense, except returning to Buenos Aires, even if
Sebastian was no longer there, and everything, I'd been told, had

changed. I clung to the memory of Evelyn's last words, as she hugged me until the taxi arrived: *The days will pass quickly and you'll be back in Argentina where you belong. The hard times won't last forever, and there will be music and dancing and... Mi Buenos Aires querido...* Carlos Gardel's voice calling to me, urging me to come home.

I believe most of us do the best we can with what *seems* to be in front of us and for me that meant carrying on with concerts and teaching; to go on with the show even if my heart was no longer in it. One night, on tour in Holland in the fall of 2003, I nearly burst out crying in the middle of a set... nearly fell to my knees to beg the audience's forgiveness for playing such crap. It's not easy to sing when you feel like that; like cement in your throat. At the break, completely out of control, I grabbed a good friend and dragged her back stage. She held me as I cried hysterically, comforting me with words that served temporarily to get me through the rest of the show. The place was packed and the owner would've killed me if I stopped playing. She helped me, and I made it through, totally surprised by the encores — I never get it that when the performer is most vulnerable, the audience most loves them. But it feels like shit.

As soon as I came home, I phoned Harold, grateful that he was still awake.

- I can't do it, I said. We have to cancel the flight to the US to see my family and I can't go on to Buenos Aires. Not alone... I'll...

- Shh... Harold said, stubborn as ever. Stick to the plan. Everything will be fine, you'll see. You always get afraid, but you always manage the flight. Don't give in to those fears. You're my brave warrior. I am always so proud of you, how you go out there and do your life when I know how afraid everything makes you. Remember, soon you'll be with Evelyn at that lovely house, and the weather will be hot and sunny and ...

- It feels different this time.

- You say that every time. Don't think now. Go to bed and I'll go to bed and this time next week you will be in my arms. Hey, I'll even pack some shrimps from Oslo and we'll have a picnic in the hotel room in Frankfurt. I booked us into a nice hotel by the airport so we can have a good long sleep before the flight to the US.

The following weekend was the Nijmegen special *Milonga*. Usually I couldn't wait for this tango event, but this time I doubted going. Feeling decrepit with age and emotionally hung-over I was sure no one would dance with me. But I forced myself out the door — I hadn't yet paid for my ticket to Argentina, which wasn't cheap and I wanted to make sure I would still dance before flying half-way across the world.

Just bite the bullet and find your way once and for all in Norway. Settle in like a bear for the winter and stop making a fuss. Accept that fate has led you there, and learn to like it. Your family is right — stop trying to be what you are not. You are a scared mouse-of-a woman, not the stuff of great singers! And you're absolutely not sexy or cool enough to be a real tango dancer.

I hated her, hated that voice of reason. Yet as I biked to the *Milonga*, my body trembled with fear as if heading to the final ultimatum. God how I needed to dance.

Just a few rounds across the dance floor and the desperate Deborah vanished. The music took over, took my body in it's arms and tangoed me until the wee hours. I kissed the tango God and swore to be faithful; that when you dance, everything really is okay. And the rest doesn't matter; it really doesn't matter. I paid for my ticket in full. Decision made, no more changes.

But in the middle of the week a strange gnawing feeling returned and with it, a terrible dream of Argentina.

I'm at the airport but cannot find my suitcases. At first this is wonderful, the complete lightness of having no things, no baggage, nothing to carry, but soon I start longing for my clothes, my books, my music… my guitar which I've completely forgotten. I have no CDs to sell… and will run out of money. It is very cold, colder than ever. There are no bananas; we cannot sit outside at Evelyn's house. But it isn't Evelyn; it is my mother. Where is Evelyn? And all the tango dancers in Holland that intimidate me are there in the studio. They have to get out so I can practice with Sebastian. But Sebastian is gone, and they won't leave. 'Get out of here, this is my place!' I try to scream, but no voice comes. Evelyn? Evelyn, where are you?

I woke up in a cold sweat. It will be impossible to find what I had two years ago. Harold is wrong; I shouldn't go. I tried to phone him, but this time he wasn't there.

The last appointment in Nijmegen was with a voice therapist, Maarten, to do an exchange. We'd been meeting and exchanging for years. He liked the Alexander Technique and I liked the sensation of his large warm hands on my back, his twist of word and phrase that helped my singing and breathing and always left me calmer, all of which was needed that day.

I worked on him first and for his part, he wanted to try something different with me, something new he was learning. I told him how unsettled I felt, but he insisted this *something new* would be perfect to ground me.

- Stand up, he said. This may feel strange and uncomfortable but I want to watch you very intensely as we work. I will take time between instructions, he continued. You will have to *be* with yourself while you wait for the next thing, and I will watch you while you wait.

- Why is this good then, I asked, if it will make me uncomfortable?

- Because it is useful to observe how and what you do when you *feel* uncomfortable, for whatever you do in this slow-motion exercise, you will be doing most likely while you perform. When we become aware of the things we do but do not need to do, we can grow and change and our voice will get more powerful. Are you ready? he asked.

- I guess so, I said.

But this was untrue. I was absolutely not ready. The downside of a friendly exchange is that you don't want to be a pain in the ass. I stood up and found myself wishing so badly for his hand to be placed on my back, for comforting strokes to reassure my self-conscious body. Instead, Maarten didn't say a word for what seemed like forever. I was dreadfully uncomfortable, growing more and more so. How terrible to just stand there and be watched and to do nothing.

It reminded me of one of my early auditions in New York, a *cattle call* for *West Side Story*, for the part of Maria. The line was enormous, at least two thousand young women all in their early twenties, all who looked exactly like me, waited outside the theater. Thirty at a time, we were ushered in and led onto the stage. It was a day with lousy weather, rain and wind, and by the time I went in, I was frozen stiff. We were allowed a brief moment to walk and stretch; then told to line up. He was a famous choreographer who weaved amongst us — as if we were cattle — sniffing, feeling, looking, judging. Many people sat in the audience, also looking and judging. Forever we stood there, with nothing specific to do. I wanted to sing, to dance, to *emote*; to be someone else — I was good at that, to be someone else — but just to *stand* inside my own skin was torture. I did notice, however, that some of the girls could just stand there and appear marvelous. It didn't surprise me when they were asked to stay and I was tapped on the shoulder and told *thank you, that was all, and please exit stage left*. I walked out into the rain-drenched streets feeling so small and so terribly unused, useless and unwanted.

- Make a sound, Maarten finally instructed.

I felt so grateful to finally be able to *do* something.

- What are you feeling? Maarten asked.

- Like I am going to cry.

- So cry, he said.

- Won't it ruin the exercise?

- No, no, the whole point is to see what happens and to let yourself do and be whatever it is.

So I began to cry, but not so hard that I couldn't sing. Maarten played some tones on the piano and instructed me to follow his lead and to improvise a sound. It surprised me how much sound came out.

- This is good, he said with his usual enthusiasm. Very, very good. Now keep going as I watch you.

It was a funny mix, his watching and coaxing. It made me uncomfortable, and yet I liked his intense gaze. Liked that my voice got stronger and stronger. He played the piano harder, looking more and more intensely. We continued building and building until the panic came and choked me. All at once the crying made it impossible to sing more.

- What's happening? He asked in alarm.

- I am not sure. I can't...

And then my knees buckled and I keeled over. Once down, I felt hopelessly ashamed and crawled into one of the corners, with my head between my knees.

- Oh my, Maarten said and then quickly looking at his watch he gasped: oh dear, but we have to stop now. I am so sorry... I have a student coming in a few minutes. Will you be okay?

- *What are my choices Maarten?* I wanted to scream. *This was shit of you to try something you haven't learned yet!*

I forced myself to stop crying and shoveled down what had erupted and prepared for the steep climb down the two flights of the very typical Dutch staircase and not kill myself.

- I feel very weird, Maarten.

- You'll be okay, he said. I promise… And he got me started on the stairs.

- See you next time, he waved goodbye.

But there never was a next time.

I returned from the session with Maarten feeling wretched and spent the rest of the day, despite the pouring rain, walking. I came back much later, very cold and unable to stop sneezing, made some soup, wrapped myself in a blanket and put on the television. While zapping, I found a documentary on Duke Ellington about his life and his music. About his mother and how devoted she was, not at all jealous of his talents, never teaching him to back-pedal nor waste time in doubting, how she instilled a steady belief and confidence that stayed with him all of his life. Even during the inevitable hard times that the most caring mother cannot prevent, he never lacked the trust in his life's purpose or talents; he was able to use all of it.

A fellow musician, whom I rented two rooms from so that I could really live and work while in Holland, came home and found me on the couch. He joined me in watching the rest of the documentary; then opened one of his best bottles of wine, and little by little my crying turned into laughter, both of us making a good party out of moaning and complaining, cursing our fate, our lives, our families. By the end of the bottle we cried out in harmony: *Oh to be Duke Ellington! Oh to have had his mother!*

PART TWO:
THE JOURNEY DOWN

1.

On yet another gray and morbid day, I leave for Groningen, in the very north of Holland, for my last gig before meeting Harold for our flight to the US.

Usually the train journey takes less than three hours with one simple change across the tracks; time enough even with more bags than hands to make it. But this is no normal day. Disaster is courting me with a scent and a howl. *You are not that powerful!* I feel Harold taunting me. *But maybe I am.* My presence, rotten to the core, has contaminated the train, for halfway there it breaks down and we must change for a bus and then another train. I am helpless, completely unable to carry all my things in the chaotic stampede. Loaded like a mule — two suitcases stuffed with winter clothes, summer clothes, tango clothes and shoes, a knapsack with computer and books, CDs to sell and performing gear, a bag of food AND my guitar — I am too tired to move, broken from all the years of touring and yearning and trying so hard to be more than I was. This train is my last vestige of hope and I can't bear to leave it. But I have no choice; the crowd is a tsunami forcing me out, out into the cold. I hold onto my guitar like a life preserver. Someone carries my luggage, but the bag of food gets lost in the current. Someone pushes me onto a bus and then onto an over-crowded train where I collapse on top of my things a slither of a second before the door closes.

The friend with whom I'll stay the night picks me up at the station. My cold is worse; I can hardly speak without coughing. He suggests canceling but I actually *need* to sing, don't know what else to do with myself feeling this odd.

It's quiet when I arrive at the club and the owner, a warm, friendly woman helps me set up a good sound, getting the best of my raspy voice. It can happen when you're sick that something switches in the brain and allows more feelings to come through: like suddenly you're Janis Joplin.

We're nearly finished, when a woman comes in. She is tiny by Dutch standards. She comes right to the table closest to the stage, as if she's waited forever to hear me. Her face beams with life, her eyes so brilliant it burns to look at her yet I cannot stop looking. She's with a man who doesn't seem interested in her, more occupied with the cigarettes he is smoking and the beer he orders. He doesn't seem to notice how intensely she stares at me. Or that she's come up to tell me her name, which is Edie. Or that she's taken my hand and is holding it in a loving way, although we've just met.

She goes back to her seat, but when the show starts it's as if she's still holding my hand, feeding me, pumping me up big and wide and mighty. The place is packed, but she's the one I sing for. She strips me naked and raw and I let her and the audience loves it. My voice pours out thick and lush and she rides me like a bronco, a wild bronco. I am open — look Bouke — I am flying! I soar across the universe because she's the sun behind the sun, the seducer, the snake charmer and the snake. The set builds and builds, the crowd is on fire: they drum on tables, they clap flamenco style, they hoot and whistle and slap their thighs. Edie, with her pigtails swishing, her hips grinding leads us directly into the *flame*. My cheeks burn red hot; my legs vibrate, my guitar roars like the Rolling Stones. Edie is so close now, nearly kissing me, and the energy whips through us and out to the audience. We ride the highest wave that ever there was and the crowd screams mad. I notice how high I am, how great this all is and then crash; fall. I swallow the entire wave in one gulp and choke so badly that I must rush off stage.

Edie runs after me. She wraps her arms around me.

- Don't cry, she says. You were so good.

I can't stop coughing and feel devastated, furious with myself. A real performer doesn't get thrown from the wave. A real performer rides the power to the end.

- I will never have what it takes, I sob into Edie's arms.

I cry about something else too, but what that is I refuse to claim. Maybe Edie knows, but she says nothing. All I can do is touch one of her long pigtails and stroke it gently in my hands.

*

Harold and I have a nice room at my brother Andy's house near Boston. The sun pours in — a welcome change from the winter gray in Europe. I am relieved that the flight went so easily. Maybe I've exaggerated the anxiety about my trip to Buenos Aires; maybe whatever has plagued me these last weeks has passed.

I'm up early, goofing around with Andy's kids — who are always happy to see me, their kooky Aunt Deborah who flies in from who-knows-where with small exotic gifts and silly songs, like an old sea captain. My brother is making pancakes and the coffee is brewing. All is going well, until the phone rings. It is my mother demanding to speak with me. The minute I take hold of the receiver, she starts yelling so vehemently that everyone hears her nasal voice bleed from the phone. Andy gives a look of wonder. What have I done? I haven't even seen her. The power she has over me is enormous. I hang up and start to shake.

- What's happened? Andy asked.

- I don't know.

- She probably just wanted you to phone the minute the plane landed. Don't worry, Deb, she's like that with all of us.

- No she's not... She'd never dare treat you like that.

I can't stop shaking and my brother looks with new concern, like something strange is rising out from the dreadful current that creeps through my bones. Like maybe something happened to me because of Maarten in Nijmegen, or the feelings I had for Edie. Like I am too open, too vulnerable for living.

- Don't let her get to you, Andy says as soothingly as he can. Just because you didn't phone her the second you arrived. Deb, you live far away, you forget how she is. You're going to see her tomorrow at the Thanksgiving dinner. Really, you've done nothing wrong.

I hardly sleep that night and dread the visit to my brother Bob's the following day. My father will also be there. All the years my parents have been divorced, I never get used to the forced feeling when they're together.

We arrive early, before anyone else, so there's time for a long walk, which helps a little. It dilutes the anxiety for goodness knows what. Of my mother yelling at me again, that's what.

Which she does the moment she arrives, so grand and theatrical, as if I, a dreadfully disobedient little girl, have seriously harmed her. She storms in with arms thrashing, her voice high and potent. I have no defense ready, because I am not sure what I have done. Only that I feel shamed. Terribly and horribly shamed. I hate her so much that I don't even know what I'm feeling. Her verbal complaint is about not phoning, yet the subtext screeches: *When are you going to be the daughter that I long for? When are you going to stop disappointing ME?*

Humiliated at being yelled at in front of everyone, friends of my brother's, people I don't even know, I run out of the room before anyone sees me crying. But of course I am seen. My brother Bob comes after me. His intention is to be helpful, yet he is the one who always gets it right so his words: *Don't let her get to you,* only shame me more, because it is too late, she has gotten to me.

After my brother leaves me I try to find Harold who has seen everything. He has gone out on the deck with a glass of wine.

- Why do I even come here? I say.

Harold, always so good and comforting, has no words to offer. Just a glass filled with wine.

*

Harold has left for Oslo and I must go on alone with the next part, to Buenos Aires. Everyone tells me that I am so lucky to be able to go off and dance tango in the warm summer sun. Why don't I feel lucky? Why does it feel so wrong, so very wrong? In the twelve-step program they teach you to listen to the pull from within and heed its' warning, yet not give over to every passing whim. What I feel now, is it whim or warning? It's been years and years since I've last gone to any meeting; have I lost all connection? Are the gods taunting me? *You think you are going to dance tango, ha-ha, just you wait girl. You are a foolish one, and you have never learned to listen.*

I decide not to drink a drop of anything in the next week; probably all this is just angst caused by having more alcohol than usual. On the phone, Harold reminds me how terrible I'll feel if I cancel this trip and come back to Oslo in the darkest time of winter, with nothing to do, no work set up. *There is no real reason not to go now. True, there has been unrest in Buenos Aires, but things are far more settled now, nothing to worry about. And your mother, forget about your mother. You've been working really hard,* Harold reassures me. *It is your fear of flying talking, nothing more.*

When we hang up, I remember another slogan: *Feelings are not facts.* There are no gods taunting me really. And yet moments later the anxiety reaches a record high and I'm forced to cancel the various things planned in Boston. My brother Andy tells me to stay in bed, to rest, if that's what's needed.

- I think you are allergic to us, he jokes. I seem to recall you getting sick the last time you came to visit!

I am grateful for Andy's kindness and yet berate myself for the role I seem to play in the family. Older than my three brothers (we are more or less a year and a bit apart), I rarely act the leader, rarely the most experienced and mature. I play the lost lamb, the black sheep, the one who can't settle down because I am searching, always searching for who will take care of me and I am running out of time.

I call my brother, Peter, the one closest to me in age to let him know that this time something *terrible* is happening, but the conversation goes hopelessly astray. He lets loose with built-up resentment saying: *You complain too much and never mention the good things, because there has to be good things. You have a great life. You only pretend to be a drowning person begging for a life preserver, but you don't really need one. You're the boy who cries wolf. Stop it,* he warns. *It is tiring.*

*

Just before leaving, I go to a doctor to renew my *Xanax* prescription. He tells me that many people fear flying, that it is more normal than we think. The doctor says it will be all right to increase the dose for the long flight from Miami, the one I'm most afraid of.

So I wait now at Miami International and I hear those doctor's words, but I can't find all those people afraid to fly. They all look so grand, so grown-up and in charge. A famous actress has just whizzed by, the one who played Frida Kahlo, in *Frida*, surrounded by caretakers. I hate her. How come she gets all those men to look after her, to carry her luggage? I smile at her and tell her how great she was in that movie and she actually says thank you before they rush her along. *She* is not afraid to fly. *She* is not afraid of her life. *She* is not an imposter.

I feel myself again. I am shaking, dreading this next flight more than anything.

So I won't go. I don't have to go. Who says I have to go?

I run to the pay phone and call Harold. He'll let me come home. He still loves me even though right now I hate him; I hate that he's not here. He answers!

- Why are you calling me? He asks. But he is not mean. He is gentle and loving. How can he do that? Doesn't he know what I think, what I dream? Doesn't he know what I'd do in half a second? Because I am trash, I am the call girl too afraid to answer the phone. I don't even listen to Harold, cause I know what he's going to say: that I am making a fuss; that in a few days I'll be basking in the sunshine having the time of my life. I hang up, but my hand is trembling. I have a disease: Parkinson's or Multiple Sclerosis. I must dance while I still can walk. I will kick myself to have missed this last chance before spending the rest of my life in a wheelchair.

They are boarding my flight. I look at the other passengers. *Help me*, I beg. But everyone looks down, looks away. I am totally alone. I take another *Xanax*; have never taken this many. But it's okay. The doctor said it would be okay.

Walk, I command myself. *Your legs still move; the disease hasn't spread to your legs. One step in front of the other*, I beg. *Just do this flight. Feelings aren't facts... feelings aren't facts...* I say over and over.

I am on the plane. I am in my seat. I have fastened my seat belt.

GET ME OUT! SOMEONE GET ME OUT OF HERE! I can't move my legs. I can't breath. HELP. Please someone help me. There must be one kind person on this plane. Why is everyone laughing? WHAT IS SO FUNNY? SOMEONE IS DYING HERE! I scream through my broken mouth, my blocked throat. But no one hears me. It is not real. This is a dream. I am not here.

But I AM here and the plane is REVVING and I MUST get out.

Flight attendants take your seat.

NO WAIT... PLEASE, LET ME OFF. PLEASE. I HAVE TO GO TO THE HOSPITAL.

We are airborne and I can't stop shaking. I search for an open window. There must be a window to jump out of.

I take one more *Xanax* and check the generic label because something is very wrong. As if having swallowed speed, my heart beats faster and faster.

The man sitting beside me sees this.

- Are you okay? he asks.

But I cannot form words and take his hand and place it on my chest.

- Oh my, he says.

He is the savior, the angel. He rubs my back; fiddles the wires and finds the switch that is stuck and disconnects the source of terror. My tears drip down, all over him. He gives me a handkerchief that smells of bread and jam and a quiet Sunday morning. He tells me where he's from, that he is going home to see his family. He knows he has to keep talking and he does.

- Come here, he says. It will be okay.

I lean against this stranger. I feel the vibration of his words…

And then the plane stops moving.

- Where am I? What has happened?

- You fell asleep, he says.

- Oh my god, we made it! Thank you, I say many times, and even once in Portuguese.

He helps me to my next gate where I must change for the short flight to Buenos Aires. I don't feel anything and collapse on a soft chair and fall asleep. A minute later — or maybe it's a year, or maybe ten — someone gets me up and leads me onto the plane. The next thing I know we have landed in Buenos Aires. Or so they say. But it doesn't feel like that. We are still flying. Why is everyone getting off the plane? My mind can't focus, but my arms and legs keep moving… claiming my suitcase, going through the passport control; my guitar straps itself onto my shoulders.

I see my name on a sign and follow the driver who *knows* Evelyn, who knows where I must go. But I don't care anymore; I just have to sleep.

- *Señora, señora*… but it is a dream. *Señora, estamos acá… Lady… we are here.*

The driver is shaking me. He is outside the car. He has my suitcase in his hand; my guitar is leaning on the side of the building. We are at Evelyn's house. I must pay him. I must get up and move.

2.

Evelyn opens the door. Only two years have passed, but the time has ravaged her face. She looks bad, hardened, with none of the charm I remember. She isn't happy at all to see me, even as I hand over a month's rent in dollars that she requested in her e-mail. I even give her more, all the money I have. I stand there frozen. She doesn't help carry my bags as she used to; instead she hands me a key and points up the stairs to my room, the good room, for Ginny has long since moved out.

- Nothing has changed, she continues. Except now you have to use the kitchen downstairs with everyone else. The pots and plates you bought the last time are down there, and everyone uses them. You are not special.

- Evelyn? I ask. Because I think I have it wrong; she can't be this mean.

I need her to help me... if she knows a good doctor, but she is in no mood to help. Although I say nothing, she gives a severe look asserting that whatever is troubling me is *nothing* compared with what's troubling her.

The panic shoots to the sky as I realize there'll be no comfort or help from her and that despite her words everything has changed. Even the banana tree looks sickly, the bananas are brown and shriveled. My hands shake as I try to unpack, hang up clothes, set out shampoo, toothbrush, creams, hoping a clear line of activity will settle me. It doesn't. I take my guitar and go down into the studio. The chairs are still there, the chairs that Sebastian and I used while practicing. I try to sing, but nothing comes out, only more tears. I suddenly miss Sebastian so much. What was I thinking? That he and Evelyn would be just as I left them, waiting for me to return. *Mi Buenos Aires querido...*

Bullshit. Everything is bullshit. All the warm Buenos Aires charm is hoax and fluff and a crock of shit. This house has become a refugee camp; it stinks and it's dirty. There's a family with a small child staying in Sebastian's room. I hear screaming and fighting and a baby crying.

Three women making food are crammed in the tiny kitchen, the one I never used before. I go in. They don't see me; they don't hear me over the onions frying.

I walk upstairs and onto the balcony just outside my room. It's almost like before, just a bit more falling apart. The view has changed. There are new buildings, but it's still beautiful.

Keep moving, I command myself. *If you keep moving this thing will go away; this horrible thing following you. Get your bankcard and get some money and get some food and get some sleep. Act as if,* the voice tells me. *You are the boy who cried wolf, nothing is happening to you.*

There are several new shops but the restaurant *El Desnivel* where I've eaten many times is still there. I am not hungry, but I should be hungry and so I will eat. I will keep doing everything that a real body does and soon I will wake up from this nightmare — because that's all it is, a nightmare. And I will wake up soon and laugh and go ha ha! And I will make it into a story and I will tell people and they will laugh and we will all live happily ever after.

The waiter recognizes me and smiles. He is so busy that he quickly takes my order. *Pechuga de pollo, ensalada y papas fritas* (it makes me so happy to remember the Spanish words) and a half bottle of red wine. I try to order olives with pits, but can't remember the word for pits, so the salad comes with shavings of olives on top. This makes me so sad; this is the cause of my anxiety.

There are two women at the next table, so close that I hear everything, but they're talking too fast for me to understand. I look for salt, for the condiments to dress my salad, but there's nothing on my table. I start to cry and stop myself by holding my breath, as if trying not to hiccup. One of the women notices me and with a big smile hands me the carrier with oil and vinegar, salt and pepper.

- Here, she says in English. We are done with it.

I want her to keep talking, but can't think of anything to say so I smile a quick thanks and return to my food. A long time passes yet I've come no further with the chicken. I put the food in my mouth yet cannot swallow. I look down at my feet. They are touching the ground, but I cannot feel them. My legs and my arms have gone numb.

The woman at the neighboring table is now touching my arm that I can see, but not feel; she is asking if I speak English.

- Yes, I say.

- Are you okay?

- I don't know, I tell her. *Act as if, act as if.* But I need her to help me and all at once I can't stop talking. I tell her that it feels like I'm still in the plane, still flying and I'd give anything to come down. That I am so scared and must get off the plane.

- You just arrived, she says. It can feel like that after a long flight...

- I am supposed to go home in six weeks, but I can't get back onto a plane. Not ever.

- So, she laughs. Live here in Buenos Aires!

This does not cheer me up. Even if I once loved Buenos Aires more than anything, right now I want to be home, with Harold. But I can't get there.

She reaches into her bag and gets a card.

- Call me, she says. I know someone who works with this...

- Okay.

- We have to go. Try to get some sleep, you will probably feel better tomorrow.

- Okay, I say again.

She leaves with her friend and I have never felt so abandoned. There are people waiting for the table, but I can't get up. And my food is still full on my plate. I look around for someone, anyone familiar, and all at once my eyes are drawn to a man who is smiling directly at me. He keeps waving his hand like he knows me, but I don't recognize him. I look down and drink the rest of my wine. When I look up again, he is still smiling, a big wide grin like he is so excited to see me. He gestures for me to come and sit with him.

I pay my bill and walk slowly past his table on my way out. He motions again to sit with him and his friends. He pulls the chair out for me like we are in a play and this is how we rehearsed it, so I sit down. His name is Luis. He is not from Buenos Aires. He speaks a much slower, sensual Spanish, so I nearly understand him. His voice is deep and rich; his skin is very smooth and brown, like an Indian. His hair is thick and black and very straight. There are dimples in his cheeks when he smiles, dimples I want to crawl into. He feeds me my lines, because I am in a play. Now it all makes sense. This is theater; this is larger than life. I will say my lines; I will stay with him.

- *Sos linda,* he says over and over. *You are so pretty.* His words wash over me as we walk through the streets of San Telmo. His words are soft waves rippling, and the anxiety grows quiet. It is very late when we get back to Evelyn's, and when he kisses me outside the door, away from the lamplight, I am Sleeping Beauty who has just awoken to the pleasure of a kiss.

We kiss and kiss and kiss some more. But he has to go. And the moment he is gone I fill out of proportion with anxiety. I'm at the edge of the world falling off. The worst is about to happen and there's no way to prevent it. My feet move up the stairs, my hand turns the key. The room is spinning and my body trembles so badly that I take another pill that actually puts me to sleep. But I wake feeling so peculiar like a *dybbuk* has entered my bones. A ghost-like being has taken possession of me.

No! No! Stop this thinking! You are filled with fantasy; your imagination has gone wild. I grab a pen and write in my diary, like I've done a thousand times, to prove that I am still me. But the nonsense that leaks from my pen is alarming: twisted lines that make no sense. And my legs, something strange is happening on my legs and on my stomach. I am a witch, a warlock, a contaminated creature. Something is itching so deeply. Where? Where can I scratch it? Where can I stop it? I jump out of bed and stare at my legs — they are red and covered in a maze of welts. A mountain range has covered my ankles. The rash grows worse before my eyes. Like watching the creation of a monster. So extreme, it can't be real. It can't be serious. *Pretend it's nothing,* I tell myself, *it will go away.*

I dress in loose clothing and walk to a familiar café and order a coffee, but can't drink it, can't even lift the cup without spilling it all. I am itching everywhere. I run to the shop and buy Valerian tablets; they are natural, they will calm me down. Think calmly, I tell myself, what have you done that is different?

Never taken so many pills in a row before! That's it. The stupid doctor didn't know that I am a fucking princess; that if one in a million get a symptom it will be me. That is the cause! Something was wrong with the pills. I forbid myself to take anymore. Now that I've discovered the source, I have something to hold onto.

I walk back to Evelyn's and feel that my body is very skinny, like I've run a marathon since leaving Boston. I need to eat. That's all it is, I tell myself. Food. You need to get some food. Then why aren't I hungry? I buy something at the shop, but nearly gag as I force myself to have a few bites.

I open up my Daily Meditation book that I've carried with me every-where since my twelve-step days. I read this:

Today is full of special surprises. We will be the recipients of the ones sent to help us grow in all the ways necessary for our continued recovery. We may not consider every experience a gift at the time, but hindsight will offer the clarity lacking at the moment.

I do not want surprises.

I want familiar.

I want this *dybbuk* out of my body.

I phone Harold but he doesn't answer. I try him at work, at home, on his cell phone and leave messages everywhere.

I get my guitar to go practice, but the studio is locked. Evelyn has never done that before and she is not even around for me to ask her why. I go to my room and try to practice there, but I am far too nervous.

Luis, the man who kissed me last night on the street, whose kiss is the only thing that for a few seconds distracts me from the panic, has given me his number. He has no work today and said I should call. He is the only person I know here; maybe he can help me get through this. But I am scared to see him again. Scared of what *I* felt when I kissed him, scared *that* I had kissed him, of what I may have started.

Impulsively, I phone him. He will come straight away to meet me.

He has a face to get lost in; his eyes so dark, like a reflecting pool. He is thrilled to see me again. I can't understand this, as I look terrible.

- What shall we do? he asks.

- I need to walk, I say.

Hoping it will calm me down we walk for a long time. It's easy to tell this is not his favorite thing to do, but he is a good sport. I want to go to familiar places like the little restaurant in La Boca where I danced tango every Sunday on my last trip. We find it and it is open, but they no longer dance. Instead, there is blues and rock and roll. I want to scream at the owner. How could he do that? How could he stop the dancing? The tango?

Luis gives a look to the owner as if to say: *foreigners, you know how they are.* He takes me abruptly by the arm and we are back on the street.

He tries to explain how hard the times have been, that I am a spoiled American brat.

- I live in Europe!

- It's the exact same, he says.

- No it's not, I yell. I want to fight; but I don't know angry words in Spanish.

- *Vamos*, he says.

We go find a restaurant. I am both very hungry and not hungry. We order food, but I can't eat much. After the meal that he insists on paying for even though I suspect he hasn't much money, he leads me down another street and then stops. I see the sign for a *transient* hotel.

- What is this? I ask. I'd heard about these places on my last visit, but never went near one.

- I want to be with you, he says. My apartment is not very nice.

I shake my head. *Oh no, I can't do this,* I tell him. *I am married.*

He begins to argue, to seduce, to convince me that being married has nothing to do with it; that I am in Argentina and my husband is very far away. The difference is — when I begin to cry, I cry so hard, so out of control that he gets scared. I fear he will leave me alone on a street that I don't recognize; that I know for certain is not safe. But he doesn't leave me. He very gently wraps his arm around me and leads me away. He keeps talking, but his Spanish is going too fast now that I can't focus on the meaning.

- *Que paso?* he asks.

We stop and I show him the rash on my legs that has been covered by my long pants. The rash is unbelievably worse — like leprosy. He takes me to a *Farmacia* and buys ointment, and we are back on the street walking faster and faster. He takes keys from his pocket and leads me into a building and up several flights of stairs to his apartment, which is as ugly and decrepit as he said. Like the skeleton of an apartment or one that has been bombed. On the wall there's a drawing of how the rooms will be. When he has time, he tells me, the work will begin. At the moment there's nothing but holes in the walls and lose wires dangling everywhere. There is a useable bathroom, with toilet, sink and shower. I go immediately to wash my hands and put the salve that Luis has bought on my legs, but the itch cannot be reached. It is deep, deep down, inside my bones.

- Does it help? he asks.

- I don't know.

He leads me into the main room (the only livable space) that faces the street. It is very noisy. Hanging on the wall is something familiar that makes me shriek with happiness.

- I know this picture!

It is a large replica of a poster I used to have in college: a photograph of a beautiful forest with a dirt path between the trees. The path is so life-like, so welcoming, so large on his wall — the entire wall — that it seems like in a children's tale the path is beckoning you to follow. If I enter this forest everything will be okay. I stand there so long, but can't find the way in. Luis takes my hand and leads me to the large mattress that lies before the forest. The entrance to the lush and healing forest is through his arms.

Luis is forty-eight, but he looks so much younger. But then so do I. God knows what he thinks with all my crying. But I can't stop as I lay there in his arms, in time suspended, feeling safe for the first time in months. And all at once I start speaking Spanish, words I hardly knew I knew: about my family and my mother and my life and my music and the flight, and this strange *dybbuk* that has taken over.

- A *dybbuk*, he says. That's a funny word.

He keeps kissing me, but he listens. Then he tells me about his family, how he was raised by his grandmother that he really loved and hardly saw his parents; about a recent motorcycle accident and the months he spent in the hospital, first in a coma, with his body in a full cast, then later, recovering, learning how to move again. Wishing his family would visit, but they never did. Before the accident he had big ideas for life, but now, he says, he is grateful to walk, to be able to work again.

- Family, I tell him. I should never see mine again. I can't be around them and act normal. But it's me that has it all wrong. There's nothing wrong with them. To help my Spanish I act out the meaning, using my hands, my face. My story and the effort I've made to express myself seem to touch him and he holds me tenderly. I push him away, but I don't want him to stop, although we do stop — I'm too scared of losing

Harold, scared of losing myself completely. Yet the terror of being alone is even greater and when he takes me back to Evelyn's we remain forever, at the private entrance, kissing goodbye.

3.

I am a train hurtling full blast through an endless tunnel, the night. At last I do sleep a bit and wake feeling even stranger than I who have tasted many variations of strangeness have ever known. This body is no longer mine. Once, with a bad case of poison ivy, I used rubbing alcohol and a hair dryer to sooth the itch. I try this remedy now but it only makes things worse, the heat causes the skin to inflame, like a forest fire. I run to buy oatmeal and sprinkle it into the bath (another poison ivy remedy), but this does little to stop the rash from spreading.

I phone Harold yet again and finally he's there. I choke out the words, explaining what is happening, that I am *really* not exaggerating this time. I beg him to come to Buenos Aires immediately. But he can't, he has too much work now, too many obligations.

- Just come home, he says gently, his voice soft and soothing, which makes me miss him so much.
- I... I can't get back on a plane.
- Maybe you are just tired... try to rest.
- I can't sleep.
- I may be wrong, he says. But I'm sure this will pass in a few days and you'll be up and dancing in no time at all, and then you won't want me around. Besides, he says. Maybe something good will come out of this. You always struggle so much... Maybe you'll learn something, a missing piece that will make your life easier. You always think the grass is greener somewhere else: when you were in Norway, you couldn't stop thinking of how great everything was in Buenos Aires and now that you're there, you're disappointed. Maybe it's time to learn to enjoy the grass just as it is.

There is no grass here at all! I scream.

Suddenly, I don't want to listen anymore. What does he know? He who mostly keeps everything so tightly in, controlled, how the hell would he know what I'm going through? He will justify and diminish.

He will make it into nothing. But it isn't *nothing.* I hang up the phone, feeling completely lost and alone and furious in my powerlessness to convince Harold to help me.

Sebastian, where are you? Come back! Please come back. If you were here we could play. Evelyn won't even talk to me without you. You would understand what is happening to me, why my bones are itching like crazy. You could make this ghost of terror go away.

Right now, even more than wishing the itch would stop, it is understanding I crave, someone to explain what the hell is happening: that I am not dying, that my body will be normal again, that I will be able to sleep and not cry at every little thing. But Sebastian isn't here... Harold isn't here... and Evelyn has lost her mind.

The rash has now spread to my thighs; it is on my belly and chest, around my neck, choking me. My skin is crawling with a feverish burn, itching like mad.

*

There is nothing about Luis that should draw me to him. He is the last tree in a forest that has been chopped down, well... besides me, the other tree they forgot to get. And the reason he has a huge picture of a forest is because there used to be a forest that we once belonged to! And that's why I can't stop thinking about him, longing for him. He is my only way home.

It's impossible to sleep — and I must stop thinking or I will explode. I have no trust in a Higher Power, never did and never will. All those hours in the twelve-step meetings, fucking bullshit. But still I pray, for I don't know what else to do...

I hear this:

With such obsessive rage there is no room for a Higher Power. You are filled up with guilt, towards everyone, for everything in your life. And look what you are doing with Luis? You don't even know him. Maybe he's a gangster, a criminal. His apartment is worse than a jail. Is that what you want? Harold, who loves you, who gave you a home, how do you think he will feel if he knew what you were up to?

God, I yell back. *You are such a fucking hypocrite! You torture us, you know, you with your high ideals. Who could ever live up to those lofty ideals?*

Not us puny humans! Why should I care about Harold? Is he here? Luis is here. He cares about me.

But God has a big mouth, and a loud booming voice: *You think you need this, cannot live without a big feeling of love. But look what's happening to you. You are so anxious. You gotta give up this game once and for all.*

Okay, okay, I say to this voice, *I will give up Luis, if you take away this dreadful rash.*

There's a knock on the door. It is the sweet girl from Colombia who I met in the kitchen. She's brought a pot of chamomile tea and two cups. She pulls up a chair like the perfect nurse. My dictionary is close by so I can look up the words as we speak.

- *No estoy cansada,* she says, and she stays for a long time, way past when the tea is finished. Her voice is soothing and I am so grateful as my body takes a respite from raging and hums along with the sound of her voice. She tells me about her life, how beautiful her country is, or was, since no one can go there, not to the mountains. There's a curfew in Bogota, everyone must be home by 1 A.M. I suddenly care a great deal about Colombia.

She is curious what's wrong with me, so I show her my skin. She gasps and this scares me, her reaction. I tell her how Evelyn used to be.

- She's completely crazy now, but lets us stay for cheap. Wait a moment, she says. She runs to get the telephone book and looks up hospitals. There is a German, a Swiss, and Italian. There's also an English hospital close by. She writes the address for me. Before she leaves she takes my hand and holds it in the way Edie did, like she has magical powers to make me well. But instead she just wishes me *suerte* and courage.

- I am so sorry, she says. I can't take you to the hospital tomorrow. But promise you will go.

I actually sleep some, and in the morning Evelyn is banging angrily on my door.

- You have a phone call, she shouts. Be quick. I need the phone.

I rush to the kitchen and it is Luis. He asks how I am, if the rash is better. I peel up my nightgown and see that my skin is even redder; been burnt at the stake in my sleep.

- You should go to the hospital, he says. Phone me when you're ready and I'll come get you.

You have given me no choice, I say straight to God.

*

What all this may lead to means nothing now, lying as I am in a hospital bed for the third time this week hooked up to an IV machine. The mix entering my system feels I've just gulped down four margaritas on top of a mountain, very fast. The doctors don't know what's wrong, but they need to calm down my system. Soon, the dermatological specialist will come with the results of the biopsy. In the meanwhile, the young English intern has promised to visit me again, after his rounds. I hear his footsteps.

- How are you? he asks, with his lovely smile that I see through a crack in my swollen eyes.

An answer forms deep inside me but it cannot surface, so I look at him with pent-up intensity.

- You have confounded the department. There's never been a case like yours. You sure you haven't gone for a quick dip in the river? It's horribly polluted.

I shake my head.

- It's probably the *Xanax*, he says. Maybe an allergy, but it could be many things, like stress. Are you very stressed?

The crying starts, again. He is a good doctor, even if he doesn't know what's wrong. The way he reaches out his hand and touches my arm, like he cares.

- Stress is a bugger, he says, a real bugger.

He holds my hand for the longest while.

- They want to look at you, he says gently. Would you mind if we wheel you into the operating room? Don't worry, he says, as he sees me spring up in resistance. They won't operate. It is just to get more opinions on what is the best treatment. The rash is not reacting to normal procedure. We do... really want to help you.

When Luis arrives at the hospital, I let him kiss me long and hard. I have no power to resist and besides it feels good, very good. With everything so terrible, good is worth any complication I may have later, and besides Harold and my life in Oslo is so far away, further than I will ever have the strength to venture back to.

Luis is now in charge. He is holding my return ticket and gives the taxi driver the address of the Airline office where I must go sort out my flight home. We arrive, take a number and find seats. The way Luis cares for me feels like a movie scene where the pregnant woman and her doting husband wait for the primary check to confirm that all is as it should be. Lost in this fantasy, I feel surprisingly light and well.

When my number is called, however, it all comes rushing back and I proceed to say the words I've written on a paper. I show the representative my skin and the note from the doctor. He shakes his head, insisting there's no way to prove the airline to blame, and despite the long letter of complaint, they will not refund nor extend my ticket. There is no way I can get back onto a plane. Ever.

We walk out into the blazing sunshine, and my first thought is relief. I can never go near another plane in my life anyhow so it is just as well not to have a ticket. No choice, nothing to question. This is the confirmation needed to decide to stay here until the end of time. Luis, a bullishly sensitive man, seems so happy about this.

- Marry me! he sings.

- ... *I am already married,* I somehow remember and mumble.

- But your husband is in Norway, he says. And I am here. You need someone here.

Think about it, he adds, taking my hands inside his warm, soft, brown ones. I will take good care of you.

As with everything else right now, I am unable to think clearly. I can only feel, and it feels good to let my body melt into his hands.

4.

Luis takes me to his apartment, to the mattress on the floor, to the forest on the wall, which is slowly becoming the only place I feel safe. All at once I understand the homeless person who insists on sleeping amongst rags and tatters in some decrepit hole in the wall, for the place offers no resistance nor demands anything in return. Luis' bare cell of an apartment is just this. Being there reminds me of nothing, nothing I have ever known or experienced, and the anxiety gets quiet. Like a movie's love scene, his mattress is the soft grass, the blanket that we lay on with food and the wine all gathered in a basket. The director knows what happens next, and as lead actress I give my whole attention to the scene being filmed. *Now* is all that matters, *now* is all that will ever be. There is no past, no future. And the music that Luis plays — Silvio Rodriguez as soundtrack — is lush and soothing. The moment the CD finishes we push *play* again and again.

Whether Luis feels himself in this movie I will never know, but it seems so. He too is a broken person; he too has been spit out from the *real* world and has found this other place. He too needs to eat and sleep, to love and to cry, but not in any predictable order. It might appear the same as the world we have left yet it isn't anything the same. In this 'other' realm of existence, there are no rules, no laws, no right, no wrong. Only sensation. And the sensation when he touches my breasts, where the rash hasn't spread — the rest of my skin is so destroyed there's no chance of doing anything more, not really — is so intense, and more than enough for me. Luis knows this. He has stopped begging for *real* sex. In a strange way, my damaged and unusable body protects me as I let myself melt in his arms. The little girl inside me, always vigilant, never knowing when her father might explode has for the first time ever let down her guard of control. Luis holds me so perfectly, that I offer him the love that I didn't even know myself to have, let alone give. We stay like this for hours and hours, suspended. We are the cubic forms of Picasso; we are swollen, distortions of humanity. I can't sleep at Evelyn's, not more than an hour or two so it doesn't matter how late it gets when he finally takes me home in a taxi, 3 A.M., 4 A.M…

- *Estás flaca*, he says, as I button my shirt and get ready to leave. I've only known you two weeks, but you have lost so much weight, you're so skinny.

I am a bottomless pit and eat and eat for I am constantly hungry, yet keep on losing weight.

- Does it hurt? He asks, as he gently touches the small black hole where they did the biopsy.

- A little, I say, but it's ugly. My stomach was nice before, I tell him. I wish they'd taken it from my butt. Luis has bought me a Spanish-English dictionary, and I'm learning loads of new words. I love the word for butt: *cola*.

On the drive back, I tell him what happened in the hospital, how embarrassing it was to have all the doctors study me like a slab of meat, except — unlike meat — I couldn't stop crying. Any little thing, any attention makes me cry. I've always cried easily, but now there's clearly a malfunction, a broken valve. I am, so they told me, having a nervous breakdown: a collapse of my metabolism, all induced by the *Xanax*. The new batch, a generic form, that I'd bought right before leaving apparently contained toxic corn starch and talcum powder, that in combination with the ingredients of the medication set off this intense reaction — a reaction that is just my body fighting for its life. In the medical literature, so they said, there's indeed a risk with tranquilizers, such as *Xanax* or Valium, that taken in excess, the reverse can occur. And the red wine that I had consumed — both on the plane and when I arrived — was the explosive element in the equation.

- *You have developed a severe allergy. A few more pills and your body would not have been able to fight the impact of the toxic elements, and you would have died. You can never take any form of tranquilizer again.* The head of the Dermatology Department has such a sweet accent in her English that at first I didn't even listen to the words.

- What?

- You can't take these pills ever again.

- But what about when I fly?

- No. Never.

- Then I can't ever fly.

- Yes you can. You will have to learn to fly without pills.

- I… it's… *impossible*.

- Here in Buenos Aires, there is very good therapy. Some say the best in the world.

- Therapy?

- Yes, you must do therapy, and then you will be able to fly again.

- But I've done so much therapy. It doesn't help with the flying. The pills have always helped with that.

- You are not listening. No more pills.

- Will my skin get better?

- Yes. (Pause) But then it will get worse again. (Pause) And then it will get better… and worse, and…

- For how long?

- For a long time. You have had a high toxic ingestion. It is deep into your system. It will take many, many months, maybe even years until it disappears completely. Try to stay calm. It doesn't help when you get more upset. Do some therapy and you will get better, I promise. Here's my number, the direct line to me in the hospital and also my cellular. Phone me if you get too scared. Phone me and let me know how you react to the treatment. And with this she gave me a shot of cortisone, antihistamines to be taken, and various salves and creams.

- Therapy! Luis says, after he hears this. Therapy is nonsense. They wanted me to go to therapy. Everyone in Buenos Aires goes to therapy. A lot of good it does!

With Luis gone, I crawl back into my bed at Evelyn's and start to shake and decide not to listen to him; that I don't have to tell him everything. I have always lived compartmentally — no one who has known me will ever know everything, not even Harold — and in this context I shall not change.

The following morning I find the card that the woman in the restaurant, Carolina, had given me and decide to phone her. And luckily she answers.

- Hi, she says. I had a feeling you would phone. So good you called! I checked to make sure I had the right number for the therapist. It turns out he can't speak any English, and, no offense, but your Spanish… Anyway, he gave me the number of another therapist, Ana, who should also be great. And she trained in the States, so her English is okay. Do you have a pen? I'll give you her number.

- Look, do you want to meet? she continues. I don't know how many people you know here.

- Just the ones who dance tango, but I haven't been able to go so I haven't...

- Tango, she says, tango is so boring. And the shoes, I don't know how anyone can manage to even walk in those shoes, let alone dance. Call me if you need anything, anything. Phone Ana, okay?

My hands start shaking, yet I phone Ana immediately, who is miraculously available to talk. Her voice opens and I pour into her.

- The fear is like a forest of beasts and uncontrollable beings inside my skin, inside my bones, eating me alive. Everything is jumbled up, like a box of a puzzle that someone has knocked over. I am feelings and emotions, a body without connection; an arm in one corner, a leg in another.

Hard to know if her English is good enough to understand what I've said, but she understands the subtext and responds in soothing words.

- I think I can help you, she says. Don't worry. You will get well.

And we set up a time to meet the next day.

I go to a *Milonga* around the corner. I can't go in with my face like a monster, my shoulders burnt red; so I press my nose against the window. I hear the music, the laughing. I watch the men slip their arms around their partners. Tango, so carefree, so phony and stupid to watch, like a porno film. Carolina is right. Tango people have no patience for the one who is not well. Even Luis hates the tango.

I meet Luis and end up telling him about Ana, that I will start therapy. He's not impressed. He rattles off his Spanish faster and faster now, as if buying me the dictionary has made me fluent, and God knows what he's saying. But the sound of his voice, so passionate, so deep and musical, is lovely. I could listen to him forever even if it seems at this moment he is furious, ranting away. I hear the word *hospital* and suspect he is not convinced of their recommendation. He is very anxious for me to get well — *and therapy, doesn't that take an eternity?* — so we can begin a normal relationship.

On numerous occasions he's moaned that our not 'having sex' is okay for now but not forever. Yet he continues to be the perfect caretaker. We go to the supermarket often and he carries the groceries back to Evelyn's, where he's allowed to sit on the terrace while I cook up something (we can't cook at his place; there's no kitchen). The Columbian girl likes to talk with him, and I make extra food so she can eat with us — which keeps Evelyn away, because she's always watching; like a hawk she watches. He is not allowed to enter my room unless I pay extra. When he needs to use the bathroom, the Colombian girl takes him to the one downstairs. Yet when I pass Evelyn in the hall she puts out her hand for the money for Luis' visits.

- He hasn't once come into my room, I tell her. He's just my friend.

And she gives me that *don't pull wool over my eyes look* and says:

- I wasn't born yesterday, and besides, these are the rules.

I am furious about this, for it seems the rules change depending on her mood, as everyone else has visitors in their rooms. She is convinced that because I live in Norway I'm very rich (which is true in a sense, as there's dire poverty all around us, but not as she thinks. And who knows when I shall be able to work again). But Evelyn needs extra money desperately for her grand scheme of building a little house on top of the roof. In one of her flamboyant outbursts, she told us all that she can't bear another moment in Buenos Aires and must return to Patagonia, her true home. But she hasn't a cent left to go there, so she's building a Patagonian shack that no one ABSOLUTELY NO ONE is allowed to contaminate. We hear her hammering and you can see it from the balcony that *something* is being built. Hardly a house, it's so lopsided that only a character in a children's book like *Pippi Longstocking* could sleep there. Every time she gets extra money she buys a piece of wood and hammers it on. I fear the house will take a long time to complete. I also fear that Evelyn, like me, is losing her mind.

5.

The medicine isn't working. Last night Luis put his hand on my head and prayed.

- You will get better, he chants. But there's something crucial you must learn first.

- Couldn't I learn it without having a rash? I reckon I'd pay better attention, but what do I know...

- God works in mysterious ways, Luis says.

- Since when are you so religious? I ask.

- Since my accident, he says.

- So pray, I tell him. Nothing else seems to help.

And again he puts his hand on my head and it feels so good. But then all at once he gets furious and I don't know why.

- *Basta*, he says. It's enough. I can't do this anymore.

I take the taxi home by myself, and doubt if I will ever see him again.

It's still two days before I can see Ana, meanwhile the Colombian girl has another idea for me. She has spoken to her special doctor who believes that everything can be cured by what we eat or don't eat, and by pouring our own urine on ourselves. I am open for anything. So I start the fast she has prescribed and I fill the vial she's bought with urine and pour it on my skin. It actually helps. And for a moment I feel sort of normal.

*

The phone rings and it's Ginny — who I haven't seen this time yet, who's fallen out with Evelyn and is forbidden to come to the house. She's working now for an English newspaper and gets free tickets for shows that she must review. She has tickets tonight to a tango gala. I jump at the chance to go, that maybe, just maybe I can manage it.

I cover my face and neck with makeup; drape a loose shawl over my rash-covered shoulders and force myself out of the house. I flag down a taxi, and my hands tremble as I hand over the address of the theater. Every step demands complete attention. When I arrive, just seeing the crowd of unknown people makes the panic accelerate. Instantly, I regret coming. At last, after the show, I find Ginny. She is so preoccupied with herself that she doesn't notice the drastic change in me. Just like with Evelyn, there's intense competition as if God has time for just one of us and her problems are more urgent. She tells me how hard things have been in Buenos Aires, for *her*; about the collapse of the currency, how she lost all her money; how lucky Sebastian and I were to have left *before all hell broke loose.*

- It is so cheap for you now, she says with such venom that I wonder if she was like this before and I hadn't noticed, or has she too gone mad. She doesn't stop: *You are so lucky... You have no idea how lucky you are...*

I listen, but my anxiety grows, even more as I try to ignore it. At one point I can hardly breathe, and tell her that I must go, that I haven't been well.

- You seem okay, she snaps. I think you're exaggerating... I remember that about you, how you could exaggerate. Sebastian said the same thing.

No he didn't, you little bitch; he absolutely did not. We loved each other, the music we made... A thing you will never know, you little twit-brain... I have an urge to wrap my hands around her throat.

- I have to get out of here. I say, pushing her aside to get the waiter, to pay the bill.

My 'illness' has given me x-ray vision, and I see everything inside out. Ginny is a nut; I am not safe around her. She refuses to see that I am not okay because she needs me to be okay. She needs money from me, just like Evelyn. I am their money tree. I leave her some extra cash and run for a taxi. Suddenly I hate her. Even if she's right, that things are cheap for me, who knows how long I'll be stuck in Buenos Aires, how much the therapy will cost or a new ticket home if I ever fly again, which I doubt. I will probably live here the rest of my life and teach English and scrape by just as she does...

I wake, feeling worse than ever. I brush my teeth and jump at the sight of my face in the mirror. Like a monster: my eyes are red and swollen, my cheeks puffed, my neck distorted. This is not an exaggeration.

I hate everyone — especially my mother. How I used to love her, ache in my bones for her. All my years living far away, I'd miss her so much. But now I loathe her; like Ginny, she thinks I am faking it.

- You are not really sick, my mother says, when I explain to her on the phone how I am. You don't even know what sick is... *She* is sick. Since when is being sick a competition? Why can't she believe I want to get well; that I'd give anything to be healthy and to sleep again? My whole life has been spent trying not to upset her. I have twisted and distorted myself to please her. But she can rot in hell for all I care. I send her a pithy e-mail telling her not to write or phone, that even if according to her I am not really sick, I'll be using all my energy and attention to get well.

My resentment grows to a large mountain — and it all comes out in the first seconds with Ana. I see immediately, gratefully, that she takes me seriously; finally someone *not* in competition, which makes me instantly love her. Her soft blond curls fall across her eyes and she looks so much younger than her almost sixty years. She really listens and looks and I can tell she's been to the dark places and back; there's no way to fool her.

After we have talked, she guides me to a mat in the center of her room where I'm to lie down and cover my eyes with an eye shade. She puts on music, loud, strong and primal music sounding older than time. She snuggles beside me on the floor and puts a hand on my sternum and makes me breathe faster and faster. My fingers prickle, the hair on my arms raise up, my head crashes in. Or so it feels with nothing to hold onto. I'm falling or flying, impossible to know. I have to stop this breathing or my body will explode, pieces of me will shatter the windows, smash on the walls.

- I can't do this, I shout and grab the shade from my eyes.
- Keep on going, she says, holding my hand. I am here.
Someone inside me is screaming.
- This is great. Keep going.

When it's over, there's a calm, an amazing calm. For the first time in weeks, or maybe my whole life, I don't feel anxious. A magical serenity.

After a few moments, the blessed calm vanishes and a rage builds up.
- What's happening? Ana asks.

I have no words; I toss and turn, I kick my legs and push her away. I push so hard yet still she's there.

- You feel terrible. But it will stop, Ana says, I promise. You've just told me how you hate everything: your life, your mother, your husband, even your music that hasn't brought the approval and fame you so desperately seek. Yet there's still so much you love even if all you feel right now is hate.

- All that love is contaminated, I say.

- By what?

- By the killer critic in me. No chance to silence it unless someone loves me directly in front of my face... but I've worn them out... everyone, there's nobody left.

- So it seems, Ana laughs, and so you think. How convincing that inner critic can be. It's brought you down, that's for sure. Let the whole show fall to pieces.

- Like I have a choice! The show has fallen to pieces. There is no show.

- Good. Ana says. But we always have a choice, even if we can't see it.

- Yeah right. Like all those new-agers who tell you we chose our family. That's bullshit.

- Maybe. Maybe not.

- IF I GET A CHOICE, I shout, HERE'S MY CHOICE: I WANT TO DIVE INTO THE POOL THAT'S IN YOUR GARDEN. AND WHEN I COME OUT I WILL BE A LITTLE GIRL AGAIN WITH A WHOLE NEW MOTHER AND A WHOLE NEW FATHER. THAT'S MY CHOICE...

- You're funny, Ana says. I'm going to enjoy working with you.

I look at her puzzled, because she seems honest.

- Your anxiety, your breakdown... it's not just from the pills...

- You're wrong! They told me at the hospital that...

- I know what they told you, and it's also true, in the physical realm, and you must attend to that part as well, of course. It won't be easy. The rash is awful, but it has given you a chance to work *this* through once and for all. This breakdown, whatever you want to call it, has been building for quite a while. Better do the work now. The longer you postpone the harder it becomes, honestly. In truth, when people get sick it's a great opportunity to learn. Think of this as a great chance.

Great chance, my ass, I think. I hate all this shit, all this fucking learning. I don't want to learn any more. I want to rub close up against Luis and feel the bad, naughty love. I want to do it all wrong. I'm sick of trying to get it right.

I walk the whole way back after the session, two and a half hours, hoping the long walk in the pouring rain will calm me down and cool the rash. It doesn't.

Still no sleep, and this, on top of everything else, is killing me. Back again in the hospital, worse than ever. *Just relax*, they all say. How the hell am I supposed to relax? They've put me back on the IV with that Margarita stuff that gets me quiet, a little bit. The doctors are stunned at how much worse I've become. This shouldn't happen, they say. This isn't how it's written in the textbooks. So typical me: others would either be dead or better by now, but not I; first I must defy gravity and go to where no *man* has gone before. The doctors haven't a clue how to help me, yet their kindness is overwhelming. It astounds me how starved I am for good care yet when I get it, I can't bear it… Real attention, this being seen for who I am, fills me with unbearable shame. Perhaps it is not gravity I must defy; it is this feeling of shame.

I have to cancel my session with Ana, for they want me to stay in the hospital. They have given me a very strong shot of cortisone. I taste the metallic ingredients in my mouth, though the shot was in my butt. They keep saying *not to worry* — such a stupid phrase, you need more details than that to stop worrying. And because I can't stop crying they get the young doctor from England. He's the best with me.

- Hey, nice to see you, he says, like he really means it.

My face is swollen, I'm unable to talk but he appears to assume what I might say and laughs.

- Really and truly it's lovely to see you again. We've missed you here. I kid you not.

I can't believe how cute he is. Surely he could have been a movie star.

- So, how's my girl, he says and takes my hand.

Not so good, my eyes tell him. *I am a lost little girl in a big scary world. It's far too much for a little child, isn't it?*

He responds with an empathetic hmmm. The only true answer.

- You're going to get well, I promise. And then we'll have a meal.

- Hmmm, is all I'm able to reply.

I am back in my room and the Colombian girl comes to sit with me despite Evelyn's look of warning, as if it's against the law to show kindness in her house. I'm completely hysterical. The terror has erupted, and I'm a big chaotic ball of hysteria. Freud would have had great fun with me.

- Shh... she says as she reaches for my hand, this sweet girl, and starts in with her lovely talking. Try to breathe, she instructs, as she breathes with me, in and out, out and in, to get a flow going.

The next day I phone Ana to set up a new appointment. I am so angry, so furious, that I want to get it over with, take the fear by the throat. One thing is absolutely certain, that I haven't a clue how to take care of myself.

By the end of the session I hate Ana as well, because she insists it's not wise to see Luis, that *that* is not taking care of myself. It is an illusion, she tells me. A dangerous, addictive illusion. No, no... I cry, for I have tricked myself into believing how much I need him.

- Is that really true? she asks.

- I can't bear to be alone, I tell her.

Which is closer to the truth. And because his touch makes me feel better than anything, I haven't the will or the strength to stop myself from phoning him.

6.

Panic like rollers, like huge waves, one larger than the previous until the size overwhelms, until the sensation of being overwhelmed has lost all meaning. Clusters of words gush into my head like discarded trash at sea. I resist these words; refuse to write them down — though in the end I do, there's no other way to quiet them. They scare me, these words, blistering, troublesome words, their jagged disorder; their razor-sharp precision. I long desperately for sleep.

The light creeps through the window and in a trance I dress and go to Ana — by taxi, the only way for me to get there. It's impossible to go down into the dark and claustrophobic subway. The money goes faster, but I also need the taxi drivers, need to hear them talk; it stills the jabbering in my head. I speak hardly with anyone since the Colombian girl moved out; she couldn't bear one more day of Evelyn. I miss her nightly visits, the sound of her voice. From her, I learned a few key Spanish sentences that keep the *taxistas* chattering for the half hour ride to Ana. And it helps; it helps so much. Because of the economic crises many highly educated people drive taxis, so listening to them is like taking a class. My Spanish is improving greatly so the drivers speak freer and freer; they need to talk and they sense my hunger for their words. When we arrive, they thank me for the money and for listening.

Ana is never on time, and I hate that. Every day I must wait. The maid has registered my anxiety, that sitting like a normal client is impossible. She lets me into the large empty room used for the bigger workshops. The walls and floor are of fine wood, no furniture, just a very high ceiling and great acoustics. Two bay windows open onto a grassy lawn, a palm tree and a swimming pool. It is a palace next to Evelyn's studio, not to mention Luis's flat. This room is so inviting that I sing and dance while waiting. Usually I'm dancing wildly when the maid opens the door, which makes me jump, which makes her jump, and then we both laugh.

- Ana is ready… you can go up now.

My heart pounds as I mount the wide staircase. Although I am beginning to believe that she can help me, it scares me so much how she *sees* everything. I have never worked with so relentless a therapist — no pulling wool over her eyes. And yet I hate when the sessions end. There is a spare bedroom upstairs with a bathroom I use before and after the sessions. I want to sleep in that room, and be a little girl with a new father and a new mother and a whole other life.

While training to be an Alexander teacher, we learned that Mr. Alexander never asked how a person was. *No point* was his reply, *as most people won't really know. Better put a hand on and find out for yourself and proceed to help them find out as well.* There's something similar in how Ana waits to *feel* me, to sense how I am, even though she does say 'How are you?' For that is so typical Argentine, that and a kiss, impossible to begin any interaction without this greeting. But she urges me to take time in response, in a way I have never experienced before, as if she holds the one and only true clock. To be with myself, to listen.

My words ramble and twist, but Ana is clever, unwearied, and somehow I manage to tell all the parts, bit by bit, day by day. Pieces, like broken pottery that have fallen hop hodge from the pantry wall; I make enough sense of the pieces so she recognizes what once was, or better yet what could be, for now is the chance to put the pieces together anew.

- If your *fear*, she says, becomes a wordless darkness that you avoid, you unconsciously open yourself up to further attacks, in the people you meet and in the situations around you. You don't realize this, of course, that you've actually *put* yourself in these situations, that you've drawn these to yourself like a magnet. How you feel you really are and what you deserve is what you actually allow to happen. Not the other way around. And this will continue repeating until you are willing to see and to change this pattern.

- But how can I, if I can't see it?

- This is what we are going to work on. What you see and what you allow yourself to see can change.

- I've done all this! With therapy, with studying acting, with Alexander technique. Maybe this is as far as I can go?

- This is not to negate the work you've done. It's led you here.

- To this? To this shit. What good did all that awareness do me if I still can't change?

- I'm not convinced you went as far as you can go. Something stopped you from seeing, stopped you from becoming who you really are. In the breathing work, we'll find out what that is that stops you, what terrifies you from going further. I'm going to help you face that fear. You've put the cart before the horse, Ana continued. You've wanted to be famous, thinking that was the answer. Then you would be loved, and would no longer fear anything. Then you'd have the permission you've lacked to be who you are. But it doesn't work like that. You cannot control the world to make you famous, and even if you were able to, there's no guarantee it would take away your fear. Mostly it doesn't. If anything, the fear gets stronger, more demanding.

- I actually know that one. It was me that wrecked my chances of getting further with my music. One of my last big concerts, I was so nervous I had to run off stage.

- We need to deal with the fear, the *cause* of the fear. That's the culprit.

- Maybe I'm just afraid that in the end I'm nothing and the idea of being nothing is unbearable. That's why I wanted to be famous. The fame would confirm that at least I'm not nothing.

- So you think, or so it seems. But it's a volatile basis. Like a house built on sand. You've lived so far away from yourself, so alien. Ana says, and yet she doesn't shame me with her words.

I feel completely overwhelmed; all the ropes that have tied me together have been snapped. I have to lie down on the floor, feeling so incredibly tired. Ana comes down as well, crawling beside me like we're in some kind of empyrean nursery school. She gives me a big loving kiss, like I've done something quite extraordinary.

- This is so good, Ana says.

- What?

- Letting go, it's the beginning.

She seems to understand how hard a time I've had in my life, even if there's been much to be grateful for. Growing up under 'normal' circumstances made it even harder for me to understand and accept why I always felt so malnourished, so deprived, so in danger.

But then, I hear my father's words from my childhood roaring: *You little shit... You have no idea how lucky you are. You want to cry? I'll give you something to cry about.* And then he'd hit me so hard, and keep hitting though I couldn't stop crying, though he never had to give me something more to cry about. And Evelyn, who barged into my room the other day screaming: *You have everything! You are beautiful, talented with nothing to complain about. Why are you staying in bed all the time?*

Session after session, Ana says so much with her eyes, with her hands that almost dance as she laughs. She seems to know the dichotomy; of what is on the outside, what we say and show the world, and what is on the inside: the stuff in our hearts and the secret forces that drive us.

- It's incredible, she says, how an entire life can be lived without ever getting the point. How easily we miss it in the rush and need to survive. So much is demanded of a person and so little time left to understand who we are, what we really need, and how to get it. It is a luxury, she laughs, like getting your nails done. Yet more people will find the time to do their nails than to do themselves.

You can tell she's taken big bites out of life, that she's not perfect and struggles, and wants you to know that you're not alone in your struggle. This makes me cry, but differently: a more calm form of weeping, more a weeping for joy than desperation. Her body is full and when she hugs me, I believe it. Like the perfect tango dance, when someone really wants to dance with you, the dance dances itself. She really wants to give this hug and that gives clarity and I get the first pop as if Ana is cooking popcorn in my head. I never believed it from my parents, so didn't want them to touch me, didn't like to have them near me. I think I have never let anyone come in so close, not even all the men I've let into my body. Funny this. So strange, this new sensation of intimacy, of reality; all at once the life I've lived, the sense of what was natural has shifted.

- If you never *truly* confront the enemy attacking from within, Ana says, you will have to fight again and again. And you have never ever trusted anyone or anything, not at least yourself. But you're here now and you have only to *begin* to trust me, just a little bit, just enough to let me lead you through. Not stopping where you usually stop. We must go further, to the place buried deep inside you. *This* is going to be *very* hard and *very* scary. I don't want to fool you and make you think it will be easy. It won't. But it will be worth it. I promise you. It will help the rash get better, and even more importantly it will help *you* get better. You have no idea just how angry you are. But anger doesn't have to be bad…

It can be incredibly useful if you learn *how* to use it. If not, it will continue to use you, like the way it's destroying your skin.

- It is not only my anger, I shout. They told me in the hospital it's an allergic reaction!

- I *know* what they told you, she says, like she's ready to get me on a roller coaster but I keep finding excuses not to board. She breathes in long and slowly, and again her acceptance of where I am right at this moment, even if she's also eager to move on, is overwhelming.

- I won't argue with you, she laughs. I am sure it's also triggered from the medicine...

- All my life, I tell her, I've guessed what people wanted from me and tried to give it to them. It served me well as a child, with my very demanding and critical parents...

- But the whole world is not your family, not everyone your parent. Can you see how you've done this, how you've turned the people in your life into mother and father? You have been very busy guessing what people wanted from you, and giving it to them. This has taken most of your energy. And the sad part is that you end up depriving the people in your life, and also the audience, of what they really want: your true and honest feelings... Of being with *you*, not the idea of you.

- Somewhere within me, I've always known this. Whenever there'd be a momentum flowing, something would happen. A look of disapproval, true or not, would slap me out of it, and in that smidgen of time I'd fill with shame and close down again... If only I didn't care what other people thought, or what I thought they thought... If only I wasn't so afraid of being exposed... Maybe I would allow myself to reveal and express... even enjoy it.

- Yes!! Ana cries out. Yes, this is it. We are going to work together to make this deep shift inside that will allow you to tolerate that vulnerable *moment of not knowing for sure*... If you don't expect and prepare for rejection, you'll see that the *slap* won't come, there won't be anything feeding it. And everything, Ana continues with her passionate enthusiasm, that you've been so afraid of, that you've protected yourself from, won't happen after all. It's true, even if you can't believe it just now.

- How can I not do this? I ask.

- Little by little, Ana says. And another thing to realize is that even when someone *does* give a look of disapproval, it often reflects their *own* fear of being shamed or made uncomfortable by whatever your voice or behavior may have triggered in them. When you begin to understand this… you will see it all around. If you didn't react immediately to Evelyn, for example, you would see it in her eyes, her own fear. It is the same for your mother, for your father, for all the people that you've been so afraid of. Listen carefully. Ana speaks very slowly now. *You are much safer than you know. Today, you are not in any danger. Not your mother, not even your father has the power over you they once had. The moment you realize this, you will see the shift, and not only in your singing.*

I listen. I can't help but listen. Ana is more than a therapist; she is the grand performer, the sorcerer. She is Merlin, the magician. Yet her words feel like stones against my brain; stones that hit and then splash and then twist and then stun.

What if I have lived my whole life with this wrong interpretation? What if I have always reacted wrongly because of this faulty interpretation of the other's reaction? The enormity of this error overwhelms, not only my brain, but every single part of my body. *Is it possible to learn everything over again from scratch? Like walking, like breathing, like thinking…*

Ana takes her time, for she knows exactly when the kernels of popcorn will be ready. The sessions last an hour, sometimes two, but unlike other therapy sessions, with the awareness of the other patients waiting outside, I have the sense that she is with me now and forever, that time has actually stopped. Eventually she continues:

- Yes, you can learn to *walk* all over again. No, it is not too late to learn to live differently. Like most people, including your parents, you have done the best you can, based on what you knew, what you were taught. In a way, with this breakdown, with this strange rash of yours, you are luckier than most. You are getting a chance now to learn it all afresh.

But maybe, just maybe Ana is right, so I let her carry on.

- There is always suffering, she says, when we are far away and disconnected from ourselves. For many people, their real self is fast asleep and either they choose to keep it like that, or they really don't know how to *wake up*. We live in a time that reinforces, even encourages this distance from self. For with this distance we are kept hungry and are encouraged to fill the need of self with things like food, alcohol, with getting famous — all the gadgets we are encouraged to buy and told we can't live without. We are shown many forms of distraction, which take up heaps of our time, but never satisfy the real need, and the gnawing within continues. It is nearly an epidemic. All the young kids here spending their entire childhood in the dark internet places, playing computer games…

She takes a big breath in and out, and I suddenly love her so much, I love her for her own realization of weakness. For this is a thing that she cares about but is powerless to prevent. As I wait for her words, as one would for good, nutritional food, I get a gush of sadness towards Harold. I miss him, but also feel the gaps in our relationship. You can be together for years and still miss the point, and still lack the connection.

I look at Ana, starved for the connection she is offering, but she suddenly seems weary, tired and I fear that I've been too much for her. I tell her that I'm sorry… that I'm…

- No, no, it's not you, she says. It is wonderful to work with you. At least you've *tried* to find a good way with all your music, your tango dancing! There is a force in you and great energy that wants to come out. There is something that you really have to do, so you mustn't give up. That's why the breathing work will be so helpful. It will take you deep inside and once there, we can work to clean out the out-dated, the unnecessary, and make a clear pathway so the energy can flow.

She explains what it will be like, the breathing workshops, called 'Respiración del Corazón,'* about the special music, that it can't be in English, or in Spanish so the text is not understandable, together with the intensive breathing — like we've been doing a little bit — can access deeper states of our consciousness. This makes *things* happen.

- What kind of things? I ask, for I *really* have had enough surprises.

- It is different with everyone. You will find out, don't worry.

Again she stops and comforts me, with her touch, her hugs, knowing how scared I am.

- You have no choice, she tells me. All the pain of your life is still there, stuck, waiting to be expressed. It needs to come out of you. Please let me help you get well. It is not only about being able to fly. There is

---

* *Respiración del Corazón* ©, which can be translated as 'Breathing from the Heart' is based on the Holotropic Breathwork© developed by Christina and Stanislav Grof. The word 'Holotropic' stems from Greek and means 'moving toward wholeness.' This self-exploration and healing therapy integrates aspects of transpersonal psychology, various depth psychologies, Eastern spiritual practices and mystical traditions. The form of the work developed by Ana includes additional forms of bodywork and differs from the approach developed by the Grofs, in which physical support is only in response to the request of the participant.

something far more important that the fear of flying is just a symptom of. Everything is connected, even your fear of singing. You know the myth of Pandora, how she opened the box and was so overwhelmed by all the negative aspects of herself that flew out. The pity was that she didn't wait to find out that behind all the terror of the dark elements was hope, a great wonderful source of hope. Instead, Pandora, scared to find out what she had within her, slammed down the lid and looked no more. To discover this hope… to feel it… is *wonderful*, Ana says, really wonderful. Let me help you go through. You will see, it is wonderful.

How she says *wonderful*, again and again. The letter "w" is rarely used in Spanish, and so to pronounce this word she puts a space of breath behind it, like a gust of fresh air promising so much. And here again, I get a big kiss on my cheek. I feel loved as I have never felt loved. For the first time in my life it is as if I don't have to do anything special to deserve and receive this love. Even now, in my terribly destroyed state, she still loves me and assures me that I can do this.

*

With Ana's support, I decide to say goodbye to Luis 'for good,' and then actually do it. He is furious. Not only will I never marry him, but I must stop seeing him. Any day now, he'll be expecting 'something' from me, something to repay him for all his kindness and patience, for my dabbling with the erotic but never really going *there*, not with him. In addition, as Ana has helped me to see, the role of taking care of people is such a strong habit that I will soon feel compelled to start taking care of Luis whether I want to or not.

I miss him. For wrong as it is, I am in love with him, or some idea of him: with his skin, his voice, with how it feels when he touches me.

*

I go with my guitar into the studio; like Santa Claus, with a huge canvas bag. Instead of there being gifts and toys, the bag is filled with feelings, all sorts of feelings and memories. I let them fall out onto the wooden floor, to be with me as I sing. I stand barefoot, close my eyes and *listen*. From somewhere deep inside I hear Sebastian playing his violin and begin to play with him. He has warmed up the room, the air, welcoming me to leap into the space; it is wonderful to play this way. It helps me sing my feelings as never before. In truth, I am not crazy and know that Sebastian is not in the room with me. Still it helps to conjure him up as I try to touch what Ana has opened in me, to not care what anyone thinks, not even about my fear that I am *too* much. Let yourself be too much! Ana had said, laughing. The part of me that has become so good at preventing more hurt, also prevents my real singing. Just go with it, the flow, the opening of the heart. When I hear the word *heart* in English, it sounds pretentious, but the Spanish *corazón* gives so much more warmth and permission. I am able to do this for the tiniest part of a moment before losing it. But for that flash of a moment it is great, perfect.

The weather is absolutely marvelous. I see the crack of a perfect sky through the broken window in Evelyn's studio, a sky that opens into the purest blue. While singing I hear the sound of children laughing outside. There is the splash of water so there must be a pool. I want to be in it, to go swimming. Unfortunately, the rash has burned my skin so severely that I can't be in the sun, can't swim, not yet. Like a child I pray that it won't take forever for my skin to heal so I can go outside and play. I've started singing again when Evelyn barges into the studio.

- You have to stop now! It's enough! Her face is bulging-red as she speaks. I am not sure why she is so angry. (She goes to two different therapists a week, but they don't seem to be helping her.)

- I spoke with Samantha (the new girl in the house), and she is going out, I tell Evelyn. She won't need the studio today.

- It doesn't matter, she shouts. We have a schedule now.

Evelyn, in her changed state, has decided it is not fair that I am in the studio so much, so she has posted a schedule in the kitchen. I am not allowed to use it for more than two hours a day. Even if no one needs to be there, she comes down and throws me out. A new woman, Samantha, has moved in and Evelyn is busy enchanting her, although nothing like how she used to. It seems Samantha likes to have a nap *in* the studio in the afternoon, and for this I have to leave, *just* in case Samantha wants it. The anger at this injustice enrages me. It crawls up my arms and into my chest. A strong urge to scream at Evelyn arises, to remind her how she used to value my practicing with Sebastian; how she loved having a musical house and that it is still crucial for me to practice. I am a child again and recall how useless it was to try and convince my own mother of some injustice; it is just as useless now.

Jealousy has its own form of reason, Ana said, when I told her about Evelyn and the change in the house. We went through the pros and cons of living there. She thought it would better if I didn't live there, but until I find another place, I have to make the best of it. It isn't easy to find a place to live where you can play music in Buenos Aires and I still love the studio at Evelyn's.

- In the meanwhile, Ana had said in her laughing way, we can use Evelyn, for she brings up the same anger in you, the anger you are not ready to admit that you feel for your own mother. You are still busy protecting her.

- That is too obvious, I told Ana.

- Good that it is obvious, she said. Right now you need the obvious to bonk you on the head. Still you refuse to see it!

One good thing has come with the new schedule — the yoga/*tai chi* class on Saturdays, with a man named Alberto. Evelyn has told all of us that we are allowed to attend this class for free and how special Alberto is. Something in the way she told us, the way her voice cracked as if being forced to share something she'd rather keep for herself, made me curious. I will go to this class on Saturday. And there's another good thing. Even though Evelyn has set it up for Samantha and me to hate each other — the way she kept sitting with *her* having tea, the tea that I am no longer invited to drink — we've become friends. I love how Samantha complains to me about Evelyn, confiding how pissed off she feels when yet another new girl moves in and Evelyn sits with *her* having tea, and how Samantha isn't invited. She also can't sleep at night and goes into the studio to watch television and likes it when I join her. At least I now have a late night companion, for the nights still terrorize me.

7.

At least Ana has not lied. She told me that I won't want to come to this breathing workshop, and this is true. The resistance to get out of bed, to move, to dress, is thick sludge in my veins. Yet Ana's words: *Force yourself to get here, that's all I ask. It doesn't matter what state you are in, just come* repeat and repeat in my head like a mantra. So in the end, I manage to get out of the house and stop a taxi on the street.

I get in and hand over the address. The driver is unusually talkative. He speaks so clearly that it's possible to understand everything. He begins with the usual questions: why am I here? Do I like Buenos Aires? But then goes on with a round of comments as if holding my palm and reading it.

- You have traveled a great deal, he says, and have seen much of the world, but I wonder why you never had any children.

- How do you know that? I demand, because I've told him nothing about myself.

- I just know, he says with a distinctive look that I can see in the rearview mirror. I am not *only* a taxi driver. These are hard times here in Argentina.

- But I...

- Ah yes, he says. It's your mother, it's because you hate your parents, but it's a pity... You really wanted children.

- It's not ...

- Yes it is, he says.

No, you are wrong. You have it all wrong. I think loudly.

He talks faster and faster. I hear the word forgiveness, but don't understand the details of his now complicated Spanish. I am grateful I can't understand more and that we are approaching Ana's street, or I'd jump out of the car. Shaking like a drunk, I can hardly get the money out to pay him. It was bad enough during my acting days when teachers saw my heart hanging open on my sleeve. Now it seems my whole life is out there as well, and is up for grabs and random interpretations. I want to run away, far, far away but Ana's voice is pounding in my head, forcing me up the last few steps to the door, forcing my hand to ring the bell. Her words, *All you need to do is get here, but get here; you MUST get here.*

The maid opens the door and leads me into the big room where the breathing workshop will take place, the room that is usually mine alone before the private sessions with Ana. Today the walls and floor are lined with cushions and mats and boxes of tissues and plastic bags are dispersed everywhere. Long rug strips have been taped to the floor, like the floor itself is in danger. And people, there are people everywhere. I nearly scream with rage — all these strange people in MY ROOM — *get out, get the hell out of here.*

Ana sees me and comes quickly, seeing I'm ready to bolt. In her rapid impossible to understand Spanish she speaks to a large man who rushes over, who takes my hands firmly and leads me to a place along the wall. I have never seen this man before. He surrounds me from all sides; there is no way to run. He gives me an eye shade, to blacken the daylight.

- You may get cold, he says in perfect English. Here's a blanket, if you need it.

- How come you speak English so well? I ask.

- I went to an International school, but I'm from Buenos Aires. Ana wanted me to work with you.

- Because of your English? Because she told you I'm…

- No, no. Don't worry, he says, as kind as a man his size can sound.

I notice how strong he seems, like a wrestler.

- I'm really afraid, I tell him.

- That's okay. Everyone is.

- But not like me.

- Because of your rash? Don't worry, Ana told me about that too.

And then he gently looks at my skin, my face, my arms and studies the rash.

- It's impressive, he says smiling.

Impressive? I think angrily, *why does everyone in this country say that?*

- Ana told me you have very powerful energy; he smiles, giving me a nod of approval. This, he says, will be exciting. You are going to be fine, really. I am here to look after you, and Ana will be close by. Good luck and have a great journey.

- *Journey?* I ask, like I am going somewhere. Or perhaps, I think in alarm, they are going to give us drugs.

- That's what it is called, he says. Have a good one.

To begin, Ana leads us through a relaxing meditation, similar to the end of a yoga class. Her Spanish is soft and mumbled, not easy to understand but with the words I catch, I try to let my body sink into the ground. Relaxing is impossible, as I am holding on for dear life.

The music starts: powerful tribal drumming, chanting. It sounds like wailing, like desperate yearning. It is very loud and gets louder. We must keep breathing deeply and fast in and out. The man sitting by me puts his hands on my chest and regulates this breathing. His hands are strong and intense but there is great comfort with his warm hands on my body. This and the rhythmic breathing make me let go. I am Alice-in-Wonderland falling down a hole, a dark endless hole. Surprisingly not scary, this falling is oddly soothing as if at last I'm able to get away from my deadly self. This is not plummeting; this is floating in another dimension for the dynamic of gravity has vanished. The deeper I fall, the more I rise above. I've never taken drugs, but it is how I imagine it could be. But there are no drugs, only the most amazing music I have ever heard.

Memories appear and vanish like strips of wallpaper, or freshly washed laundry flapping wildly in this unusual breeze. Suspended, I realize this is *my* laundry and it is fresh and clean, the colors brilliant. Something so pleasantly familiar and then like a jolt, like a sudden earthquake, there's horrific screaming in the room. It terrifies me, I want out, I want my FEET ON THE GROUND. I leap up and remove the eye shade from my eyes. I can't bear all these slimy, screeching bodies around me.

- No, no, you can't stop, my helper whispers firmly. Keep going. Keep breathing!

He puts the eye shade back on, takes a soft scarf and wraps that around my head, gently, all of it gently. I feel my heart fluttering like I am a small bird he's rescued from a storm. He lays me back down, guiding my breath. He knows I'm at the edge of the cliff, the cliff of familiar, before I plunge into the unknown. He holds me in a way that gives support but yet doesn't hamper the descent, for it is this descent I must make, that Ana has been preparing me for, that leads the way to getting well. It is so bizarre, this free falling, this borderlessness of both nothing and everything. Everything I have ever wanted, have ever feared is in this space. Yet I have never been this afraid and this courageous at the same time, because he, my helper, won't allow me to fall *completely* through the stratosphere and out of the world. Instantly, I comprehend how impossible it is to be completely free. Walls, enclosures, even a prison gives security, and without this we humans become disoriented, like ants whose line of direction is broken.

All at once, as the music builds in intensity, the room fills with more screaming. A new level of terror crashes in, and I can't stop my own screaming. It isn't even me: I never scream like this, ever! A scream surges out, and another and another... from somewhere far in the distance someone is shrieking in terror — but it is me. How can it be me? What power has taken over? I no longer have control of this terror, even worse than the last weeks together. I will die, I want to die; the sensation is horrible. It will kill me. Just then, Ana comes to my side. She places a hand on my head and whispers: Go on, you are doing great, go with it!

She puts another hand on my chest, below my sternum and presses so hard. It hurts like hell; she is crushing me to death.

- Make a sound from here, Ana says. Even if it hurts now it will be fine in a moment and you'll feel much, much better. Trust me.

I can't believe how strong she is, I can't believe how much this hurts, and yet she is touching the valve, of this I am sure, the valve that's impossible for me to reach. The sound that surges out of me as I fight for my life is a volcano erupting. I am boiling lava. I shall destroy everything in my path. My arms flail. I kick and punch and break and tear and rip. Any minute I will kill Ana. Maybe I have already killed her.

She shouts in Spanish and instantly I feel her team surround me, like a group of skilled pirates invading a small island. They hold me in a way that prevents injuring Ana and the others and myself, and yet still allowing some part of me to smash and bang and kick. They have put pillows under my feet, under my fists. I cannot see anything, but I imagine I'm pounding these pillows into small pieces of foam that fill the room. I nearly tear the blanket apart in my attempt to destroy the world. My arms wrench upwards, trying to reach the unreachable. I must get out of myself, away from this horrific fury.

I sob convulsively; an unbelievable amount of fluid, muck and snot sprouts forth from this body that is no longer mine. In this raging storm, my tears have flooded the room. Where the hell is this coming from? The others, I think, all the others will drown.

- Don't care! Ana whispers. Keep going.

The volcanic eruption peaks: all the shit stuffed inside me, all that has been shoveled in, swallowed down, compressed in muscles and bones, all the years, my constant insecurity, my loneliness, the terror as a child, the little girl who longed for her mother — her powerful, successful, wonderful mother — who was rarely there. Who was always so busy with her millions of important friends incessantly phoning, incessantly stealing her attention. Goddamn her, convincing me how important those conversations were... Bullshit, complete bullshit! She needed them, she needed them to tell her how great she was.

I am eight years old. I am calling my mother from the downstairs extension to our other number. My hand is shaking.

- Who is this? my mother shouts.

- It's me...

- Hang up immediately, I'm expecting an important call.

I was a good girl and hung up, but the moment the phone rang again I picked it up silently and listened, listened to her *important* conversation. I heard her laugh, exchanging all sorts of nonsense with her friend.

Nothing could interfere with her busy life.

We followed along, me and my brothers marched to her orders. She scared me... the fragile setup at home. How quickly I became the one my father hit when he was infuriated, intimidated by my mother, frustrated with his powerlessness.

How desperately my parents clung to the need for control, an elusive control one can never obtain... In order to help a child feel safe, the parents have to feel safe themselves... And they never did. Ever.

I keep falling and falling, and as the music changes, the sensations change. Suddenly, my brother Bob is before me... I see him holding his first-born daughter... So beautifully he rocks her, so soothingly... How jealous I am of that. A father's little girl; a thing I will never ever experience, no matter how hard I try to make it happen.

While vomiting up my history, the more recent words of the taxi driver — about not having children — reverberate through me, and all hell breaks loose again. God, Ana is strong, for I am using all my power to damage myself.

- Hit the pillow! Ana yells, as she pulls my hands away from my body, for my anger has turned inwards, and I am trying to break my limbs.

- Make a sound!

And I scream and scream... And out of the blue rises something that I have not thought about for a million years... I scream for my lost baby that I once wanted so badly. I hate my mother so much... It was her who took me to get an abortion... Surely for the best, she had said. But still I wanted this baby. She said I'd have one later, at a better time... that it wasn't the right time... She had just gotten divorced; there was no money to take care of me *and* a baby... I would have to leave school... Who knew it would be my only time; that I would never get pregnant again.

I toss my body frantically on the mat as I try to flee from these thoughts, and again I want to stop more than anything. I get up. Instantly my helper is there with his hand, getting me back down, getting my breath going again... and the memory comes back... how much I loved being pregnant; loved the sensation of something in me, of not being alone.

The memory is so piercing, so actual, that I suddenly *feel* pregnant and give birth. Now, completely out of control, I wrap up one of the blankets as a baby and rock it in my arms. And then abruptly the blanket, which was just my baby, metamorphoses into a hobos' bundle, my entire life dangling from a stick. But it's too much for one stick, the bundle swells over — like a refugees' bulging sack, containing all their worldly belongings, possessions they refuse to let go of no matter what — and everything spills on the ground. This is my life that I've carried hidden in me... Nothing... nothing ever thrown away.

As if the volcano has at last run empty, I get quiet, very quiet and become aware of someone else crying in the room. It reminds me of the sound my brother Peter made when my father would hit him (giving *him* something to cry about). I hated that my mother didn't stop my father, either with me or with my brother. How she pretended it wasn't happening, or maybe in her means of survival she really didn't know. I hated my father's rage. I could never understand what made him so angry, and yet I tried to make sure we all behaved, that we all were good. It infuriated me there was no referee, like in sports; someone to tally up the score and see the real sequence of events. So much of my life I have spent yearning for the truth and yet how unattainable, there never was anyone who dared speak the truth.

Finally here in this breathing session there is an arena for *my* version, with neither censor nor interpreter, like my mother who might yell out: *No, no it didn't happen like that.* Perhaps God in his/her infinite wisdom created people and their memories in such a way, allowing them to alter or entirely forget the past, and with it, the truth. If not, life would be unbearable. For the truth, the unadulterated truth is just too much for a person to contain.

The breathing sequence lasts two and a half hours, but feels like two and a half lifetimes. Like sitting in a movie theater, so shocked from what you've just seen that you can't move. When they start the next showing you're still sitting there and end up watching the whole film again. But this time you see it differently; you notice the parts missed in the first viewing.

All at once, I begin to weep for my entire family, for all the episodes that no one had ever, ever dealt with. Everyone was so busy, always so busy, there was never time. All these tears make me think of a Mexican movie I once saw where everyone was chopping onions and soon began weeping. *First it is just because of the onions,* the voice-over said: *but once you start crying you can't stop and before you know it, you are crying for your whole life.*

I cry up all the times when something felt too strong to express, when I lacked the confidence in my own seeing... for all the overeating and the lost years and the people I hurt because of it, for all the wrong men I spent the night with, and for all those who have tried to be close to me and I could not let them, could not give them what they needed.

It shifts again and now my mind is a cacophony of shrieks and revulsions. The way I've survived by holding on, by getting anxious, is pathetic. I am pathetic. This current of thought leads straight to the rash that is suddenly itching like hell, burning like an inferno.

I scream wildly again, hitting and kicking, literally choking on myself, furious at how my fear messes me up, time and again... all that I've lost. I realize with what feels like an electric shock, that despite the rationale — that I've always been a person unable to make a commitment — I have all the while been completely committed to my fear. So devoted to it. And this is why I have been unable to love: not myself and not another person. Like a sailor, never leaving the watch, keeping one hand on the rudder and one eye at sea, it's impossible to live life fully, impossible if forever on guard for danger to arrive. You actually *want* the danger; you need it, thrive on it, as that's all you've been trained for.

When the last of these insights penetrate my awareness, I cascade through layers of consciousness and collapse in exhaustion. The landing back into the now — into the room, onto my mat — is surprisingly gentle, as if falling onto a bed of downy feathers. I actually feel calm, as if finally I have stepped off the plane and have at last arrived in Buenos Aires. I nearly am asleep when I feel Ana by my side. She wraps me up in the blanket that has just been my baby and my bundle and whispers in my ear:

- How are you?

There are no words. I am not sure if I am alive, or what form I am alive in.

- You did really great. I am proud of you.

And then words come.

- It has to be wrong, I say too loudly (for not everyone has completed their 'journey'). It has to be too indulgent, all this feeling *of me*, all my sadness, my anger. It can't be right.

- Shhh… Try not to judge, Ana says. And I actually believe her.

The music is softer, more subdued. A voice is chanting in a foreign language, maybe Indian, Hindi, I am not sure. But it is so beautiful, so tender, like a gift that comforts, even more than Ana's words reassuring that what has just happened can only be positive. That it is not indulgence. For I have not hurt a single person in these last three hours, and remarkably, the itch has stopped. This brand new experience is truly wonderful, just as Ana had promised. I reach out to check if she is still there; her presence is so powerful that I am both surprised and not, that when I feel with my hands, she has gone.

The chanting continues, and it fills me so completely that I am overwhelmed with gratitude. A prayer forms inside me. I've never felt so profound a connection. *God help me go through. This is the music I yearn to create, this deep in the belly singing. Help me find the courage and trust I lack.*

Neither my mother nor my father gives this or takes this away from me. It is me depriving myself of this. Please, please help me stop.

The music ends and there is a lovely quiet, a perfect peace that fills the room. This must be what God intended when creating life; this ease of perfectly timed breathing, ribs opening to allow the lungs to fill with nourishing air, no struggle, no resistance. Life doing life. My eyes are still closed, the eye shade still on, but the darkness lifts as if morning has come. I feel a change in the air; hear the soft chirp of birds outside. Someone must have opened the curtains and windows. The man who has been my helper sits down on the edge of my mat and enters my sphere so delicately that it doesn't startle me as his hand comes to my face.

- You can take this off now, he says as he helps me remove the eye shade. His hand shields the excess light and lifts it ever so tenderly.

- How are you? he asks. He puts a soft hand on my cheek and strokes it, the perfect parental stroke that is just enough and doesn't ask for anything back. It is so lovely, so giving; I have never experienced such love.

- Nothing is how we think it is... Is it? I ask.

He laughs, for I have asked a convoluted question that doesn't need an answer.

- Each of us has so much inside... that we think is not right, nor good. It is a heavy load... all what we carry around. You get so used to carrying it that you no longer feel it, until you put it down. It's incredible when we get the chance to lay it down and to let it go, all the extra room you get. It's like having someone in your house that has stayed too long. When they finally leave... what a relief!

- I want to believe in something, I say, and new tears begin to fall. How can I cry more? I ask. I must have used up a carton of tissues. Do I have to pay extra for all the tissues?

- No, he says laughing, it's included in the price. Just cry, if there are tears, it doesn't matter. And you will discover what you believe in. It may take time, that's all. But we all have more time than we think we do.

- Maybe I don't even like to sing, I say. Maybe I have grown so used to the struggle of trying to prove myself...

- I don't believe that, he said, you know you were singing at the end.

- I was?

- Yes, and it was beautiful. I think you have a great voice, but talk about it with Ana. She knows you better. I only know that for myself, this work has changed me so much. I had no idea what I really felt, what I loved, not at first. Give it time. Don't think too much, and don't talk it away. Let it be how it is inside you now, whatever it is.

And he hugs me again. I can't believe this, this being hugged — even if you don't get it right, even if you have no clue. For me, love was a thing to be earned, to deserve; you had to be very, very special to get this love. I've spent most of my life trying to figure out how to be that special.

8.

A few days later the rash is worse than ever and I desperately want to see Ana. I have no appointment, and her line is busy, busy. Finally, she answers and tells me to come immediately and to bring my guitar.

- My guitar? I ask. Why?

- You'll see.

I hurry to get there, yet when I arrive she slows me down. *Wait*, she instructs, just wait. This infuriates me. It is New York style action I crave: fast, swift moving wings that swoop down and take the bad away. With Ana, when not doing the intense breathwork, it's like floating on water as we wait for the *real* issues to drift by on the current. She refuses to focus on the seemingly urgent I am so attached to, like how much worse the rash has gotten, which is even more upsetting now after feeling so cleansed from the workshop, so cured. Once again, I am the miserable, abandoned child with no one to help her. This too is part of the training: I must tolerate this feeling of being denied.

- It is not unusual, she says, to get worse after a breathing weekend. So today I have another idea for you and someone else I want you to work with. Please... be open.

She gets a look from me like: *I am open for God's sakes, what more do you want?*

- I understand that this *feels* very open for you, and it doesn't diminish how well you did in the workshop, but trust me, you still have no idea what being open is like.

- Look at me Ana! Look at my skin... I can't stand it.

For a moment I think I've trumped her; that I will go down in her archives as the failed case, the girl too sick to help.

- No, no, no, she says, I won't let you go *there*. We've just begun our work together. You *have* to get worse before you get better.

The way she sees straight through, forces me to at least *attempt* the motions of trust, and right now that means gathering my things, my guitar, and following her out of the room. It hurts that she passes me on to someone else as if now even for her I am too much. Like a person who has finally found an oasis after years in the desert — *she* is the water, and I need to drink and drink her. It is not just a matter of thirst but also the fear that soon there will be no more water.

I am trembling, as she takes my hand and leads me back down the wide staircase and into the big room — that has totally changed yet again. It is now set up like a new-age church. Laid out in the center of the floor is a huge cross, made of string and tiny crystals, with enough space for a person to lie within its form. There is a big star on top where the head will be. What is this? This symbolic Jesus-on-the-cross gives me the creeps. A new terror overtakes me with the notion that I am in the wrong hands. But the rash is so frightful, and I don't know where else to go... Once again Ana feels my thoughts.

- This is Luis, Ana says. He is *wonderful*, and no... he is not part of any cult. Don't *worry*.

Another Luis, but so different from my Luis, the calm and centered way he greets me, that immediately I think of him as Louie, like a white 'Louie' Armstrong, round, warm, and kind, with soft brown eyes. He sits in front of six Tibetan bowls of various sizes with a small perfectly shaped piece of wood in his hand, a pestle, the kind an alchemist would use. He carefully puts the pestle down as if part of the ritual and stands up. He observes me, like he's reading my face, and when he's finished, he leads me to the center of the room. Holding my hand, he guides my body inside the cross. Touching the outside line of crystals are flower petals, giving off a delicate smell of jasmine and lavender. It is so pretty, I fear my manic body will destroy the design, distort the fragile aroma.

- Lie down, Louie says softly. Try not to touch the string, and do not move.

Already he has asked the impossible, yet when we begin, a stillness takes over that is both relief and blessing. My legs touch each other and my arms stretch out like Jesus, yet unlike him, I am being brought to life.

- I must leave you now, Ana says.

I start crying, like a child left at the nursery school on the first day. Foolish is what I feel, but am too intimidated to say anything.

- Lie back, Louie tells me again, and close your eyes. It doesn't matter if you cry... Just try not to move. Pay attention to your breath... Let the sounds I make come to you, like waves of the sea.

He sits with such presence, like the Buddha, and begins moving the pestle on the bowls creating different frequencies of soft and sometimes stronger vibrations. I begin to vibrate, almost rattle as the sound comes into my bones. The tears quiet down, which is a small miracle. It is so lovely, whatever he is doing, whatever these sounds create, that my only wish is to remain here on this floor for the rest of my life. The tones cover me in a soft glow of vibration that soothes the itch, the anxiety, and fill me with a sensation of wellness so profound, so healing. But when he finishes, I can't bear him to stop.

- Can you do it more? I beg.

- A little more, Louie consents, and then we will chant together.

It is astounding how calm I feel, and when he leads me in a repetitive mantra, the sound that emanates *is* from someone else's body. After a while we finish chanting, and he takes me outside, barefoot, onto the grass behind the house. There is a gush of gratitude towards him and Ana. And then, as he lets go of my hand and I'm standing on my own, the spell is broken. The delightful sensations leave, and I plunge back into my old self. A tumble of obsessive thoughts come as I try desperately to recapture those good feelings and only hear a part of what he's telling me.

- Love? Louie asks, leading me back into the room. Do you know what love is?

I think I say *No*, but the rest of what he says gets jumbled. There is something about connection, how important it is to stay connected.

Connected to what? I want to ask. But he has already answered while I was not paying attention. This brings the panic back with a powerful swing and with it the full package of anger and shame — I am furious that I can't even focus when someone is right in my face helping me.

Ana comes into the room just then and notices my distress. She says something to Louie in a fast, mumbled Spanish, and shakes her head.

- You are so hard on yourself, she says to me. Isn't it enough that you have a terrible rash, do you have to beat yourself even more? *Try,* she says, *not to judge so hard.*

And she does the thing that she's so good at — she comes and holds me, knowing that at this moment I can't help being a broken record that skips and skips on the same spot.

- It's okay that you need us, we are here to help you, but you must *let* us help you.

They have to see me, Louie and Ana, and I have to let them see me in order to be helped. And for a moment I almost trust them, far more than I've ever trusted anyone. This sensation of reliance, of confidence, is so extraordinary, so completely opposite the unsettling notion I had as a child. How unsafe I always felt then, somehow knowing that my parents hadn't a clue what to do with me, the child who seemed to have thoughts and feelings so alien to what they expected.

If you do not know what trust feels like, you can't fall back on trust when the going gets rough. In a river blocked by a dam there can never be a flow... All that has unleashed in me these last weeks and months... it has been there all along, always threatening to come up and out of me. This, it suddenly dawns on me, is the root of my fear of flying (and all my other fears). That no one was able to manage this unexplainable fear in me only left me more and more terrified. The times, for example, when it manifested as a severe stomachache or a sleepless night, the best my mother could do was to hush it away. And my father... his choice was anger. If only all the terror inside me could have been hushed away so easily. And I tried; I really tried. But it was always there. To control all that 'hushed away' stuff at the moment of takeoff on a plane, or alone on stage was impossible, and manifested in unbearable fear.

I hate it, but I see that Ana is allowing, demanding, for all that stuff to come forth, in the daylight. Exposed, with this understanding attention, *it* diminishes, it really does. This fear of self is just a *feeling*, not a *truth*, and denying its essence has made it into a monster. But it is not a monster and I'm not a monster, and I'm not crazy (as I secretly feared all my life), just different and filled with other emotions and needs than my family could deal with, than the people around could deal with. I get a glimpse, a blessed moment of belief that I *can* learn to tolerate and manage these feelings, and that they will pass. Or maybe they don't have to pass; maybe I can live with them.

When Ana asks me what I'm thinking, I tell her my new revelation.

- Great! They both say. Can you be here with us... like this?

Then they ask me to stand in the middle of the room... to be *there*, the center of attention.

- Will you sing us a song? Ana asks.

- *Now?* One of my songs? (I'd completely forgotten about my guitar.) It feels impossible to sing with this unfamiliar, confusing, yet maybe promising sensation of freedom. That it should not be necessary to do my normal over-preparing, pumping myself up, leaves me in a vacuum. I have no idea how to begin.

- No excuses, Ana says laughing, just sing for us.

My voice comes out surprisingly open and easily. The power in my voice is so startling, so foreign that I can't tell if I'm singing in tune or have made a total mess of it — as if something *other*, like in the chanting, is singing me. When I finish, they clap and say how beautiful, how wonderful.

- This is how you must sing! Ana exclaims happily. This is your real voice, and this is what touches the listener, the listener that is open to be touched.

- But it must sound bad, out of tune, I squeal. Unprofessional.

- It may *feel* like that, Ana says laughing, because you're not used to being in yourself, but that's not the same thing.

Back at Evelyn's house, the anxiety returns with a vengeance. But this time I manage it better, riding my great pounding fears like a rodeo cowboy. I try to stay mindful, as Louie advised, but because of his name, it makes me think of Luis number one and *that* makes me long for him so much. I ache to phone him, to see him, to tell him all that I've been learning, but have promised Ana that I won't. Instead, I force myself to find a way to dress so that my damaged skin is not noticeable (my face has dramatically improved after the session), and decide to go dance tango. This is the reason, for goodness sake, that I came to Buenos Aires, to dance. Not to see Luis.

*

A few days later I go to the dermatologist that Carolina has recommended for a second opinion. It is quite remarkable how my body has improved since the breathing workshop and the session with the Tibetan bowls. The inflamed red has lessened to a soft pink. And yet this doctor, as he checks my skin closely with a magnifying glass, also uses the word 'impressive', like it's something I've labored hard for, this horrific rash.

- It's much better now! I pronounce proudly (I have truly labored hard for *this* improvement). I just need to know if I am going in the right direction, or if it will get worse again.

- Hard to tell, this doctor says. But probably yes it will get worse, for your body is still reacting to the medicine in your system.

And then instead of a different opinion, I hear the exact same words as in the hospital.

- Therapy, he says, you must go to therapy. Drink lots of water, eat well, and don't *worry*. Remember, you must never *ever* take *Xanax* again or any other tranquilizer. You really have developed a severe allergy, and you are lucky to be alive.

- I'll never be able to fly without medicine, I say. I'm terrified to get back onto a plane.

- Work through your phobia. It is the only way, not with medicine.

It is a gorgeous day, and the office is located in an area I rarely visit so I take the time to walk through a nearby park. This is a rich and fancy part of the city, hard to believe that this is the same Buenos Aires that Luis lives in. Hard to believe there's really a crisis in Argentina walking amongst these well-dressed, overly-pampered citizens.

It hits me how many layers of reality exist at the same moment. And how, while in one realm you hardly have a clue about the others. I think of my old friend Karen from my time in Holland who first convinced me about *Xanax*, and wonder how she is doing, and how she'd react if given this ultimatum — no more *Xanax*. I think of the obese woman sitting next to me on that long flight so many years ago, even if a specialist in phobias at a great university, how wrong she was. Maybe that explains why she was so overweight; she followed her own advice and did not confront the real issues behind her eating.

I walk past the glamorous shops and notice the busy important people with their briefcases, their shopping bags — the self-appointed aristocracy of our time — who usually make me feel inferior, a failure. Today something is different. The sun caresses my face, my face that is gratefully so much better, and for a moment I don't feel left out or diminished in my non-life. I actually feel relief to not be a part of their life, their competitive race where nothing ever is enough, with the relentless fear of lacking behind. Struck with awe, it comes clear that I no longer need to be a slave of that life. A glimpse of a new truth emerges: a freedom, another way of existing... and *this* is what I've searched my whole life for.

In the past, my way of coping was to give up whatever caused or stirred my inner demon of anxiety — acting, my music, even people. Now I'm learning not to give up so fast the things I love (well, besides Luis), but rather go deeper; to really be committed to the activity at hand and be *mindful, to focus on the process and let go of the end result.* Ironically, this is the essence of the Alexander work I've been teaching others for years but rarely managed myself; the desperate need to be safe made that impossible. Ana, with her bountiful supply of love, is helping me uncover, tolerate, even include the untouchable and unlovable parts of myself *and* have the courage to stand in my own fear.

Perhaps this allergy and rash have been useful after all as if burning off an old layer of skin to a new self. The trump card is finding out that my all-powerful mother and father are no different than the Wizard of Oz. Like Dorothy — who discovers that the Wizard is just a humble being after all, that it was his *room* full of levers and buttons magnifying and manipulating his voice that gave the image of power, and without that room he was nothing more than a frightened old man — I begin to fathom that my parents' all-powerfulness is also just an illusion. They have no *real* power over me, not anymore. A shock, but if I can take this in, really take this in, I will be free. And then, as I continue to walk home, I hear Ana's words in my head. *Herein lies the work... The hardest part about freedom, is realizing how scary it is to be free, even if we think we want it.*

I am definitely getting better and decide to call my brother Peter in this window of wellness and tell him my good news. I tell him about how kind and understanding the doctors have been, about the therapy, but notice that he isn't really listening. He's distracted. If only Louie could teach *him* to be mindful, if only Ana could visit with my whole family and teach *them* to pay attention. All at once, I realize that this too is part of my journey, this difficult art of acceptance, that being mindful also means allowing others to be just as they are, giving up the desire to change them.

I don't get to tell my brother much after all, for he has bad news to convey: my mother is in the hospital with cancer. What I instantly notice is that I don't crumble with terrible guilt. This is new! Before, no matter what, I'd feel guilty just for not being at her side. That I don't, is truly remarkable.

Before hanging up, my brother gives me the number of the hospital and her private line, urging me to phone. Not surprisingly her line is busy, busy, busy. Finally I try the hospital's number, and they can put me through (calling from Argentina gives priority). First we speak at length about her and her operation, and then she asks about me. This is our first conversation in almost a month, and I give a brief version of Ana, the breathing, and the work I am doing; how much of it involves her and our relationship.

She has upstaged me (again), being in the hospital with cancer, but I am truly sorry that she is sick and that I'm not able to be with her. It seems the operation has been successful and she will be fine. Plus, with all the attention from the doctors and everyone phoning, she hardly needs anything from me. Perhaps she too has been learning, for she actually says that she understands what I am trying to do and wishes me luck.

This is so astonishing, that it comes with the sensation of my brain burping. Ana has told me that as I begin to really change this will be reflected in how others treat me. I just didn't think it would include my mother.

9.

It would do me a world of good to have a walk in the woods, amongst cool, dripping trees, but here in Buenos Aires there are no woods, not really. There's only the big picture of a forest on the wall in Luis' horrid apartment. In my still distorted thinking (change is slow, one step forward, three to the side and many slips back), I tell myself that going to see him would be more about being near trees (that wonderful forest of his). And besides, Ana who is after all human, cannot be right about everything, so I decide to phone Luis, Luis number one. And my clever thinking continues: if I were meant to be alone, there wouldn't be so many people in Buenos Aires that look just like him, that keep reminding me of him. Impossible to *not* see him; the pull is too strong, and a pull that strong must not be denied or there'll never be connection. And isn't that what Louie told me after the sessions with the Tibetan bowls, to find *connection*? There is a connection (and attraction) so powerful, between Luis and me, that it can't be bad. (Right?)

What tricks I play, convincing myself that sleeping with Luis would be a good thing; it would really free up my voice, and spending time with him would be fine, perfectly fine. Completely convinced, I phone him. When we meet to have a meal at the restaurant where we first met, it really seems like we're perfectly fine; just a normal happy couple, with every right to go out on a Saturday night.

I am laughing and joking, speaking Spanish remarkably well, when suddenly I look up and notice the cute English doctor from the Emergency room sitting at the table in front of us.

- Is it you? He asks, for he'd never seen my face without the mask of rash.

- Yes it's me!

- My, my! So there *was* someone underneath all that after all!

- Yes, I laugh.

- You look good, my sweet doctor says. He is so charming that I have

to be careful not to flirt with him in front of Luis. I introduce
tell Luis (in Spanish) that this was my helpful doctor.

- Aaah, Luis says, nodding his head and singing out the Ah, as if to
express what he'd say if he spoke English. He is obviously thanking him.

- It was my pleasure, says the doctor in English (he doesn't speak a
word of Spanish), but in such a way that Luis can understand. It is
amazing how one hardly needs words if the subtext is clear. It's also
amazing that Luis is not jealous, but he *seems* to be fine and proud that
he too has helped in my getting well. I begin thinking even more as-
suredly that Ana has to be wrong about Luis.

The next day, Sunday, while practicing in the studio, I impulsively
stop — sensing that Evelyn is about to barge in and force me with some
cockamamie excuse to leave and convince myself that *anything* is better
than a conflict with her — and go phone Luis to ask if I can practice at
his house. I've never done this before, and he seems delighted with the
idea.

We meet halfway, at Plaza Dorrego, and stop to watch the tango dancers that are always there on Sundays, before continuing on. It is so nice,
so quintessential Buenos Aires that I forget entirely about being ill, about
Harold, about my other life. We stand and watch for a long while, when
all at once the weather, which started out fine, changes rapidly. The
wind picks up so we hurry to leave before the *tormenta* starts. *Tormenta* is
a fitting word, for it doesn't just rain in Buenos Aires, it comes down
passionately. Luis takes my hand, and we start running as if in a movie.
And I, like Gene Kelly, break into song.

I'm singing in the rain
Just singing in the rain
What a glorious feeling,
I'm happy again...

We make it to his apartment just as the enormous drops of rain begin
falling and laugh and kiss as we climb the many flights of stairs to his
flat. My guitar is damp but okay, and I begin to play. The sound of pouring rain gives an atmosphere of intensity. Luis, who has never heard me
sing before, loves it. I sing for hours, filled with inspiration. So many
songs I want him to hear. I explain the meaning of every song in my all
at once impressively fluent Spanish. Finally he takes the guitar gently
from my arms and hugs me. He puts on a CD of flamenco music and we
dance around his room. He has never danced with me, though he's men-

tioned wanting to teach me the *Chacarera*, the Argentine folk-dance that he loves. He puts on other music and we start doing this lovely, partner dance, this *Chacarera* that I pick up quickly and I am so happy I could burst. Just at the moment when it seems that we are having the grandest time, he stops.

- *Basta*, he says. He sits down to roll a cigarette.
- Why did you stop?
- You sing so well, he says. You're stupid to waste time dancing tango…
- But we weren't dancing tango…
- Just practice your singing.
- I can do both.
- But you shouldn't, Luis says. You should only sing.
- You're jealous, I laugh. Just because I'm getting well and will start dancing again…
- Don't laugh at me, he snaps. I don't like you dancing with all those stupid men at the tango…
- I don't ever have anything with those tango men. I just dance with them.
- And that doctor of yours, Luis went on. I don't trust him.
- He isn't my real doctor. The real doctor is a woman… from Argentina…

But Luis doesn't listen. I go over to gently touch him on the shoulder. His mood has shifted, but I don't care; I'm not willing to abandon all the good that has just passed between us.

He lets me hold him, and for a brief respite even seems happy with this attention. But then what he really feels takes over. I'm asking for the impossible with this distorted love. He declares that he deserves the whole show, not just this girly dancing, hugging, and pushes me away.

- Please, I beg, we had it so nice. We…
- I can't do this anymore, Luis says, you're killing me… And for god's sake, please don't start crying.

And once again we vow to never see each other again.

Back at Evelyn's house, I find Samantha curled up in the studio reading a book. We've become good friends and chat whenever we meet. Samantha wants to hear the whole story, luckily for me, as I can't think or talk of anything else. When I finish she bursts out laughing.

- What's so funny? I ask. This is serious, Samantha. He won't see me any more and it feels like shit. I don't even want to dance tango. I just want to be with him, but...

- Fifty pesos, she says.

- What?

- I'll bet you fifty pesos that you're gonna see him again.

- No, I say to her, it is really over now.

- Yeah, yeah... Wanna bet?

I feel guilty and rotten, and it falls out of my mouth immediately when I next see Ana, who also laughs when she hears the saga of Luis. She isn't stupid, and probably knew I'd sneak and start seeing him again.

- When I said to be *open*, I didn't mean about sex. It will do you no good to sleep with him.

- I haven't slept with him! I shout.

- Sure, but you will.

- Anyway, it's not how you think. He broke up with *me* this time.

- That means absolutely nothing. He will take you back in a second if he thinks there's a chance for sex. This is Argentina, not Norway, and the men are different here. It will just confuse you and break the connection with Harold, and *that* connection is the important one.

- Harold is not here, I bark. She knows how angry I have been at Harold for not coming to help me.

- I know, she says, but it's not so bad that he isn't here. It is good that you find a way on your own.

She burns her pretty blue eyes into me, like she too is making a bet, daring me to be alone. So we sit in silence and I look at the clock; I want it to stop when our talking stops so that I don't lose the precious time... For what feels like forever I refuse to say a word.

- I will have to forfeit my ticket, I finally say. They won't let me change it. I can't fly now, that's one thing I am sure about. I'll never be able to get on an plane again.

- Stay in the moment, Ana begs. You are living way ahead, and that just feeds your anxiety. Do you know that you make yourself worse with your thinking?

- Yes, I say, I know and I don't give a shit.

*

It is Christmas 'Eve' and I am at Carolina's house. Since giving me Ana's number, she's called time to time to see how I am and insisted that I join her for Christmas. It is my first attempt at anything this normal. I fear that I won't behave sanely for the duration of the dinner party. Carolina insisted that I come, that she'd look after me. She had told her friends about my illness and promised that they'd be sympathetic. *Besides,* she said, *my friends are all actors. They adore all things dramatic. If you break down and have a scene, they will love it.*

Indeed everyone is being nice and attentive, speaking a slow and clear Spanish so I'm able to follow the conversation. Once the food is served, I'm amazed how hungry I am and how delicious the food tastes. I eat voraciously, as if the food slips out a trap door in my back. One woman comments on how lucky I am to be able to eat so much and stay so skinny. I look at her, somehow triggered by what she's just said, as if her flippant comment holds far more than the words intended. Anxiety rises up fiercely, startling me with its potency, as if this time I *truly* am in danger.

Be in the moment, I urge myself, but can't. I leap ten paces into the future: I am forced to get on a airplane... but I can't fly, I can't... I rip the seat belt off. I run down the aisle and use all my power to push open the door... I will have to stay here forever in Buenos Aires... but where? Not with Evelyn... How will I support myself? My Spanish is terrible... I will never see Harold again... A boat? What about a boat? ... I could go home by boat, but it will cost a fortune... I'll get a job singing on the ship... and David Letterman announces me... *Ladies and Gentlemen please welcome...* The nerves are strangling me; I can't breathe...

Carolina leaps up.

- It's okay, she says. Come on.

I hold her hand like a little girl who is walked across a large busy street. She leads me to her guestroom.

- You did better than I thought, she says.

- I did?

- Really, just until the last few minutes you seemed quite okay.

- Really?

- Really. And this is the best news I've had in a while.

- I am so tired, I say.

- I can imagine, Carolina says, with such kindness that I stop holding my breath and burst out crying. She squeezes my hand and gets me a towel, an old tee shirt to sleep in, and pulls the curtain across the large window.

- It faces the street, she says, but it's really quiet. Sleep as long as you need. We can have a brunch together tomorrow. It is good for me too. I hate being alone on Christmas day.

- Thank you, I say. I mean it, you are being so good to me. I really want to get well, but it may take more time than I have.

- Then take the time, she tells me.

- I have concerts booked in Europe, students, things to do... And I will run out of money. But... I want to get well.

- Then stay here and get well. Stay as long as it takes. Don't worry about all the parts, the money, your career, your husband. I bet you will look back some years from now and know that you did the right thing. You are really ill. I mean, if you had a bad car crash and all your bones were broken you wouldn't be able to leave, couldn't you see it like that? You should respect your illness. Ana is a great therapist. You're lucky she has the time to see you.

I look at her with fresh tears of gratitude that it can be that simple, that I can *lay my burden down by the riverside and stay by the river as long as it takes.*

I get into the small bed where I feel perfectly safe, hearing the distant voices of the party, the laughing. It brings a sense of comfort, normality. My exhaustion, like a heavy knapsack carried for so long, slides from my shoulders, and the tiredness holds me tenderly like the sweetest of lovers. I fall into a deep, dreamless sleep, the first good sleep I've had in months. When I awake it's as if a year has passed and all things have fallen into place.

In the morning, Carolina has prepared a feast of a breakfast for just the two of us. Once again I'm famished. While we eat she tells me about her life, the hard choices she has had to make, the hard times in Argentina. To survive, she will start renting rooms in her apartment for tourists. We talk, eat and drink tea and indulge in the gift of this warm and sunny Christmas day and I feel completely free of anxiety, which is the best Christmas gift.

Before leaving, she gets a guitar and asks me to sing a song. I'm astounded to *still* not feel an iota of discomfort as I begin to pluck chords and a song flows out of me with grace. It feels even stronger than the best moments with Sebastian, for it isn't his violin drawing my voice out, but something within me.

Once back at the house, everything seems different. Even Evelyn, who normally has something mean to say, looks at me differently.

- Merry Christmas, Evelyn.

- Okay, she says, the same to you. (Even soldiers take a break from fighting at Christmas.)

A bit later, Samantha barges into my room.

- Fifty pesos, she says, you owe me.

- I haven't seen him! Honestly.

- But you will. I am sure you will. Here, she says and throws a box wrapped in tissue paper at me, he came by when you were away and left this present for you.

10.

Buenos Aires — how great this city is, with its creaks and cracks and everything slightly broken or falling apart. How magical! Just as anything can fall apart, anything can happen, and never the way you think. There's no way to prepare, which gives great relief and great freedom. Fascinating how all things rise up out of order, in *disorder*. I feel incredibly alive. The summer holiday in Argentina has begun. It is sweltering, and the streets are a pandemonium of shrieks and yelps. The children are no longer dressed for school with little white coats like miniature lab technicians, but out in shorts and tee shirts, leaping around the wild-spraying fire hydrants. Suddenly I'm back in the hot summer days of my childhood running in and out of the sprinkler. I can almost feel the sensual pleasure of the cool refreshing water, and just have to walk in amongst them, to let the water spray and soak me, to laugh with them.

I phone Ana, who is leaving for a few weeks on vacation, to tell her that I've decided to forfeit my return ticket and stay. She is delighted, for this means I can continue the private sessions with her and even more importantly attend the *weekend* breathing workshops starting in February. Before we hang up, she urges me to trust this choice.

I immediately phone Harold to tell him the news.

- I'll miss you, he says. But you're doing the right thing. Better for you and *me* when you get completely well.

- Oh, I gasp, both relieved and hurt. Even if it makes sense to stay, I'd hoped Harold would insist upon my returning. Determined to not let my positive mood sink, I quickly change the subject and tell him about the classes on Saturdays in the house with Alberto.

- It's a combination of yoga, relaxation and *tai chi*, I tell him. Evelyn invited us all to come… and it's great.

- Evelyn? I thought she hated you.

- She does, but she doesn't come to the class. Nor do any of the people in the house. Just a few come from outside and they're really nice. Alberto gives each of us a massage at the end and because we're so few, he has time to give me a really long one. It's the most amazing massage you could ever feel, and it's for free. He told us that he's in training and needs students to practice on, so I told him he could practice on me all he wants. So now he comes on Sundays as well to just give me a massage!

- And that's okay with Evelyn? Harold asks.

- Alberto said so, that it was okay with her. And he knows her better than anyone.

- What's he like… this Alberto?

- Don't worry, no one you need be jealous of, I tease Harold. I won't fall in love with him.

- And he with you?

- I don't think so. He's like someone outside this world, like a Dalai Lama. You can't imagine him having a crush on anyone.

- Okay, he answers, not sounding completely convinced.

- What's the matter?

- I… just wish I could be with you, Harold adds. I didn't realize how bad you were, honestly… And I've been thinking… I can come in March, if you'd like. I could take the whole month off, and we could fly home together. What do you think? Can you manage two more months on your own?

- I suppose so. I've managed so far… And I think the worst is over.

- Let me know as soon as you can, then I'll book my flight.

- Okay, I tell him in a voice that sounds bland and not very enthusiastic. Do I feel guilty about Luis, or resentful that this amazing experience with Ana and Alberto will come to an end? I'm relieved that Harold doesn't seem to notice.

- I think, Harold says, that you'll come out of this so much better. You've been brainwashed by the American way of life with its frantic pursuit of fame and fortune and all the competition. You've been so hard on yourself that you didn't 'make it,' whatever that means, those words you always use. It's a pity, for you have so much even if you're not famous. I probably wouldn't even like it if you were. It would change you and we'd never see each other. I'm not even sure *you'd* like it.

- I'd like some of it, I say, like a good sound system and not having to work so hard to get work. Ah, it's so stupid… I should just give up the music once and for all.

- No! Harold shouts. You should give up *thinking of giving up* once and for all!

- It just wrecks things, I say. I want too much.

- But it also enriches your life… Well, not the *wanting*, but the music. And besides, without the music, I never would have met you. Maybe the key is to want less and to play, just play for it's own pleasure, and not care what happens.

- You sound like Ana, I laugh, suddenly loving him so much. Harold laughs too. He has a great laugh that resonates in me long after we've stopped saying anything.

- Well… Happy New Year, Harold.

- Happy New Year to you too.

- It's funny how many New Years we *haven't* spent together. We could be in the Guinness book of records.

- Ah, Harold says, I've never been so fond of these holidays anyway.

We hang up, and instantly I feel the void. I hate it, how nothing lasts more than a few seconds before shifting again… before I'm back feeling vacant and alone, that something must be there to fill the vacancy. I am tempted to phone Luis, but instead phone Carolina who has invited me to go with her to a New Year's party, and tell her that I will join her after all. I dress in my tango clothes and shoes, the only nice clothes I have with me, and wish that I could dance — but my skin is still too raw and painful.

After the party (okay but nothing special), my plan to take a taxi home proves impossible, so I drive back with her and once again sleep at her house. She's rented out the guest bedrooms now and leads me to a tiny alcove at the end of the kitchen.

- You can use the bathroom here, she says whispering.

Perhaps my imagination, but she seemed disappointed that I suffered no lapse of sanity at the party, that I didn't need her like before. Instead, I noticed the creeping in of competition, a thing I loathe between wo-men. Perhaps she was also disappointed that I hadn't moved out from Evelyn and rented a room from her. No longer needed as my savior, she had no use for me.

- Carolina…

- What? she says.

- I… Thanks so much for everything. You really helped me a lot when I… umm… Can I give you some money for staying tonight?

- No, that's okay. The house is full, and they pay me well. Join us for breakfast tomorrow.

The little room was clearly a maid's quarters in better times. Carolina, who works as a translator, has filled it with loads of books, many of them in English. It's been ages since I've seen so many books and it is like being amongst old friends. Maybe books are easier to be with than people and I take a bunch off the wall and bring them to the small sagging cot that is my bed for the night. One book, filled with inspirational texts, gets my attention. I read a couple and then there's one that I recognize; it's exactly what Ana has in Spanish on her table.

Each indecision brings it's own delay and days are lost lamenting over lost days…

The moment that you truly commit, then Providence will also move
Things will occur to help you…
Whatever you think you can do or dream you can do, do it
For courage contains genius, power and magic
Begin Now! — Goethe

The last thing I read before falling asleep is:

Our deepest fear is not that we are inadequate. Our deepest fear is that we are powerful beyond measure. It is our light, not our darkness that most frightens us — Marianne Williamson

In the morning I awake to the delightful smell of coffee and the sound of people laughing and talking a mixture of Spanish and English. I find Carolina in the kitchen and offer to help, and without saying much she gives me some platters of food to carry in. The shift between us is now so obvious and confusing that I have no clue how to react. I'm not sure what I have done or if I have done anything; if I should speak about it or follow her lead, which seems to pretend that everything is fine, albeit a forced and pretentious fine. It could just be that she is not pleased with having all these people in her house, and yet with the last of the platters set out, she sits down next to one of the guests and goes immediately into rapid, overly cheerful and impossible to follow Spanish. She appears to be having a grand time, and if I had never seen her before, I wouldn't question the authenticity of her laughter.

Which segues into my thinking that I probably should leave. But it's so nice and *normal* sitting here like this, chatting away. And the others, her guests, are so friendly and welcoming that I stay. When I finally do get up to leave, one of the guests, an Argentine woman now living in the US, asks me if I've ever been to a *Parilla*, the traditional barbecue. I tell her no, that all I've ever seen in Argentina is the tango. She insists that I join them on their planned outing for the day to a farm where there'll be a traditional *Parilla* and a show of folk dances from the North.

- You, a musician, she adds, you have to come hear the music. It's so beautiful.

What choice does Carolina, who also seems to be going, have but to say in a voice shrill with conflict, *yes of course you must come!* Just then the door opens and a few more people rush in. Amongst them is a musician, who I'm guessing Carolina may be interested in. His behavior, the way he starts flirting with me (which I don't encourage), is not helping my case. I am not sure how to read the situation and look at Carolina for a clue.

- It's okay, she says pulling me aside, I am not sure I like him anyway. Come, you'll enjoy the day.

But the day goes badly. This musician friend is persistent in seeking me out despite efforts at avoiding him, at putting myself down, despite bringing the conversation repeatedly back to Carolina. My efforts are still not enough to avoid looks of disapproval from her. I get anxious and feel the rash coming back with a vengeance.

I go and check my skin in the bathroom mirror; it is incredible how quickly the rash is spreading, like red wine spilled on a white tablecloth. I try to calm my anxiety, even more to observe it. But it doesn't help. What's happening? Why is this vaguely familiar? Am I afraid of upsetting Carolina, of losing her affection as I used to with my mother? Then I think of the last inspirational quote from last night and wonder if my deepest fear is that I am both inadequate *and* powerful beyond measure.

Whether I like it or not, the dynamic has turned bad with Carolina, and by the time they drop me off at Evelyn's, I realize I won't be seeing much more of Carolina. This makes me sad. This, and the relapse of my rash awaken the powerful ache of loneliness. I give in and phone Luis, despite promises to all and sundry that I won't see him again. It is only to wish him Happy New Year, and what harm can come from that? Nothing, until I hear his voice, his deep resonant voice, his long beautiful *Hola... Oooohhhh... llllaaaa Deborah!* And my name, my name sounds so good... that the time it takes for him to sound out the vowels is all the time needed for my knees to get wobbly, and for my mouth to become like mush, unable to form the word *no*, when he asks to meet me.

I pass Samantha on my way out. She gives me a look and then a grin.
- And you? Where are you off to?
- I'm going to take a walk.
- I could earn a living from you.
- The rash is back.
- And he is your medicine to get rid of it?
- Maybe.
- Have a good time, she says. I hope he's worth it.
- We don't... It's not what you think.
- Yeah, yeah, she says.
- You sound like Evelyn.
- Please, don't say that, Samantha begs, and then adds: I wish I could come with you — does he have a brother? I am going crazy here today.

Then I feel so grateful, so amazingly grateful that Luis wants to meet me. No judgment, my thinking assures me, you are not a bad person. There's a weak-in-the-belly sensation: this being human makes me so happy there's a skip in my step as I make my way to the park.

*

The rash is so bad (the encounter with Luis only helped delay the inevitable), that back in the hospital they give me another shot of cortisone. The doctor tells me this new development isn't at all surprising.

- It will get better and then worse, remember? The good news is that each new outbreak will have less strength and won't be as bad, I promise.

Pain and discomfort are hard things to remember for it feels as bad as ever. This getting worse undermines my courage to get well. I miss Ana terribly, who will be away a full month and Alberto, who has canceled class until after the holidays.

What I'd added so as not to go completely loopy, with Ana and Alberto away and the feeble structure of my days broken, is tango lessons.

Since beginning the dance, I haven't gone this long without dancing and it seemed wise to do something until my body recovered sufficiently to go to a *Milonga*. The rash is ugly but not contagious, and when I explained my situation, the teacher was very sympathetic about my fragile moods. The private class is just around the corner in a gorgeous hotel with the grand feel of old Buenos Aires. Right outside the street is a mess of trash and broken bottles, but inside we enter another time, another world — an exclusive world, like a vintage wine chilled to perfection. The lesson is truly marvelous, and we are dancing well together until the teacher touches me in the *place*, the place where the rash is the worst. He can't see it, for it is under my dress; it is around my waist where his hand comes to hold me firmly. He takes my ribcage and moves it up and holds it, inviting me to be present, to be *there*. This was already hard for me in the tango, the demand to be fully present. But now with the rash magnifying this vulnerability it feels unbearable. The tears squirt out of my eyes as if water guns lay behind my skull.

- Why are you crying? the teacher asks in surprise. You are dancing so well.

I tell him that it's part of my illness, these sudden tears, and to please not mind it. The best we can do is to keep dancing. I only apologize that his shirt is getting wet.

- It's okay, he says.

What I don't tell him, is that being present is so hard. That it leads straight back to shame, the shame of being seen or noticed. But we keep dancing, and as we pass the big mirror I see that we look very good, almost in love, which we aren't. It's just the tango danced well. Startling, how different what I see is from what I feel. So startling that I wonder if I may be well enough to go dancing after all.

- Do you think I can go to a *Milonga* now, I ask the teacher. Would anyone ask me to dance?

- You look very beautiful, he says.

What could he say? Every man in Argentina tells every woman she looks beautiful; it is one of the charms of being there, yet the dancing feels so good that I actually believe him.

11.

Today I am the only student in Alberto's class. He seems delighted with just one body to focus on, as if at long last he can make sure that at least one of his students gets it right. The exercises are tricky and so specific that he often uses his hands to correct my position. They feel so good, so calming I almost prefer to get it wrong. We are deeply involved in a very hard exercise with Alberto wrapped all around me when suddenly Evelyn pokes her head in. It gives completely the wrong impression, but Alberto neither stops nor says anything. He is so focused he doesn't even look up, which infuriates her all the more. She makes a loud huffing sound and looks as if her eyes will pop and storms out. She runs up the metal staircase making a racket and a few seconds later, besides the thumping of what seems to be combat boots, we hear heavy pounding like thunder, followed by rapid hammering. That house of hers! Amazingly, Alberto doesn't seem to notice this either. His concentration is impressive. I, with the attention span of a flea, have lost it completely.

- Alberto, I interrupt. It's Evelyn up there… she's pretty angry that you're working just with me…we should…

- Try to pay attention to this, the exercise, not to her. What Evelyn is doing is not part of this class.

- But the noise?

- Try to ignore the noise.

I'm so angry with Evelyn, angry that she is interfering with this precious time with Alberto. And I'm furious with myself for letting her get to me. This awakens a feeling of being powerless that has been there so long; like a crotchety old woman who I will never, ever be rid of.

- Why are you crying? Alberto asks.

- Evelyn, she's such a…

- Evelyn is not well. She could come to this class if she wanted. She's choosing to be on the roof building her house.

- What house? That thing will never be a house.

- Still, it is her choice, and we must allow her that.

We do a few more exercises, but all I can focus on is Evelyn and the noise.

- Did she have a hard childhood? I can't help but ask.

- She did.

- Me too, I say.

We do some more moves, and this time Alberto stops, as if realizing he has left out the most important ingredient. He takes both my hands in his so that I not only hear his words but feel them.

- And yet, he says, we must be grateful to our parents for they have given us life.

- But they…

Alberto shakes his head and speaks very slowly.

- They are no longer responsible for how you feel, for how Evelyn acts. It is you, and how you decide to think that determines your life. All I ask of you now, even if you keep crying, is that you don't think of anything for the next ten minutes. Try to clear your mind of *everything* while we do the *tai chi*. It is so good to have a rest from thinking, from worrying. Allow yourself to experience the opening and the closing, the *yin* and the *yang*, just let it move through you.

We do this as tears continue to stream down my face.

- Your muscles are so tight. Alberto says, when we have finished. Just let yourself cry, it is good, it releases the tension.

- What about you? I ask. Isn't it too much for you, all my tears?

- Why should it be too much? It is not me who is crying.

Then he bursts out laughing and gets me laughing too, even with the tears falling steadily, like rain. After the *tai chi*, he takes the huge exercise mat and places it down in the corner of the studio for the massage part. His hands feel so confident and so well trained it's hard to believe that he's doing this for free; he could earn a fortune in Norway. Such a huge gift that I almost don't know how to receive it, except by doing my best. Doing my best to not be distracted by the intensity of the hammering and my thoughts about Evelyn, who I'm sure is not even looking how she hammers in the next piece of wood… She'll never be able to live in that house of hers, ever, especially not when it rains. Which segues into realizing that what Alberto has asked of me — to not think of anything — is impossible. And yet when he finishes, he seems pleased.

- Very good, he says. You are letting me in more, and you are beginning to trust me.

I hardly realize how on-guard my muscles are, it is so habitual. All I know is I've never experienced such relaxation (especially after the hammering finally stops). Before we end, Alberto takes my hands in his again and says again how well I've done. He gives me a soft kiss on top of my head like a pleased parent, a wonderful parent, and goes upstairs to drink tea with Evelyn.

With Alberto by her side, giving *her* attention now, she changes dramatically as laughter ripples through the house. Shielded by the banana tree, I watch them; it is intriguing, almost miraculous to see how the evil, poisoning look on her face transforms, and she becomes beautiful. Alberto has brought her flowers. She has cleared the weekly clutter, just as she did for each of us when we first came, and has spread out a freshly ironed tablecloth, a plate of *media lunas* and her finest tea set. I want to run to her, to embrace her, to tell her how happy I am to see *her* again; that we actually have so much in common and there's no reason to hate me, that Alberto is committed to a spiritual life and there's no way I could take him from her, ever. And yet I know if I dared interfere with this moment with him, she would kill me. So I tiptoe with my guitar around the tree and down the stairs — the good thing is that she won't stop me practicing in the studio now, she wouldn't dare yell at me in front of Alberto. It is the best to sing, after he's worked on me.

The time with Alberto is rich and full and his words repeat in my head like a mantra: *focus on the nourishment that is good for your energy.* He is the perfect complement to Ana, who has asked me while she's away to be alone a little bit every day without doing anything special — *even if you must sneak and see Luis,* she laughed, *try to be alone in a mindful way as much as possible, to experience yourself without judgment. For instance when you sing, try not to watch and judge if it is going well. If you are able to notice that, you have lost concentration on the singing itself.*

I take the guitar and watch my posture in the mirror. The work with Alberto is amazing, like being back at my Alexander training with hands carving and sculpting my body. Ah, to have such hands on me every day, how well I'd sing. With the vibration of Alberto's touch lingering, I hardly recognize the voice that pours like velvet; so free, so lusciously free.

While practicing the telephone rings and I rush to pick up the extension in the tiny kitchen next to the studio so that Evelyn is undisturbed. It is my brother Andy. He tells me that he will be able to transfer enough of his free miles and get me on a new flight home to Oslo, the same one as Harold has booked. But he has to do it very soon, as the miles will expire.

My brother's generous offer almost feels too much. Further, just thinking of getting back on a plane again causes terror to rip through my body so the fruits of Alberto's hard work instantly vanish.

- Deb... Are you there?

- Yes, I... I'll tell Harold to phone you directly so you can coordinate flights.

- As soon as you can.

- Andy... I...

- It's okay Deb. It's my pleasure.

I phone Harold and leave him a message to contact my brother before the panic makes everything impossible.

I go back to the studio, to my guitar, to the song sheets that just a moment ago filled me with joy. I kick them with my feet and feel the urge to smash my guitar. *Alberto is a complete nut, and Ana's promises about me flying are bullshit;* nothing and no one makes any sense.

I change my clothes; then change them again, and again. I don't know what to do with myself. I can't phone Luis — the last time we were together we had a terrible fight, our worst one yet, and once again broke up for good. He even made me scratch out his number from my address book.

- *Por favor,* Luis had begged, stop crying! People will think I hit you. Can't you just walk down the street like a normal person? You're like a little girl... It's stupid. And I am a man who needs sex, not all this shit. Don't call me anymore, I mean it!

He was right, of course. If we'd had sex — real, grunting sex, we wouldn't have had so much energy left over for a fight.

It is not easy to trace the number (as Luis forced me to cross it out with a dark pen), and I'm not sure if I've figured it out correctly and have to try several combinations, but I do get through in the end. He's furious that I have the nerve to phone him. After he rants and raves for a justifiable amount of time — his angry voice is so resonant, so musical, it's like listening to a Spanish opera — he finally agrees to meet me after all in our usual place in Lazama Park. Like me, he is a broken person, and having someone, *anyone* to be with, is better than the dreadful nothing that reminds you of what you are: nothing. He won't come to the house now, for he also hates Evelyn. The way she looks at him like a low-class workman, and because he refuses to charm her in the slightest, she treats him like human trash. And he won't meet me for dinner for macho as he is he insists on paying and hasn't a cent left with all the going out we've done. He does, however, allow me to buy us each an ice cream cone which we lick voraciously as we walk, the ice cream giving a *clear line of direction* (don't ask me why I think of Lee Strasberg just now, but I do) so we don't have to look at each other, don't have to say anything as we find our way to a bench, *our* bench so it seems. Despite the awkwardness (we are after all broken-up), it is good to sit here, such an undemanding perfect thing: sitting on a park bench on a warm summer's day.

- I want you to come live with me. Now! he blurts out.

I give the look that tells *we've been through this.*

- You're not really married if Harold isn't here.

- Well... but he... and anyway your apartment, it's ...

- I know. I am going to fix up my apartment, soon.

I look at him with a mouthful of delicious ice cream, knowing absolutely that soon will never come, that he's never going to fix up his place, and yet as I swallow down the sweet texture, I believe him. I want to believe him and don't mention that Harold will be coming to Buenos Aires soon.

- You'd never let me dance tango, I say laughing, catching the ice cream from dripping. It is so warm outside; you have to concentrate on all sides of the cone.

- That's right, he says.

Like Meg Ryan in the movies, I bite my lower lip and think guiltily of Harold re-arranging his work to fly here and be with me. What I want is both these men, to have Harold, who loves me consistently and allows me to dance tango — he allowed me to come to Buenos Aires in the first place — and to have Luis, who loves me bad and naughty and dangerously close to the edge of everything that is wrong.

We finish the cones and with his hands free he wraps his arms around me. For a few moments there's absolute perfection. *Slow down time, please slow down. Really, there is no hurry to get well, no hurry for Harold to get here.* This indulgence in myself, this time-out from everything is precious and marvelous, a miracle how everything is changing. Why can't this go on forever?

For an instant, I stop caring about my brother and the new airline ticket; I don't have to get on the plane, simple as that. I don't even have to go see Ana again. I can just stay like this, floating on the ether of becoming.

I suddenly think of the play 'Equus,' about a highly neurotic, mesmerizing boy brought to a therapist for treatment. In a stunning moment, the therapist realizes that he's jealous of his patient's neurosis; that the boy has more passion and fire than anything his own personal life contains and what right has he, the therapist, to remove this passion? In his own bleak despair, the therapist wonders if having a passion, albeit neurotic and dangerous, is still better than having none. Maybe I shouldn't get well. Maybe if I got well, there'd be nothing but a blank emptiness.

No! I won't let anyone take my passion, no matter how wrong or sick. I don't care if I lose everything, but I refuse to have a boring and empty life. I won't go back to Oslo. I don't fucking care if Norway is number one in all the statistics. For what? The wealth? The functionality? But life there is so boring, so incredibly boring.

Then in the rumble of confusing thoughts, I remember the surprising conversation with Samantha the other day when she told me about her husband and kids back in California. I hadn't realized that she had left her family, that she even had a family, and that she'd had a brutal love affair in Brazil.

- Brazil? I asked in amazement.

- It's a long story... but it didn't work out and I can't go home. In the meanwhile, it's cheaper to hang out here in Buenos Aires.

- Will you ever see him again?

- Probably not... Anyway, you know how that goes, how you can be *willing* almost eager to ruin your life because of how someone touches you, how someone makes you feel.

- What do you mean? I stupidly asked.

- You know exactly what I mean.

Sitting with Luis on the park bench, we slip outside the realm of time and reason, like we're on a broken-down train, far, far away from anywhere. Unsure how long, before the *stalled* train moves again, still we're delighted, Luis and I, to be stuck here, suspended in time. I, for one, just now, right here, hope the train never moves again.

*

Not everything is as unreal, and Samantha who has become a sort of sister urges me to renew my visa in time so there'll be no trouble staying longer in Buenos Aires. The easiest and nicest way is to cross the border by boat, into Colonia, a little town in Uruguay three hours across the river. I had done it before, on my first visit, so I knew what to expect and how nice it was. I asked Samantha to join me, but she can't and since I don't feel secure in my precarious state to go alone, I persuade Luis to come. I insist on paying; he's had so little work, yet knowing he'd rebel I manage to convince him by saying that he'd be helping me and that he could bring our lunch.

We meet at 7:30 A.M. at the harbor. The weather is gorgeous, with a piercing blue sky and not too hot. All is perfectly fine as the boat slides gracefully away from Buenos Aires. We sit on the open deck, with the refreshing breeze, drinking coffee, eating *media lunas*. Me, as happy as a lamb, the rash relatively quiet, my mood as open and hopeful as the stunning vista before us. Schemes of how to stay forever in Buenos Aires fill my head and heart. It all makes beautiful sense. I imagine myself, with sleeves rolled up, with paint all over my face, fixing up Luis' apartment. Together. We can live there. I can teach English, music — like Sebastian was in the process of arranging — even the Alexander Technique. The hard times won't last forever in Argentina. I will get well enough to work again. I don't have to go back to Europe. Harold will let me go. It will be better for him to find someone who loves Norway, who can do the life he wants.

Luis seems happy as well with me all calm and behaving normal. No tears. He can't read my thoughts, but he sees my face, sees how content I am to be with him. He takes my hand when we've finished our coffees and holds it, lovingly. I think of the end of García Márquez's book, *Love in the time of Cholera*. How the two thwarted lovers spend the remainder of their lives traveling back and forth on a boat. Sometimes, when there seems no real choice the most creative solution arises. As the charming town of Colonia rises in the distance, I feel again as I did sitting in the park with our ice-cream cones, wanting time to stop. But as always the time doesn't. It moves and moves and moves again.

We arrive, and Luis, who is wearing city shoes, insists we take a taxi. Bursting with enthusiasm for the marvelous day ahead, I spontaneously ask the driver to take us to a *beautiful* beach, one that has been recommended. Luis rams me on the thigh — he had warned me not to talk, to not let the driver know that I'm a foreigner, a *yanqui* (pronounced 'junkie,' meaning Yankee), and when we are dropped off at the wrong place and have been over-charged, Luis is furious.

- You and your stupid accent!

Even after I apologize profusely, he won't drop it, and instantly I fear that I've crossed an invisible line of safety and am now in unknown territory with a possibly violent man.

In the middle of nowhere, and no taxi in sight we start walking. After a while, we get directions to the correct beach, which is another two kilometers.

- I hate walking, Luis moans.

But we have no choice, so he does. At last we find the beach, which really *is* nice, with an endless stretch of soft sand and settle on a good spot under a tree. We unpack our towels, water, cheese and crackers and a tin of mackerel. Luis takes out a bottle of wine, our favorite, and opens it in a most peculiar way, with his teeth. The violence in this action and the success in removing the cork seem to relieve his tension.

The water is brown, not dirty, just brown from all the soil that is traveling from Brazil towards the Atlantic Ocean. It feels soothing on my skin. The rash is still fine, and the day is again on track, like a day straight from the movies.

- Come into the water, I yell, it's fabulous.

- I can't swim, Luis yells back.

- Doesn't matter, I say, you don't have to swim.

The water is very shallow, there are no waves, no rip tides: it is water for children. He enters tentatively, yet after a short time seems to enjoy how nice and refreshing it is. He can't say that I've done well after all in finding this beach; those words are not in his mouth. But he strokes my back soothingly and this is more than enough; I don't need words. We stay for hours at the beach swimming, eating, kissing and laughing as if we haven't a care in the world until the sun begins to set.

Luckily there's a restaurant at this beach where we phone for a taxi back to the harbor, and all continues well, my passport is stamped, no problem. Once on board, Luis insists on sitting inside. Never afraid or anxious on boats before, yet this time — with the first rev of the engine speeding up and the rumble of movement awakening the claustrophobic sensation of being trapped, like on the plane — the panic flares with terrifying ferocity. I leap up.

- What's happening? he asks.
- I have to get out.
- Don't start, he warns.
- I can't help it.

He gets up and rushes past me. I cling to his arm.

- Where are *you* going? I shriek.
- I don't know, away from you. When you calm down come find me.
- Don't go… please…

He frees himself with a force that stings, and runs off.

All at once I am invisible. The people nearby can't see me. I want to scream, but can't breathe. My skin turns an angry red, a new rash threatening. I stumble over people in my way, rush out, not thinking where, just up, just out. I make it to the open deck; my heart is racing.

The night is dark, the stars brilliant like in a planetarium. I lay down on my back. The amazing sight of the southern hemisphere's starry sky stuns my panic. I have never seen such a sky, so many stars. A blast of sacred embraces me, like the arms of God — what Ana hoped I'd feel at the end of the breathing, which I hadn't, not yet — powerful, far more powerful than me, than my skin, than my rash, than Luis, than anything I could imagine. This essence is so much stronger than my fears, my schemes, my plans. As the boat moves and the stars shift, I realize I don't know what I'm supposed to do, that I don't have to know, not now, not yet. Only, that I will and must continue working with Ana.

After a while, I get up and see Luis sitting against the railing. I walk over to him. He doesn't push me away, and I lie there in his arms and we fall asleep for the rest of the trip.

When we arrive back in Buenos Aires, we are both tired and hungry. We look at each other with a desperation that is new and honest and impossible to push away. We both realize that we long for a thing that cannot happen, not now, not ever. All at once, I long for Harold; after such a full day it is the comfort of familiarity that I want. But Harold isn't there, and Luis and I are still on this *stalled*, existential train, and we just can't part yet, so we buy *empanadas* at the corner shop and go to Evelyn's to sit on the terrace.

It is late, yet still she is up, waiting like a panther for her prey. She has moved the table on the terrace so she can keep an eye on who's out there (namely me) while sitting on her couch across the hall. I take money out of my knapsack, storm across the landing and pay her, just in case Luis needs to come into my room to use the toilet; I can't bear to see Evelyn one second longer than necessary. And because I have already paid her, he *does* come into my room (for the first time). We don't feel free, so we lie on the bed with all our clothes, even our shoes, and just hold each other with all our might, like if we could just squeeze hard enough we could stop time and the train from ever moving. But we can't defy the gravitational force of the universe, and we know that the day spent in Colonia was 'it,' the best we could do.

12.

Ana is back from her summer holiday, and like a teacher at the beginning of a new school year, she's busting my ass. No mercy. We toil away searching for me, who I am, and all I discover is tension, the tension I've spent my entire life fighting. So what's the bloody point? I feel like one of the lost souls during the Gold Rush, who wasted their lives digging for gold, but all they ever found was dirt, nothing but dirt.

I am hopelessly sleep-deprived again, for I am dancing tango like crazy to make it easier not to see Luis. It seems there's a ratio: the more I long for Luis, the more men ask me to dance. And because I long for Luis worse late at night, and the tango is the best then (the ones lingering are the ones who really need to dance) I come home later and later. And Evelyn, goddamn her and that ridiculous 'penthouse' she's building, wakes me early every morning with her incessant, insane hammering.

I am actively looking for another place to live, especially for the month of March when Harold will be here. I don't want Evelyn to meet Harold, afraid what she might tell him, do to him, to us. Unfortunately, with so many travelers in Buenos Aires now, the cheap rooms are all booked. The places available are cramped little cubicles, with no place to practice music, let alone move. Alberto said we could continue privately if I found a suitable space for us to do the exercises and the massage. It is crucial for me to continue with Alberto. He is as much a part of my recovery as Ana. She helps my mind, but it is Alberto who is helping my body. The way his hands melt my anxiety, the way he's teaching me to breath and to move *mindfully* in every day life. It's Alberto who helps me put into practice what Ana teaches. After a session with him, I feel more grounded, more present and trusting in my body. Happier. Able to love myself, as corny as that sounds and I feel so grateful to have found such a unique combination in these two.

To find a place to continue with Alberto has been fruitless, so I remain in the insanity of Evelyn's house. And that insanity, alas, is only worsening. She now keeps the studio locked all the time and only opens it when Alberto comes. She's set it up so that it's entirely my fault, and everyone in the house is angry with me. This is unfair and completely ridiculous as I only used it a few hours every day, the hours allotted to me. Besides, I was the only musician really needing it. Samantha used it to nap, and the others to watch television.

Ana laughs when I speak about Evelyn.

- Like a caricature of your mother, she says. Can't you see how you've drawn the same energy to you?

- Why would I do that? I ask Ana.

- Ask your deeper self and find out, she says. Find out why you have drawn someone like Evelyn into your life.

Luis has hurt his back badly and smashed some ribs; he fell off a ladder at work and can't move. He has phoned me to ask if I will take care of *him*. How could I not, after all he has done for me? So I go visit him in *his* sick bed. To distract Luis from his pain, I talk about Evelyn and Samantha and the new girls who have moved in, how crazy the house has become. Luis explains that I am in a house of lonely women, all in need of a man, all jealous of me because I have one — him. We laugh so hard about this that somehow we start up again.

*

I have a strange dream where everything is distorted and uncertain, and yet I feel so unbelievably alive. There is a man, not a clear face, and we are in an amazing house, colorful and complex. We start cooking a meal, but it takes forever and the man grows impatient and goes to the bedroom. He is very aroused and calls me, letting me know that he wants me now and will not wait forever. I continue cooking, but suddenly change my mind and decide to find him, but cannot. The house has become a maze of endless hallways and rooms. I frantically search for this man, but wake up before I find him.

*

The closer we get to Harold's arrival and my flight home, the worse the therapy becomes. Ana seems brutal but so is my resistance; it scares me to death just waiting downstairs for her. She viciously leads me straight to the point, forcing me to acknowledge my part in the problems, problems created because I cling to the past, to my idea of how things should be. Like my family, my music, my relationship with Harold, living in Norway, even the studio and Evelyn.

- You are trying to find your way back to Sebastian and the time you had a few years ago, when Evelyn was different, when the house was different, when Argentina was different. It won't work, Ana says, you must be *here and now,* with the situation *now.*

- But the studio was magical for me. I've never sung so well anywhere. It really helps me open up.

- No, Ana says, it's your *idea* of the studio and how you once were open there. That, you can find in another place. If you go deeper down, if you are willing to open up more, the place will be in you. It will not depend on the outside. And that's a good thing, for the outside is always changing.

- But, but...

You can *but* all you want, Ana says with her laugh, *but* you won't seduce me. You give away your power to people like Evelyn, who will only abuse you. And Evelyn, like you, is addicted to the chaos around her. Evelyn, she continues, will never see you, and yet you beg her to not only see you, but to love you. It is not any better than bashing your head against a wall and begging the wall to heal your broken head. Let's make a deal, Ana says, one more insane move from Evelyn, and you get out of that house. No more going to beg her understanding or forgiveness. I promise you, when you get *clear* about leaving there, you will find another place

- What about Alberto?

- If your intention is clear, you will not lose Alberto. He has offered to continue the class with you in another space. There will be another place.

- But I've looked! I've looked so hard. I've looked everywhere.

- I know, Ana says, I know. But you have not looked hard in the right way. It is the *unconscious intention* that still takes you in the wrong direction. You still *want* to live at Evelyn's, you are drawn to the distraction that she and her house provide, and the hope that things could go back to how they were, the lost paradise, and that makes it harder. You have to be *willing* to move, not at least for your self-respect, even if that means not practicing for a short while.

When I get back to the house there's a note from Evelyn pinned on my door. She has written in large capital letters:

IF ANYONE MOVES OUT BECAUSE OF YOU, I WILL KICK YOU OUT.

I feel the impulse rising, like bile, to explain to Evelyn that *I* want to move out, that she's so stupid because the others, besides Samantha, only stay a few days, and I pay a much higher rent! I nearly choke on the urge to defend myself, to make it fair, just.

On my way to Evelyn I stop and realize what Ana has said. No, I won't speak with her. Instead I go to the phone and check if there are messages. There is an angry message from my mother. She has tried to call several times:

WHY *ARE YOU NOT THERE*, her message screams through the phone. This is so embarrassing as everyone checks the messages, including Evelyn.

A well of hate rises, mixing up with my mother, my father, Evelyn, Luis, Harold. I go back to my room and do what Ana has instructed: I am supposed to *feel* it. And boy do I feel it! I pound the stupid pillow on the bed with all my might. It is not a feather pillow but cheap foam, otherwise feathers would be flying all around the room.

There is a breathing workshop this weekend, and I am terrified. Terror has taken on so many new dimensions that I need more words. Like how they describe snow in Greenland: there must be fifty words for it: wet, coarse, old, crusty, icy, slippery…

I can't bear one more moment: the confusion about my life, about Harold and what the hell I've been doing with Luis, about ever giving a concert again, and about ever getting back on a plane, which I still can't imagine. Easier to give it all up so nothing matters. The only thing I want is relief from the cruel itch of the rash.

Ana thinks the breathing workshop this weekend will be important for me. Like an alcoholic, knowing this is my last binge before sobriety, I phone Luis. We are addicted to each other, he and I, and we're both in terrible shape. My skin is red and swollen, and he can still hardly move after his fall from the ladder. He needs a real bed to sleep in, so has arranged to stay at a friend's apartment while they're away on vacation. When I arrive, it feels odd to be in a normal apartment instead of his ramshackle dwelling — our broken love needs a broken house to thrive in. In this standard two-bedroom, taken straight from the advertising catalog, with its bulging furniture, knickknacks, generic paintings on the wall and *functioning* kitchen, our relationship seems pathetic. He insists on cooking me dinner for the first time. He's a lousy cook, and it's nearly impossible to eat what he's made but I do my best. We even watch television, a thing we've never done together. Luis seems proud to offer me this, finally, yet this is absolutely not what I want. It's what I've loved about being in Buenos Aires, of being with him, to be away from the typical, soul-degrading activities of our time. I suddenly see that Luis would love to have an apartment like this with television, toaster, microwave and everything, if he could afford it. Not that I don't want these things, but I don't want them as center of attention, the goal of existence. All what I crave to be away from is exactly what he loves. After dinner and watching television from the couch, we fumble around, but the eroticism is missing in all this normality.

*

The rash is so bad — this time the shot at the hospital doesn't help — and I beg Ana not to make me come to the breathing workshop, the final one before Harold arrives. I feel too anxious.

- You have to, she says.
- I will go crazy.
- It doesn't matter.
- IT DOES MATTER, I scream.
- You can do this, she says. PLEASE just do this. Just get here, like you did the other times. That's all. We can take care of you. Please don't worry.

The music starts and I am more afraid than the other times. I don't trust my 'sitter'— the one that stays by your side during the journey. He doesn't seem to care, or even notice me, not like the man who helped me the first time. The music pounds, the effect of the hyperventilation begins. It isn't my first time, I know what's coming and I don't want it, not today. I resist giving over to the forced and rapid breathing; refuse to fall down the rabbit's hole. Today, it feels manipulating and false. I lie still, like a crate of resistance. Ana comes to work with me with her usual pressing, hugging, and loving. But this time I don't love her. I don't want it; don't trust it.

Still, she gets something moving, something out of me and I hate her, hate her saying fine, and good, and more. Fucking hell, still more anger that needs to come out?

- Fuck you, fuck you, is all I say.

- Fine, she says, and presses her hand even harder into my sternum. It hurts like hell. NOW, she yells, put all that into the sound.

Instead of anger, I get in touch with the fear of the anger, with my fear of showing my anger. My mother is telling me over and over: *'You're just like your father! You're so angry like him.' And just as she left my father, she will leave me. I love my mother. I need my mother. I cannot manage alone. I must do whatever it takes, even deny who I am, so she won't abandon me.*

Ana keeps pressing; her assistants rush over and surround me on all sides. I am exploding. I will die. The rope holding me down gives way and fear and anger surge forth like a tsunami. I rage and fling and scream.

- Go on, go on, GO ON. Ana is relentless. She presses inside places I didn't even know I had. She tears me apart, throws me out the window, over the cliff. *I am falling. This is the fear of flying: this terrible sensation of nothing containing you, of nothing taking care of you.*

- Go on, this is great, you're almost there.

I have ten arms, ten legs, and with all of them I am beating and killing my whole family. My father looks at me with sad, tragic eyes, telling me he knows he has let me down, that he was never strong enough.

And my mother, as she lies there dying — finally, she listens. I tell her: Please look at me, please see me, and if you can't, please let me go, let me do my life. I see that she can't do this, so I yell: leave me then, abandon me. I don't fucking care anymore. I am too tired.

Take it. Take it away.
And then it is all so quiet.

Ana keeps holding me, and slowly a body forms, with just two arms and two legs, and one head, and one very sore torso.

- Great, she says, great. I am so exhausted that nothing in my body can move, and I let myself lie in her arms.

13.

We arrive at the airport with plenty of time. I am doing surprisingly well until they announce the boarding for our flight. Hoards of people spring up and crowd the gate; I suddenly start to choke.

- I can't do this, I gasp to Harold. I can't go.

- Yes you can, just breathe.

There's something different in his voice, something deeper and more convincing, more secure; he has changed a lot in the month in Buenos Aires, in the breathing weekend he did and the private sessions with Ana. Yet I don't want to need his help, not anyone's; I want to manage myself.

One foot in front of the other and breathe… That's all life ever asks of us. In doing that, the rest takes care of itself. I squeeze hard on the stone in my left hand — the stone Ana's assistant Hernan gave me before leaving — a sort of talisman with profound meaning for me because of the work I've done. *Squeeze it,* Hernan had said, *to reassure the child in you that she's taken care of, because you can now, you can take care of her.*

I follow the queue. I know I can run back, can decide to stay in Buenos Aires. No one is forcing me on this plane. Yet, I want to go. I am ready.

Before Harold arrived, with the fear crawling all over me, I told Ana how much I wanted to stay in Buenos Aires. In truth, it was not only getting back on the plane that troubled me but where I was flying to — and I dreaded the return to Norway.

- Tell me, I begged her, what is best? What should I do?

- There's no right path, Ana said repeatedly. Each one has its good and bad. Staying here, going to Norway, back to America, no path is guaranteed, none easy. It all depends on what you do with your choice.

And neither could she promise that I'd be okay on the flight — as she said laughing: *I am not God.* But she felt it was time. That at one point one must take a leap and trust what one has learned.

During the last months, I began to understand how the panic and flying phobia were based on more than just a run-of-the-mill childhood fear but on a fundamental and far deeper root of never feeling safe. Convinced all my life that something dreadful was wrong with me, I had kept it secret. But it's nearly impossible to hold in just one secret. Lee Strasberg used to say, if you shut the door on one emotion, you shut the door on everything. Before you know it, you've shut the door on a huge load, a load without inventory — invisible, put away, forbidden memories, unexpressed feelings and impulses. You fear them, you hate them; they wrench you with shame. So you convince yourself they never existed or if they did, you insist the story is long-gone without importance or power today.

But still they were there, behind the closed door, living their own life, haunting like ghosts, brewing up to who-knows-what. Threatening to explode one day — you never know when nor how it will hit. You can never be free of this bondage; the deadly tick-tick-tick is terrifying. It would be better to open the door, if you could, if you had the courage, if you even knew there was a door.

It was more than courage I lacked to open that door, more than strength.

Previously, whenever I encountered a frightening situation like flying, like performing, like being in love, like driving through a long tunnel or across a high bridge — all things I could not control — the thought of what might happen (the gruesome inventory hiding behind the door) the fear of the fear, the panic of the panic became itself a monstrous panic.

I didn't believe Ana at first, that all the screaming and crying during our sessions and workshops was in fact opening the doors and off-loading this inventory. Growing up, I never dared to really oppose my parents, never dared say or show what I really felt or wanted, didn't even realize what was behind these close doors. But as long as those doors stayed shut, unconsciously mostly, I remained a child, frozen in time, forever needing protection.

To alter this powerful pattern, to find trust that I could, was essential in discovering and developing the adult, me, who could take care of herself. I needed help for this, to see it, to allow it, to change it and they helped me so much, Ana and Alberto.

Though they never met each other, Ana and Alberto, they became new parental role models. The experience of their loving me — with all my bad, ugly and terrible secrets — helped me to not hate myself as much, to catch a glimmer of that other thing (I still had trouble saying), that corny self-love.

There was still a long way to go, still many dangling pieces and un-answered questions but at least the panic, the terrible unrelenting panic, had withered. And I actually began to trust that *if* an attack of fear should occur there'd be far less 'fuel' to burn, not enough to ignite the full-blown panic. That whatever had once made me so afraid, so viol-ently afraid had grown quiet. Still I dreaded the approaching flight. The child, the adult, even the *grandmother* in me didn't want to go.

- Of course you don't want to leave us, Ana said. We took very good care of you, and you will miss this attention.

I held Ana's hand, felt her warmth and closeness, her abundant caring while she reassured me over and over that I could manage the flight, that I was doing so much better, that the journey home was a proving ground, a rite-of-passage. Of course there was more work to do, and yet, she firmly said, let the work we've done be integrated. Stay in touch with me, don't disappear please. Maybe you can return one more time.

- Come back? You mean get on a plane again and fly back?

- Yes, she said. You will manage this flight, and you will take more flights, you will even go and see your family.

- My family? How can I ever see my family after what I did, and thought about them… and killed them!

Yet again Ana's response was laughter:

- If only more people would work and heal the *image* of their family in their heads, then they could actually be with their family and love them for what they really are and have to offer. Once you no longer need your family as you once did, you will see *wonderful* things in all of them.

I didn't want to start crying, not then, but just the thought of never hearing Ana say *wonderful*, never seeing her lips move in a burst of life, her face vibrant with love made me determined to do the flight home, so I could come back. I would come back, it was my destiny to keep work-ing with her, with Alberto (who'd also encouraged me to return to con-tinue with him) — because there wasn't, I profoundly realized, just one closed door but several, layered like onions, each impossible to access until the one in front had opened. More than any other therapist, Ana had brought me closer to my true house, my true self. But she'd repeatedly said that I came to her ready. As bad as I thought I was, it was just the darkness before the dawn. All of it had prepared me — my earlier therapists, Lee Strasberg, the Swami, the Alexander Technique, the 12-step program, even Bouke and every single person along the way. Not at least Harold, who was more willing than any other man I'd ever come close to, to delve into the unknown. Who had his own hunger and need to open his own doors.

Even Oslo, that would never be my favorite place or my ultimate destination as home, was an important part of the story. For Norway was a country and culture that left you on your own, that demanded you claim without reaction or confirmation who and what you were or being there would kill you. (Not for nothing it ranks high in suicide and depression, but it also has impressive nature and powerful poetic individuals.) I was lucky, I now realized, just as Ana had said at the start. The terrible episode on board the plane, the toxic *Xanax* had been the catalyst, just as the Thanksgiving debacle with my mother, just as all of it had been. I needed to fall off the edge, needed to crash apart, to almost die before becoming willing to change. It just goes like that. We humans are not just lazy, although that's part of it, but most of it is out of our view, our reach, in our blind spot. It really can be a journey, this being alive, yet it's so confusing. So confusing to know what to focus on, pay attention to, have faith in. That alone — in this excessive time where so much demands and calls out for attention, the masquerade of faith — is a challenge.

Ana, like Houdini, like the finest magician, had moved aside the locks and chains, the noise and the muck, enabling me to be discerning, to see and focus on a deeper level of vibration, of awareness so that it wasn't just her words but my actual experience, like the tuning of a guitar — the A 440 tuning in the orchestra is not illusive, it is actual. That I could for seconds at a time have a glimpse of a spiritual connection, a deepening of what had begun that day, years ago, in Golden Gate Park while driving home that senile man. And maybe because it was not just her but Alberto as well (that desperate need of mine to be convinced), together they brought me across the threshold, through the Baptism of Fire into a whole other order of the world. A world I had suspected but never believed in, not consciously.

I'd had a recurring dream since childhood, of coming into a cave-like room, dark but for a crack of light that came through a door, slightly ajar. In the dream I rush to the door wanting so badly to break through to the light. I push with all my might but the door never opens. I can only stand at the crack, longing for the colors, the landscape that lay beyond, the lush greens, the vibrant hues of wonder. I had this dream again. This time the door moves but it is not me pushing it.

Life is hard — the foolish notion that life is easy or that there's just one enemy outside to be slaughtered and then we shall be safe and happy is a vicious and destructive myth.

Ana and Alberto, they helped me see this, and they were both so genuinely happy when I began to get well. Yet for me, that my skin actually healed and became normal again, that my puffy and distorted face completely recovered was nothing shy of a miracle. And I miraculously found another place to live, just as Ana had said — once my inner intention had changed — in a building directly behind Evelyn's, with a large spacious room to practice and do my class with Alberto, available on the exact day of Harold's arrival. With beaming satisfaction, I left a note for Evelyn that I'd be moving out.

Relieved to have found another place, relieved that Harold would never have to meet Evelyn, still I felt terrified for his arrival, frightened to be with him, frightened of the guilt I felt. We'd spoken on the phone about Luis — he knew and I knew, I could never hold a secret like that — and even if he seemed to understand that Luis was also a part of the process, I felt afraid. I think we both were scared to see each other, so much needed to change in our relationship.

I knew I had to give up Luis for real. Even if I were to crave him, to feel him, smell him, kiss him *one last time*, I knew that would be insane, would push Harold past his limit, unfair for all of us including Luis.

It hurt to give him up, but I'd finally come to realize that he was an *archetype* of my longing — the longing I'd had my whole life for protector and savior, for the father, an obsessive need to be with whomever was providing this protection — and a life with Luis would have unfolded into a worse misery than any I'd ever known. The frustration with his life and his unconscious turmoil would probably have made him increasingly hard and critical, focusing more and more on what was to blame outside of him, namely me. Very similar to my father's behavior, which I tried my whole life to escape.

The whole breakdown that had ignited the *child* in me, that had made me all child, was at first charming and erotic with Luis — being so small and skinny, crawling inside his arms, sitting on his lap, dancing around his room (things I also did to avoid having sex). But as the therapy intensified and I started to grow up, I was no longer as drawn to him. If anything, our last meetings were a desperate search to re-find the past, those first inflamed days together. Luis stubbornly refused, but at last I saw the choice: to learn to take care of myself, or spend the rest of my life searching the world round for the one to do it for me.

I hope and actually think that Luis learned something from me; he'd listen almost hungrily to my tales of Ana and Alberto, despite macho words against anything therapeutic — as the anger towards his family, life, even towards me was his *raison d'être*. Yet there was more between us than just the pull of longing, even if it would never fit into any form, any box. He had helped me and I had loved him and he, in his own way had loved me and we needed a good ending. So when Luis asked me to meet him for something special on the last night before Harold arrived, to dress nicely, but not, he begged in tango clothes, I agreed.

We met at six thirty at the bus stop on the opposite side of the Lezama Park, through which we had walked so many times. It was a Friday evening, mild and breezy, the wind coming straight off the river. He wore brand new slacks and a newly pressed tan shirt, his luscious brown skin shaved clean and his hair so black it shined blue in the light.

I sat across from him for the forty-five minute ride and watched him: this gorgeously handsome man with his lost inner child that he'd never get to know. His poverty, his anger, his education, his pride, whatever it might be would not allow it. It made me guilty and grateful at the same time. Although I'd not grown up rich — and perhaps his early years in a small tribal village in the North of Argentina were better, more wholesome than mine in New York — the last years in Norway had graced me with enough savings to stay in Buenos Aires all those months. That I had the means to pay for all the sessions and workshops — noticeably cheaper because of the devaluation, but still if all this had happened in New York, I'd never have been able to do it. Alberto had never charged me a cent, though I begged him to take money. (In the end, to thank him, he let me take him for a meal. And to accept money to buy Evelyn flowers, from *him*. I am glad I did, for I would never see her again; she would die later that year.)

We arrived at our stop and Luis led me to a large Spanish colonial-style building. A huge crowd had gathered outside, everyone dressed finely, the children squeaky-clean and behaving. Through a loudspeaker we were told to gather, to enter in if we could — the rest would spill onto the street. Everyone began to sing. Luis took my hand, ceremoniously. I'd never heard him sing before. He had a good voice, rich and deep and expressive. He led me closer and closer to the pulpit of this rare church. Luis refused to say the name of the religion or the group, or whatever it was. *No importa, estamos aca, ahora. Ahora.*

The sermon was in fast Spanish, too hard to understand. I watched the faces of the congregation, envied their innocent devotion. I couldn't see Luis, who had moved to stand behind me. He pulled me close to him, held me against his chest. I felt his beating heart so strongly as if his heart was the heart, the one heart of the world. I turned around and he looked proud and brave and happy, happier than I'd ever seen him. He was here; he was *now*, the only thing of importance.

On the bus ride home, both of us filled with the powerful chanting that I'd understood enough to join into, I thanked him with all my heart. We came to our stop and got off the bus. In the awkward moment of parting, I noticed Luis kept more distance as if claiming his territory, his boat to sail away in. It had to be *him* leaving me. He waved goodbye and started walking but then stopped and said:

- I couldn't do what you are doing. I could never get back on a plane. I only flew once, and in order to do that I had to drink a whole bottle of whiskey.

When Harold arrived the next day I felt distant and cold. I didn't want to be, but I was. I could force myself to never see Luis again — and I truly never did. I could force myself to get onto the plane, but I couldn't force my cells to open and let Harold in. I just couldn't. It would take time; we would need time.

I recall, once he'd arrived and Ana had met him, moaning to her that I didn't really love him, that I wanted something more.

- We all want something more, Ana said. (And yes, she laughed and I wanted to slap her.) Love is not the movies. But you have a good man in Harold. If you don't want him, I'll take him. There's so much love in and between you, not just history and connection but something stronger that would be a pity to give up.

- But what I did with Luis? How I felt?

- We've been through this… it's not that important. What happens now is important.

My last breathing workshop before leaving Buenos Aires, the music pounding, the intense breathing again ripping me open. This time it wasn't Ana who came to my side, but Harold. I didn't even know he was allowed.

- Shh, he said. It's okay.

The way he cared for me, laid the blanket gently over my body, stroking my back felt different. He was more there, more present. It was a thread I could never share with Luis. Harold had a breakthrough himself, earlier in the session. He, always afraid of the soft side taking over, of losing his protecting strength, had cried for the first time in 46 years. I had heard his crying; it had touched me, it had shown me who he was, who he could be. He wouldn't stop me from changing and growing, and I wouldn't stop him. That was important, maybe the most important of all.

Alberto had taught me, and I taught Harold the simple counting of breath. Alberto had said it was normal to be afraid, that we should be afraid, a little. But if you have to fly then know, if you keep breathing the fear won't take you over. *The key is the breath. As soon as you enter the plane, even before movement on the runway, start the steady count of your breath slowly in, slowly out. Just keep on doing this, no matter what, and you will be okay.*

Two days before the flight, Harold and I went walking in the *Reserva*, the national park beside the river. On the way out, in a state of pre-panic — convinced that I'd be even worse, would have a heart attack on the flight — I didn't pay attention and banged my head terribly, banged it so hard that I feared a concussion. A good reason not to fly home! On our way back, I became more and more furious and anxious that I hadn't been able to pay attention, not even while walking. A clear sign that I wasn't able to take care of myself. I was so bad that it scared Harold. He'd never seen me as Luis had, this wanting to rip off my skin.

- Let's do the breathing now, Harold commanded, once we'd gotten home. It will calm you down, come on.

We got onto the bed. Harold wrapped his arms around me, and I imagined wrapping my arms around the little girl.

- In — two, three, four, five and out — two, three, four, five, six, seven. And in... and out... Harold's voice became rich with resonance, almost song-like. With full attention now, full commitment, something clicked, something shifted. I tried not to focus on the change but kept right on listening to his voice, to the counting in, the counting out.

- It works! Harold said clearly relieved.

And it had.

Ana had asked Harold to join us at the end of my last session, the day before leaving. We had done so much work with her, alone and together not just about me and the flight but to find a way back, or rather a new way towards each other. Without words, Harold followed Ana's motion as they embraced me from two sides, holding my hands. It was a wonderful feeling for me, to be loved and held in such a natural way..

- God, I wasted so many years! If only I knew how simple it was to change after all.

- Shh, Ana said, shh, it doesn't go like that. It seems simple now because you've shifted and moved all what was buried deep down, but until you're ready it remains invisible and it isn't at all simple. It is the hardest thing a person can do.

It was just after the session when Hernan, her assistant, who had come to say goodby had given me the special stone to hold in my hand whenever I felt afraid

Perhaps silly and corny, but I keep squeezing this stone with one hand and holding onto Harold's with the other, and somehow, one tiny step in front of the other we board the Iberian jumbo-jet headed for London. We find our seats and right away begin the slow pattern of breathing, just as Alberto had shown us: one, two, three, four, five counts in and one, two, three, four, five, six, seven counts out... again and again. I wait for the panic, but it doesn't show up.

The plane starts to move, the engines rev, the captain announces: *Cabin crew take your seats* and still no panic.

Ana was good, damned good! And so was Alberto.

When we begin to level out in altitude, Harold falls asleep while count-ing. I could wake him; he'd open his eyes and say, *oh sorry, where were we?* There is something calming in how he sleeps, something reassuring that he can. As I watch him, on the amazingly gentle and not scary flight home, it is this new sensation of love, of sitting beside someone, separate yet together that I will most remember.

And maybe that is not so bad after all.

EPILOGUE

It is not like I love to fly, or that I never *wish* the pilot could stop the plane and let me out just at the point of take-off, but I *can* do it now without *Xanax* and without holding the hand of a flight attendant or a fellow passenger (although I dearly miss the stories I used to hear!). It still feels remarkable, when the rumble and roar starts up that I'm able to manage what once was terrifying. And even when the fear comes back — as it does from time to time like an old companion visiting — it never develops into a panic and it always passes, sometimes faster sometimes slower.

I still mention my fear of flying before boarding so that the flight attendants, if they seem friendly, will come and check on me, just in case. And they usually do come round in a gracious way while closing the overhead bins and adjusting seats to see how I'm doing.

Not long ago, having a bit of a rough time before take-off, I noticed a young woman crying hysterically in front of me. The flight attendants were occupied helping *her*, and no one was left to attend *me*. I hesitantly rang the bell, and one of them instantly came over.

- Yes? he asked urgently as he clearly wanted to go back to the young woman in distress.

- I am also afraid! I also have a fear of flying.

- *You!* You're doing fine. *She's* having a terrible time.

He was right! I was doing fine — fine enough. All at once I wanted to go to this young woman and wrap around her just as Ana had done with me. I didn't; one doesn't do such things on a plane out of the blue. Everyone will think you're crazy. Instead, in a moment of gratitude, I realized yet afresh how much I had learned and changed. How I wished for the grace to tell all of it, each thing learned, each piece realized, as if in the telling it could free the young woman from her own prison of panic.

And even with all the dangerous things in the world (my original fateful flight to Buenos Aires was not long after 9/11) it was in the end not the danger itself from outside, but the fear it triggered which lived its own life, the panic that ultimately scared me to death. It is, after all sometimes frightening to be alive, but if we're able to hang in there and breathe, if we're able to tolerate the dreadful discomfort, the energy of the once terrible and threatening can shift into life-enhancing power, like laughter, like the gorgeous vibration of tone in song.

There are times, walking in a forest or up in the mountains when my voice rings out freely, that remind me of the acoustics in Evelyn's studio. From the distance I see her and feel forgiveness not only towards Evelyn, but my mother as well.

I get a picture of the happy little girl inside me: *I am eight years old and have gone away for the first time, alone, without my family, to a Girl Scout sleepover camp, and am so relieved to be coming home that when I see my beau - tiful mother with her big Panama hat, her brown summer skin, her smiling face, I run very fast and leap into her arms. We drive home and she tells me all about the new swimming pool in the backyard and all my friends that are coming over to see me. I am so happy to be home, to be near my mother again, that I put on my favorite bathing suit, the one with a little skirt that ripples as I turn. I am so happy twirling in my room that I almost forget about going swimming.*

The idea of getting famous, that Ana worked so hard with me on, that fame would force my mother to love me, is no longer as urgent. Under- standing, well more than understanding, *accepting* that my mother (and the world for that matter) is never going to love me the way I want any- how, and forcing the music to provide this just contaminates the music.

My mother (like the world) is capable of loving me in her (their) way, and without a desperate need or special demand, I am more open to see and accept and enjoy what is available. Then the music can become its own force; not a thing to force in order to be loved, but love, itself.

At my best today, I am able to mix it all in, no longer ashamed of what may come up. Rather, delighted when elements rise up in me: so much richer is the texture of my voice. I imagine the touch of the wooden floorboards in Evelyn's studio on my bare feet, I see the cracked ceiling and overhead fan with its swish-swish as it slowly moves the air just enough to create a breeze. I sometimes add strands of Sebastian's violin. I immerse myself in the singing — the amazing curl and wave of sound.

A year ago, while accompanying Harold to a conference in Italy, I stayed behind in our room, which was part of a beautiful villa nestled in the hills of Umbria. With everyone gone, I took my guitar out to the small amphitheater that was built in the garden. I warmed up my voice and found the acoustics to be incredible, not to mention the stunning backdrop of lush green hills and scattered poplars. So inspired, so blessedly alone, I let out full throttle and sang with all my heart. My voice resonated freely; nothing blocked the gush of music in me, and tears filled my eyes. I went on, song after song, even making new ones up on the spot.

Out of nowhere I heard clapping. The Italian caretaker, who I had run into several times, came running with *bravo*, with *encore*, and lastly in English: *I must call my friend* — *Sergio, Sergio*, he shouted. And Sergio came running, and the two of them sat down, like eager school children, on the ancient steps.

- Sing, sing! they shouted

I became a little self-conscious, but not enough to stop the flow, the geyser in me, loving the singing so much that nothing could stop me. I sang and sang for them, and they clapped and leaped about and cried, and finally both men circled around me and hugged me.

- You are in love!! Sergio sang out

- Well I do love Harold, but...

- No! No! Sergio exclaimed, I'm not referring to love like that... Although it's nice that you love your husband... I'm talking about something much bigger. You are IN THE LOVE when you sing like this, and you fill me and my friend with love. This is how you must always sing!!

AFTERWORD

Huge thanks to Bill Greenwell who got me started, to my dear friend Marilyn Raider, there through all the versions, to Kevin Cook whose jumping out of his seat with genuine enthusiasm was crucial in early drafts and desperate moments of doubting, to Naomi Leimsider whose sharp insight gave the final focus, and to my husband Harold, who listened, read and contributed to the numerous drafts with a monk's worth of patience, to friends, early readers and various editors who supplied inspiration and wisdom along the way. To all the agents who said *no* ever so kindly with the human touch to keep me going. It is the willingness not to stop that does in the end get us there and I am so grateful for the help I was given to do just that. To Kenneth Sloan of Stream of Experience Productions who said *yes* and for his diligence and patience in supporting my birthing of the book into the world.

Many thanks to my brother Andy whose comments on an early draft gave invaluable feedback, to my brothers Peter and Bob for their support, to my mother Rose Foster and her partner Harry Galinsky for letting me winter at their home in Florida to write. To my father, Joe Weitzman, who in his own way has always been supportive of his daughter's unusual life. And to George Singfield, my first therapist and life-long friend who, although not mentioned in this story has always been hugely important as guide and mentor. If not for the early work with him, I'd never have been ready for the intense work with Ana. I am very grateful to Ana Maria Aguirre, Silvia Quagliano, Hernan Penido and her marvelous team and to Alberto Antonio Rossi with his magical hands and heart.

It's a hard thing to write a book where scenes may be hurtful to others, a very hard thing to own one's version of truth. First, while working with Ana, and then in the growth that continued with writing Pandora, my relationship with every single person I have ever known has changed. Special thanks to my parents who were willing to change along with me and for allowing me to go forward and publish this book. Thank you, all of you, for all you have taught me.

For further conversation, please contact Deborah at
www.deborahjeanne.com.

About the cover art: *She Who Knows*

This image invokes the feminine spirit roots of the world's oldest forms of ceremony and healing. It is a celebration of indigenous shamanic practices all over the world. It is evocative of, and dedicated to, all that we as wounded healers have survived, created, become.

From the cover artist, Rowan Farrell:

My mother is a painter and sculptor as was her mother before her. Somehow we all managed to survive the social confines of the deep South and to nurture eccentricity in our children. My studio, about 30 minutes south of Asheville, NC, is hidden at the end of a long dirt road tucked into tall poplars beside a creek on our farm. I first began establishing myself in 1992 by exhibiting as well as working as an assistant with well known artists in Atlanta.

My work is both a rich exploration and a celebration of The Wise Woman Tradition and indigenous shamanic practices around the world. The image for the book cover is from the series, *Deeper Than Dreams; Archetypal Visions.* My work is bold, bright, pulsing with intensity. They are mixed media paintings on paper grown from layer upon layer of adventurous collage and mark making, packed with unexpected iconography and delicious details. Huichol artistry, medieval tapestries, Egyptian iconography and indigenous healing traditions all have their say in the outcome.

www.rowanfarrell.com

Made in the USA
Charleston, SC
11 October 2015